THE TRUTH ABOUT (M)OTHERHOOD
CHOOSING TO BE CHILDFREE

edited by Helene A. Cummins, Julie Anne Rodgers, Judith Dunkelberger Wouk

DEMETER

The Truth About (M)Otherhood
Choosing To Be Childfree

Edited by Helene A. Cummins, Julie Anne Rodgers and Judith Dunkelberger Wouk

Copyright © 2021 Demeter Press

Demeter Press
2546 10th Line
Bradford, Ontario
Canada, L3Z 3L3
Tel: 289-383-0134
Email: info@demeterpress.org
Website: www.demeterpress.org

Demeter Press logo based on the sculpture "Demeter" by Maria-Luise Bodirsky www.keramik-atelier.bodirsky.de

Printed and Bound in Canada

Cover artwork: Desireah Lascelles
Cover design and typesetting: Michelle Pirovich

Library and Archives Canada Cataloguing in Publication
Title: The truth about (M)Otherhood : choosing to be childfree / edited by Helene A. Cummins, Julie Anne Rodgers and Judith Dunkelberger Wouk.
Other titles: Truth about otherhood
Names: Cummins, Helene A., 1961- editor. | Rodgers, Julie Anne, 1977- editor. | Wouk, Judith Dunkelberger, 1945- editor.
Description: Includes bibliographical references.
Identifiers: Canadiana 20200375628 | ISBN 9781772582840 (softcover)
Subjects: LCSH: Childfree choice. | LCSH: Childfree choice—Social aspects. | LCSH: Childfree choice—Psychological aspects. Classification: LCC HQ755.8 .T78 2021 | DDC 306.874—dc23

Acknowledgments

A task of this magnitude involves many people who have worked with us from around the globe. We are grateful for the hard work and commitment from all our authors. Everyone cooperated at a time of unprecedented change and global challenge, as the COVID-19 pandemic has reshaped our personal lives, our families, and our communities.

Demeter Press and Andrea O'Reilly, our publisher, went the extra mile to guide and assist us from the beginning through to the completion of this book. Brescia University College provided a publishing subvention through their faculty research grant provisions. We are fortunate to have this financial assistance to bring the book to fruition.

Our anonymous reviewers offered solid and expert advice for reworking and rethinking different parameters of our work. Their academic and scholarly input have resulted in useful revisions to the final draft.

We are also grateful to Desireah Lascelles, who graciously granted permission for the use of her artwork on the cover.

This journey has also involved the university students of the editors and authors of this volume. They have helped us understand how we can better equip society to honour new and diverse social realities. We are grateful for their input and experiences.

Our close network of kin, colleagues, and friends were the touchstones that we needed from the start of this project to its completion. Their love, goodness, compassion, and resolve made all of us bigger and better and helped us to see the project through to completion.

On a personal note, Helene is grateful to her beloved parents, who taught her that anything was possible in life. Their love, support, and care and that of her siblings—Michelle, Michael and Bernard—are constants in her life. She also cherishes her students and colleagues at Brescia University College, which allows her the opportunity to teach, research, and develop in numerous ways.

Julie would like to express her thanks to the Motherhood Project at Maynooth University for the supportive community that it provides for her research.

Judith thanks her friends Diane Finkle Perazzo and Gillian Alban, who read earlier versions of her chapter and her late husband, Jonathan Wouk.

Lastly, Judith, Julie, and Helene forged new academic and personal relationships, as they undertook this project together coming from diverse academic and vocational backgrounds. In our life's work, we are grateful to have had this time and experience together.

Foreword

Helene A. Cummins

The understudied social experience of women who are childfree is interesting, given that many more women are pointedly choosing this lifestyle around the globe. Childfree women also may not necessarily choose it but find themselves without children resultant from all different types of social experiences. Perhaps they have advanced education and have not found a suitable partner, or they are too late in their reproductive cycle to foster children in a timely fashion, or they feel they cannot financially afford to bring children into their world. Other reasons around challenges with their own process of socialization in their family—including forms of molestation and witnessing or being physically and/or psychologically abused—can also lead to choosing not to have children. Climate change has also factored into this social issue; researchers are suggesting that climate change and global warming trends may create conditions whereby women may choose to remain childfree. Given that the world is overpopulated and that human suffering continues, some may suggest that it is wise not to bring more people into society. Clearly, there are many reasons why women may choose a childfree future.

Women can choose not to have children, despite the stigma that has long existed—that childfree women are selfish and immature. They may be culturally represented as desperate, as unnatural, or as an embarrassment to womanhood. However, as women move forward against pronatalist trends and sociocultural structures and either choose or find themselves in this childfree social space, they can find freedom, social mobility, happiness, higher incomes, and increased leisure. They may be able to entertain in the role of sister, friend, or aunt or have loving and caring relationships with children of their friends, relatives, and coworkers rather than with their own children. I argue that there are many ways to mother and be on the mommy track without being a mommy in the normative way of carrying a child to term and bearing that child.

As the world has industrialized and more and more people move from rural to urban spaces, the need for an extra set of hands to work the land may be less needed nowadays. Children were valued as an extra set of hands for the purpose of work on the farm, and, in turn, they would care for their ageing parents. Furthermore, now that contraceptives and abortion have become more available for women, the number of children born, as well the size of families, has become more limited overall. Although fewer children are being born, the cultural norm is still built upon the nuclear family.

This interdisciplinary manuscript focuses on the childfree experience in many different contexts, including a childfree professional Black woman's experience of empowerment, biblical depictions of women in the Hebrew Bible, the abandonment of children in Ethiopia by low-income, childlessness in contemporary French women's writings, as well as how women, and sometimes men, define their childfree experiences. With a few exceptions, however, the current childfree research focuses on the experiences of white women and tends to negate the experiences of racially diverse women and Indigenous women young and old across the globe.

Although women may be able to choose to have or not have children, there are few to no existing supports for those who choose to be childfree. The term "childfree" was coined in 1972 in the United States by the National Organization for Non-Parents, yet there are still only a few organizations that support childfree women. One example is the NotMom Summit, which is a conference that aims to help childfree women around the globe.

In moving beyond pronatalist values, cultural norms, and delimited options for women, this anthology focuses on childfree women, and some men, and looks to refashion old and outdated beliefs, roles, values, lifestyles, definitions, and cultural understandings concerning childfree women and men across the globe. Our 16 authors from around the world embrace and identify different ways of being in the twenty-first century—ways that do not view women only as mothers and that respect women's and men's diverse ways of experiencing otherhood.

Contents

9.

Childlessness among Women in the Hebrew Bible:
Reframing their Stories
Judith Dunkelberger Wouk
201

Afterword
Judith Dunkelberger Wouk
227

Notes on Contributors
235

Contextualizing the Choice to Be Childfree

Julie Anne Rodgers

Pronatalist Pressure

Despite the increasing numbers of women choosing voluntarily to remain childfree in the twenty-first century, the decision to deviate from the expected female life trajectory remains largely underarticulated, poorly understood, and often invalidated. Even after multiple waves of feminism, contemporary society continues to position motherhood at the core of womanhood, conflating the two to such an extent that women who choose not to become mothers find themselves marginalized and subjected to a whole host of injurious stereotypes. As Renée Ann Cramer observes, we are living in a society that is obsessed with bumps and babies, and this is particularly evident in popular culture. We are either speculating on the pregnancy of a celebrity or, if already pregnant, closely following the event through to birth and into new motherhood. This constant focus on the pregnant body, Cramer argues, shows us that far from having attained reproductive freedom, women are still subject to idealizing and normative views of femininity, and at its core, this includes the idea that all women should aspire to becoming a mother (2-3). If this is the case, where then do we position the woman who chooses of her own free will to be childfree?

Based on the overwhelmingly negative media coverage of American actress Jennifer Aniston's childlessness, one could easily assume that her childfree state is neither a wilfully chosen nor desired life trajectory.

Aniston, like many other female celebrities of a certain age who have no children, has been persistently harassed with "whens" and "whys" in relation to her reproductive status. Indeed, so relentless was the scrutinizing of her unused womb that it led her to publish a detailed statement in the *Huffington Post* criticizing the tabloids' "perpetuation of this notion that women are somehow incomplete, unsuccessful or unhappy if they're not married with children." Childless women are regularly depicted by the media in a pitying light; these sources are unwilling to recognize that their nonmaternal state may, in fact, be a chosen life path.

As Laura Carroll informs us, the regulation of women's reproductive choices is closely aligned with policies of pronatalism, which is the idea that bearing and raising children should be the central aim of a woman's life (10). She continues her definition, describing pronatalism as "a strong social force [that] includes a collection of beliefs so embedded that they have come to be seen as true" (11). Pronatalism, according to Carroll, "furthers the agenda of power structures such as the church, state, and industry—not individuals" (12). The predominance of pronatalist policies in many cultures and societies worldwide renders it difficult for any woman to act outside of these prescriptive structures and, furthermore, have their childfree state validated. As Madeline Cain remarks, choosing to be childfree continues to be a misunderstood choice, as it "confuses us and challenges our set beliefs" about society and, more specifically, femininity (2). Subsequently, it is much easier, she notes, "to ignore childlessness rather than face it" (2). Carolyn Morell is highly critical of the conflation of femininity with fertility because it suggests that there is only one right way to be a proper woman. She writes as follows:

> A woman is a person. She may bear children; she may not. She may rear children; she may not. She may be deeply concerned about the lives of children or she may not, whether or not she is a mother. Yet since the nineteenth century, motherhood has been seen as the reason for women's existence. The collapse of womanhood in motherhood ... is inaccurate and morally unacceptable. Maternalism splits the category of woman into good and bad, successful and failed, based on the primary reproduction role. (140)

Following on from this idea that a good woman is mother and a bad woman is a non-mother is Lisa Downing's theory on the childless woman as perhaps the ultimate selfish subject in the eyes of society: "The willfully childfree woman and selfish woman occupy the same cultural imaginary terrain" (107). Given that females are socialized from birth into the role of motherhood and taught that it is their nature, the childless or childfree woman inevitably ends up being branded abnormal. Downing states, "The allegedly 'natural' association between women and the loving, caring work of motherhood means that to refuse this role places the individual woman in a position of being aberrant with regard to social expectations" (105). Downing's work on women without children incites us to reconfigure our negative conceptualization of this particular life choice and instead view it as female self-realization and affirmation rather than failure and self-centred egotism. Elisabeth Badinter also draws our attention to the widespread trope of the childfree woman as selfish but goes even further than this: She highlights the overt pathologization of women who choose not to have children. Women who are voluntarily childless, Badinter informs us, are often (wrongly) deemed to be suffering from unresolved psychological and mental health issues (143). This erroneous and highly negative labelling of women without children is commented on once again by Natalie Edwards in her study of the childfree woman by choice in French and Francophone women's writing. In a similar vein to Downing and Badinter, Edwards uncovers the numerous pernicious stereotypes that are associated with not having children: "It is time to change such attitudes and assumptions that underpin our definition of femininity" (4).

Adjusting the societal mindset in relation to the childfree woman is crucial when one considers the steadily rising numbers within this particular demographic worldwide. As Olivia Petter highlights in her article for *The Independent*, fewer women are having children than ever before. Petter cites the following example: For those born in 1946, just 9 per cent had no children, whereas for those born in 1970, this figure has risen to 17 per cent, nearly one fifth of women. Badinter makes a comparable observation, noting that the phenomenon of childlessness is becoming more and more widespread, particularly in English-speaking countries, almost doubling in figures since the close of the twentieth century (131). Whereas some of this childlessness, Petter admits, is connected to circumstance, at the same time, there is a growing number of women who are freely choosing not to have children for one reason or another. It is vital, therefore, that we, as a society, accept this life choice as legitimate and overhaul the prejudicial way that the woman without child is configured in the cultural imagination. Becoming a mother, as Badinter remarks, is not necessarily the summit of all women's aspirations (131).

Articulating the Choice to Be Childfree

The first two decades of the twenty-first century have witnessed a marked surge in the number of publications by women on the topic of voluntary childlessness. A common thread in these texts is the way in which the woman without child continues to be viewed as suspect by society and is the victim of countless unfounded stereotypes. However, far from simply being a lament for the despicable state of the childfree/childless woman, these texts are also empowering manifestos that sketch out the fruitful possibilities of alternative trajectories for women which do not include motherhood. In the following paragraphs, I will identify and discuss a selection of these texts so as to demonstrate how the discussion on non-motherhood is evolving and making itself heard in the public arena.

One such text is, of course, the now widely popular collection of essays entitled *Selfish, Shallow, and Self-Absorbed*, edited by Megan Daum. The writers who feature in this book (and who share their own personal experiences of nonparenthood) carefully reflect on why not having children is more often than not met by sharp criticism and incredulity from mainstream society. Together, they make a convincing case for why parenthood is not necessarily the right option for everyone and show the reader that what it means to live a full life is much more diverse and nuanced. Daum's text is concerned with exposing and correcting the misconceptions associated with the voluntarily childless and challenging "the taboo of a life other than parenthood" (10). As one of the contributors to Daum's collection remarks, it is wholly "unreasonable, not to mention sexist, to suggest that because all women have the biological capacity to have children, they all should; and that those who don't are either in denial or psychologically damaged" (Houston 171). This is one of the key points that emerges across the body of essays—that is, the questioning of the so-called maternal instinct and the idea that all women naturally long to have a child. The overall tone of the book is one of self-assuredness and refusal to apologize for not conforming to societal expectations. As Jeanne Safer explains, choosing to be childfree means acting "authentically in line with your own feelings.... It is an act of willed self-assertion, of standing your ground on your own behalf" (192).

Cailtin Moran devotes a chapter to the childless/childfree woman in *How to Be a Woman*. Deploring the fact that women are constantly harassed about their reproductive status, she writes: "For some reason, the world really wants to know when women are having children. It likes them to have planned this.... It wants them to be very clear and upfront about it" (235). When a woman reveals that she does not, in fact, want to have children, "the world is apt to go decidedly peculiar" (Moran 236). The decision is not accepted as final or resolute; instead, it is patronizingly presumed that the woman will "change her mind when [she] meets the right man" (236) and will end up having babies.

Moran remarks with sarcasm: "[Women] might go through silly, adolescent phases of pretending that it's something that they have no interest in—but, when push comes to shove, womanhood is a cul-de-sac that ends in Mothercare, and that's the end of that" (236). She also notes that given the prevailing societal expectations concerning women, deciding not to have children can be a very difficult lifepath to take when the overall atmosphere "is worryingly inconducive" to saying no to motherhood (241). Similar to Downing, Moran observes that women who choose not to have children are branded as selfish, and it is inferred that their life is fundamentally lacking. Moran underlines the societal tendency to "make women feel that their narrative has ground to a halt in their thirties if they don't finish things properly and have children" (241). She develops this further: "Men and women alike have convinced themselves of a dragging belief: that somehow women are incomplete without children.... As if a woman somehow remains a child herself until she has her own children—that she can only achieve 'elder' status by dint of having produced someone younger" (241). Moran's intention is not to devalue motherhood in any way (indeed, she is a mother herself) but rather to show that non-motherhood, is not a lesser way of living. She emphasizes the importance of being true to oneself and valuing alternative pathways to fulfillment. To believe that no action will ever be the equal of giving birth is to betray the immense capabilities of the thinking, creative, and productive woman (Moran 245). Moran calls on feminism to have a zero-tolerance attitude towards the ostracizing of women without children. She advocates a valorization of each individual woman's "becoming," whatever direction that may follow, and defends freedom of self-actualization: "In the 21st century, it can't be about who we might make, and what *they* might do any more. It has to be about who we are, and what we're going to do" (Moran 246).

L'envers du landau (*The Other Side of the Cradle*), a convincing and powerful treatise on non-motherhood and penned by Québec author Lucie Joubert, also merits attention in our discussion of emerging voices on voluntary childlessness. A discursive essay comprised of five succinct chapters, *L'envers du landau* effectively exposes and subsequently deconstructs many of the prejudicial myths associated with non-motherhood. As the title itself indicates, it is a text that aims to oppose and reverse received notions and social discourse concerning motherhood by speaking from an alternative position. In line with the scholarship cited so far, Joubert argues that the non-mother continues to be viewed as an aberrant figure of femininity in society (16), possibly more so than ever before, given recent turns towards new momism and postfeminist retreatism with their emphasis on the reprisal of traditional feminine roles. In order to highlight the extent to which the non-mother is rendered "other," Joubert, a voluntary non-mother herself, likens her open admission of this choice to a "coming-out" (19). Her text then serves as an example to other voluntary non-mothers who have been silenced by the dominant pronatalist discourse that currently presides in Western advanced-capitalist society and who have had their life choice denigrated to what Joubert describes as "the unspeakable" (18). The first line of attack that Joubert adopts in *L'envers du landau* is a rigorous deconstruction of the injurious myths and clichés associated with the non-mother. She skillfully takes each one and exposes how it both distorts and misrepresents the reality of the non-mother—for example, immaturity, egocentrism, child hating, dysfunctional, substitute mothering, and so on. Astutely, she turns the questions that are fired at non-mothers on their head. Subsequently, "Won't you regret not having children?" becomes "What if there are women who regret having children?" and, similarly, "Why don't you want children?" becomes the rarely asked "Why do you want children?" (39)

This question of "Why do you want children" as opposed to "Why don't you have children" resurfaces in Sheila Heiti's formidable

Motherhood. Heiti asks if the desire to have children is sometimes aligned with a fear of not belonging. She wonders, "Do I want children because I want to be admired as the admirable sort of woman who has children? Because I want to be seen as a normal sort of woman?" (22). Heiti urges women to live by their own rules rather than conforming to someone else's idea of how they should be: "Ask only whether you are living your values, not whether the boxes are ticked" (28). At the same time, she recognizes the difficulties involved in transgressing the norms and that sometimes the path towards voluntary childlessness can be suffused with ambivalence: "There is a kind of sadness in not wanting the things that give so many other people their life's meaning. There can be sadness at not living out a more universal story—the supposed life cycle.... There is a bit of a let-down feeling when the great things that happen in the lives of others—you don't actually want those things for yourself" (23).

Heiti makes a number of salient remarks in relation to societal motivations for keeping women enmeshed in motherhood and caregiving. Most strikingly, she asserts that society is afraid of the potential power of the woman without child: "A woman must have children because she must be occupied.... There is something threatening about a woman who is not occupied with children. There is something at-loose-ends feeling about such a woman. What is she going to do instead? What sort of trouble will she make?" (32)

This is a point that is reiterated by Jacqueline Rose, who boldly purports that "by refusing to be mothers, women have the power to bring the world to its end" (48). Meanwhile, Heiti elaborates on the pervasive sense of pressure felt by women to reproduce and "of life standing by, twiddling its thumbs, waiting for me to have a child ... tapping its foot, waiting for me to give birth" (42). Heiti also adds that because it is often seen to be the ultimate deviation from the norm, it is never enough for a woman to simply announce that she does not want to have children. Instead, "You have to have some big plan or idea of what you're going to do instead. And it better be something great. And you had better be able to tell it convincingly—before it even happens— what the arc of your life will be" (Heiti 51). Like Joubert, Heiti reflects on the articulation of the choice to childfree as resembling a "coming-out" moment, making reference to a suppressing of the true self for fear of reprimand or rejection: "For how long am I expected to live as though there is a second me, hiding somewhere inside? When will it finally feel safe to prioritize the me I know?" (190). Indeed, Heiti makes an overt comparison between choosing to be childfree and queerness, thus heightening the image of non-motherhood as a "coming-out" experience. "Why don't we understand some people who don't want children as those with a different, perhaps biologically different, orientation? Wanting not to have children could even be called a sexual orientation, for what is more tied to sex than the desire to procreate or not?" (161)

Perhaps the most feminist aspect of Heiti's text, however, is the work that it does to undo the division of mother from non-mother and the pitting of women against one another based on their life choices. Heiti makes it quite clear to the reader that choosing to live one way is not necessarily a criticism of every other way of living. For this reason, the mother and non-mother should not be positioned as threats to and polar opposites of one another. Of the mother and the non-mother, she writes as follows:

> We both have everything and nothing at all.... Neither one of us has more than the other, and neither one of us has less. It is so hard, I think, to see this: that our paths equal something the same; that having a child reflexively or not having one doubtfully are equal lives ... the childless and the mothers are equivalent ... there is an exact equivalence and an equality, equal in emptiness and equal in fullness, equal in experiences had and equal in experiences lost, neither path better and neither path worse. (239)

Heiti is hopeful that, in time, improved dialogue and better under-standing will lead to a more supportive relationship between women who choose to have children and those who choose not to become mothers.

Terminology and Title

I would now like to briefly consider some of the terminology employed in this collection as well as the title of the book itself. As has been noted in numerous scholarly publications, the terms that are used to refer to those who have voluntarily chosen not to have children remain largely problematic and indicative of negative social attitudes. The main ones in current usage include "non-mother" (also seen as "nomo"), "unchilded," "without child," "childless," and "childfree," not to men-tion the now outdated but still iterated "barren." As Natalie Edwards reflects in her study of voluntary childlessness in contemporary women's writing in French, "It is unfortunate that so many of these expressions insist upon a lack; the suffix *less*, the prefixes *non* and *un* and the conjunction *without* are all predicated upon something missing and proclaim the non-normativity of this choice" (8). Indeed, even the term "childfree," coined as a more positive alternative to the negative labels listed above, carries, as Edwards notes, "the potential to aggravate tension between the childless and the child-bearing majority" (9). Edwards continues: "Part of the stigma to which the voluntarily childless have been subjected is due to real or perceived accusations from parents that those without children cast judgement upon their lifestyles. In view of this, the label 'childfree', despite its originally good intentions, may be greeted as superior, smug or glib" (9).

Amy Blackstone (a contributor to this collection) also comments on the dispute surrounding the terminology. Blackstone explains that the term "childfree" came into circulation to distinguish voluntary nonparenthood from involuntary nonparenthood. Although the term is useful in this respect, Blackstone does recognize that it is not without its critics, as some compare it to common expressions, such as "smoke free," thus imbuing it with a desire to be rid of children. However, Blackstone argues that the term can and should be employed in a positive light: "It's an affirmative take on a contested identity.... It's about joyfully claiming our own life choices. It's about embracing the conscious and intentional choice that those of us who've opted out of parenthood have made" (48-49). What is clear from the ongoing debate concerning the terminology, however, is that there is no one ideal term to describe the position of opting out of motherhood or parenthood more generally. Subsequently, in the chapters that follow, the authors use a wide variety of terms, with their justification for the choice of term given in each case.

It is worth commenting on the title selected for the overall collection of essays: *The Truth about (M)Otherhood. Choosing to Be Childfree.* The initial inspiration for the title stems from Melanie Notkin's 2014 publication, *Otherhood: Modern Women Finding a New Kind of Happiness.* Notkin uses the term "Otherhood" to refer to a growing demographic of women without children, a demographic, she argues, that lacks visibility and definition. Although the text concentrates on those who are childless not through choice but through circumstance, Notkin does recognize the rise of this new lifestyle through choice as well and aims to mount a challenge to the prejudicial stereotypes associated with women without children. In contrast to Notkin's text, the key focus of this collection is the examination of both the process and state of voluntarily choosing to be childfree. Until recently, freely articulating such a desire had mostly been a prohibited topic. However, as this collection demonstrates, given the growing number of women choosing this particular pathway in life, it is no longer possible or ethical to continue ignoring these "other" voices. This brings us to the coinage of the term "(M)Otherhood" and its use in the context of this collection. The reference to "Otherhood" is intertwined not only with the affirmative idea of choosing an alternative life path but also the negative way in which society persists in "othering" women without children, rendering them abject for opting to exist beyond the expected confines of femininity. Including "(M)" before the term "Otherhood" has the double function of allowing these women to simultaneously situate themselves outside of the institution of motherhood while retaining a connection to the dialogue around the subject. It is important to realize that women who decline motherhood have often thought long and hard about their decision, engaging with theories and examining their choice from every angle and, therefore, have much to offer to and should be part of discussions on the topic. As Badinter remarks, it is usually the case that women who choose not to have children engage with and assess the responsibilities of motherhood more rigorously than those who take them on with little reflection (144). Subsequently, one of the key aims of this book is to listen not only to what these women's stories can tell us about not being a mother but also to what they have to say about the institution of motherhood itself, particularly in relation to mothering ideals and expectations.

Navigating (M)Otherhood

The essays gathered together in this collection represent a diverse and interdisciplinary range of perspectives on the decision to remain childfree. The contributors examine this life choice against the backdrop of society, literature, cultural norms, television, race, the workplace, poverty, religion, and legal structures. Although the articles adopt variegated approaches to their analyses depending on their specific discipline, the shared objective of the collection is, nonetheless, sharply defined and always to the fore of the discussion. Underpinning all the contributions is an ardent desire to challenge the dominant perceptions of the childfree woman by choice and, alternatively, present this stance as an empowering and positive experience.

The collection opens with a coauthored chapter (Clarke et al.), which questions both the "motherhood imperative" (the notion that all women must and should want to have children) and the concept of innate "maternal instinct" (that is, that all women naturally desire and know how to care for children). Victoria Clark et al. also draw our attention to the lack of clarity that exists around the childfree by choice phenomenon and our poor understanding of the motivations involved in choosing this lifepath. It is assumed, they argue, that the childfree woman by choice can be easily categorized and reduced to a singular definition when, in fact, the reasons behind this lifepath are often complex and disparate.

Following on from this chapter is Helene Cummins's rich discussion on what she labels WINKS (single women with income and no kids). Cummins provides us with a broad overview of the global statistics for the childfree by choice, which clearly demonstrates the growth in this particular demographic which, in turn, strengthens one of the core arguments of this collection— the need to devote more critical attention and accord more visibility to this sector of society. As Cummins asserts, it is no longer acceptable to brand the childfree by choice as socially defective. She, thus, deconstructs the stereotypes of the childfree woman by choice, particularly where the expectation of regret later in life is concerned. In addition to this, Cummins alerts us to important issues surrounding the childfree woman by choice in the workplace.

In the next chapter, Stuart Gietel-Basten et al. concentrate their discussion on a close study of the terminology employed in referencing the childfree by choice. Based on the results of a survey carried out among childfree meetup groups, the contributors carefully dissect the semantic differences between childfree, childless, voluntary childless, involuntary childless, and childfree by choice as perceived by the members of these groups themselves. The experience of not having children, they contest, is acutely individual, and it is wrong to assume homogeneity within this demographic. Again, this finding points to a key objective of this overall collection— the intent to highlight the diversity of motivations and contextual factors involved in the decision not to have children.

The fourth chapter, authored by Amy Blackstone, shares many of the same aims as the opening chapter by Clarke et al. in that it questions systems of pronatal heteronormativity and ideologies that naturalize motherhood. Blackstone rightly highlights and denounces the ongoing stigma of deviance associated with the childfree woman by choice and is highly critical of gender norms that expect women to procreate.

Cassandra Chaney's contribution to the collection introduces a personal perspective, which she describes as an "autoethnographic gaze." By adopting this unique approach, Chaney can reflect on her own position as a childfree woman by choice, specifically as a Black African American academic. However, she also turns the gaze outwards to society, asking pertinent questions regarding women's reproductive rights. Most importantly, though, Chaney's chapter considers the choice to be childfree against the backdrop of race—what it means to be a Black African American woman who does not want children in a culture that valorizes motherhood so strongly.

Victoria Team's chapter asks us to expand our definition of the childfree woman by choice to incorporate the abandonment of infants by domestic servants and beggars in Ethiopia. Deprived of adequate contraception and access to abortion, these women are forced to proceed with unwanted pregnancies, and it is only after birth has occurred that they can execute the choice to be childfree through abandoning the newborn. Subsequently, Team's chapter incites us to reflect on the privileges of middle-class, white, Western women, who although still suffering from stigmatization, at least have the possibility of choosing not to have children, even if it is not always socially sanctioned.

The two contributions from Joselyn K. Leimbach and Nathalie Ségeral bring us into the domain of textual analysis and the fictional representation of the childfree woman by choice, which, of course, has much to say about social constructions of femininity and the broader cultural imagination. Leimbach focuses on screen representation and explores a popular television series. She contests that there is a dearth of positive televisual representations of childfree women by choice and uses her example to illustrate the need for more onscreen characters and scripts that disrupt normative gender standards. The character on whom she focuses her analysis has unambiguously embraced the childfree path and is depicted as accomplished and satisfied in all aspects of her life, thus demonstrating that procreation is not always necessary for self-fulfillment.

Ségeral discusses the choice to be childfree from the perspective of contemporary French and Francophone literature. Using two texts for her analysis, Ségeral, like Leimbach, questions the trope of motherhood as the pathway to ultimate fulfillment for women. The texts that she has chosen overtly challenge ideas of maternal instinct and instead portray motherhood as a social construction that demands women's adherence and is punitive to those who deviate from this trajectory. Ségeral also interrogates the various layers of meaning attached to the choice to be childfree, again reiterating one of the main points that emerges from this collection—that is, the importance of respecting diversity in definitions of the childfree by choice stance.

The concluding chapter, authored by Judith Dunkelberger Wouk, ventures into the realm of religion, specifically Judaism. Wouk astutely observes the impact of religious beliefs on the choice to be childfree. Through close analysis of the depiction of motherhood and childfree women in the Hebrew Bible, Wouk exposes the difficulties involved in transgressing the norms associated with traditional womanhood within a culture that is so heavily family orientated and convinced of every woman's innate desire to procreate. How then, Wouk asks, can the woman who wishes of her own free will to remain childfree situate herself within such a pronatalist culture?

Together, these chapters function as a feminist testimony for the right to be childfree and to have this choice validated by society. By unveiling the persistent stereotypes and challenges faced by women who do not wish to have children but also pointing to this growing demographic in society, the contributors make it clear that negative attitudes to alternative reproductive stances must be dismantled.

Rethinking (M)Otherhood

By placing these contributions alongside each other, this collection intends that the decision to remain childfree be viewed as an active, determined, and self-fulfilling choice; it cannot be reduced, as is typically the case, to an existence associated with lack. As Blackstone remarks, "Childfree people—those who have made the explicit and intentional choice not to have kids—are not incomplete and they're not missing out, at least not any more than any person who chooses not to do something because they have no interest in it" (27).

The deliberately wide scope of the volume highlights the diversity of experiences contained within the childfree by choice pathway. Non-motherhood and, by extension, nonparenthood are entirely valid life choices, and in the current global context of extreme environmental crisis, it could even be argued that, in some instances, it is the most ethical option. Where pronatalism is concerned, despite falling birthrates and ageing populations in some countries, it is wholly inappropriate to coerce women into motherhood by depicting it as the ultimate life goal and, worse, as inseparable from natural femininity. Choosing to be childfree is an empowering decision that exhibits intimate self-awareness on the part of the individual. It is also, however, genuinely revolutionary on a broader social level in that by confidently opting for a reproductive choice that continues to met by disapproval, childfree women by choice pose a challenge to traditional definitions of womanhood and are paving the way for more nuanced and inclusive reconfigurations of femininity.

Endnotes

1. Retaining the hyphen in the terms "non-mother" and "non-motherhood" denotes a specific theoretical position. The hyphen importantly indicates both separation from but also involvement with ideologies of motherhood. Given that the choice not to mother, as illustrated in this collection, is often bound up with careful reflection on the practice of mothering itself, it is essential that the terms used to signify those who decide against motherhood effectively convey the double-coded nature of this particular identity, an identity which is at once outside but also connected to maternal discourse. To remove the hyphen from these terms would, I feel, collapse the non-mother into the dominant figure of the mother, whereas the hyphen, on the other hand, preserves the destabilising potential of the non-mother with regard to normative constructions of womanhood. Finally, the hyphen is suggestive of an identity in transit or in flux, an identity that is still evolving, establishing its own voice and gradually claiming its own space, as is the case for the wide range of non-mothers discussed in this volume.

Works Cited

Aniston, Jennifer. "For the Record." *The Huffington Post*, 12 July 2016, www.huffpost.com/entry/for-the-record_b_57855586e4b03fc3ee 4e626f. Accessed 4 Jan. 2021.

Badinter, Elisabeth. *The Conflict. How Modern Motherhood Undermines the Status of Women*. Translated by Adriana Hunter. Metropolitan Books, 2011.

Blackstone, Amy. *Childfree by Choice. The Movement Redefining Family and Creating a New Age of Independence*. Dutton, 2019.

Cain, Madeline. *The Childless Revolution. What it Means to be Childfree Today*. Perseus, 2002.

Carroll, Laura, *The Baby Matrix*. CreateSpace, 2012.

Cramer, Renée Ann. *Pregnant with the Stars. Watching and Wanting the Celebrity Baby Bump*. Stanford University Press, 2015.

Daum, Megan. *Selfish, Shallow and Self-Absorbed. Sixteen Writers on the Decision Not to Have Kids*. Picador, 2015.

Downing, Lisa. *Selfish Women*. Routledge, 2019.

Edwards, Natalie. *Voicing Voluntary Childlessness: Narratives of Non-Mothering in French*. Peter Lang, 2015.

Heiti, Sheila. *Motherhood*. Henry Holt, 2018.

Houston, Pam. "The Trouble with Having it All." *Selfish, Shallow and Self-Absorbed. Sixteen Writers on the Decision Not to Have Kids*, edited by Megan Daum, Picador, 2015, pp. 163-84.

Joubert, Lucie. *L'Envers du landau*. Trytiques, 2010.

Moran, Caitlin. *How to Be a Woman*. Ebury, 2012.

Morell, Carolyn. *Unwomanly Conduct. The Challenges of Intentional Childlessness*. Routledge, 1994.

Notkin, Melanie. *Otherhood. Modern Women Finding a New Kind of Happiness*. Seal Press, 2014.

Petter, Olivia. "More Childless Women Than Ever Before." *The Independent*. 9 Aug. 2017. www.independent.co.uk/life-style/ childless-women-rise-more-ever-fertility-crisis-menopause-career-study-reveals-a7882496.html. Accessed 1 Sept. 2020.

Rose, Jacqueline. *Mothers. An Essay on Love and Cruelty*. Faber and Faber, 2018.

Safer, Jeanne. "Beyond *Beyond Motherhood*." *Selfish, Shallow and Self-Absorbed. Sixteen Writers on the Decision Not to Have Kids*, edited by Megan Daum, Picador, 2015, pp.185-96.

Section I

Literature Review of Childfree Women

Chapter One

A Critical Review of the Interdisciplinary Literature on Voluntary Childlessness

Victoria Clarke, Nikki Hayfield, Naomi Moller,
and Virginia Braun

Introduction

This chapter provides a critical review of the interdisciplinary research on voluntary childlessness and examines some of the problematic assumptions underpinning the literature and the image of the childfree woman that emerges as a result. This review is not intended to be a comprehensive overview of this literature, but rather a feminist engagement with the frameworks and ideology that shape and limit it. One of the reasons why the motives, characteristics, and personality of women who choose to be childfree have been of interest to researchers is because there is a social assumption that having children is a natural human instinct. Pronatalist social ideologies frame parenting as deeply fulfilling, as essential for human happiness and a meaningful life, and as a marker of a successful adulthood (Morison et al.; Moller and Clarke). Furthermore, a connection exists between motherhood and femininity—sometimes referred to as the "motherhood imperative" (Giles, Shaw, and Morgan; Gillespie, "When No Means No") or the "motherhood mandate" (Russo)—that results in a social expectation that all women naturally desire motherhood. In this chapter, we explore assumptions relating to pronatalism and coercive pronatalism, fixed categories, women's social responsibility for reproduction, and heteronormativity, and we show how feminist researchers have begun to problematize some of the pronatalist and, arguably, racist, heteronormative, and sexist assumptions underpinning voluntary childlessness research. We conclude by outlining a framework for future research that avoids perpetuating these problematic assumptions and the associated view of childfree women as regretful, lonely, and depressed.

Defining Voluntary Childlessness

Pronatalist assumptions have shaped research on the childless population. One example is the preoccupation shown by early researchers with determining who exactly counts as voluntarily childless (Houseknecht, "Voluntary Childlessness"); arguably, this focus was driven by the assumption that those who choose not to have children are unnatural. Yet despite this early focus, research has been plagued by a lack of definitional clarity (Park), with certain groups of women, including single women and lesbians, assumed to be childless by default rather than through choice. Furthermore, assumptions about who is responsible for reproductive choices and who should reproduce have resulted in a selective focus on particular—often socially privileged—groups. A reliance on marriage in early definitions of voluntary childlessness reflected a presumption that only married heterosexuals make reproductive choices (Moore). For example, Houseknecht's ("Voluntary Childlessness") pathways to childlessness reflected this heteronormative assumption. Her early articulator "expresses the intention to remain childless relatively early in life, *even before marriage*" (our emphasis, 370), whereas the postponer "arrives at a childless decision through a series of postponements *after marriage* (our emphasis, 370). Research from the United States (U.S.) indicates that only 53 per cent of childfree people have been married (Abma and Martinez). Consequently, definitions that rely on marriage exclude almost half of this population. Despite this, the focus in voluntary childlessness research has been almost exclusively on the motives and characteristics of married (or, more recently, partnered) heterosexual childfree women. Studies that include, or focus on, single and lesbian and bisexual women are rare (Addie and Brownlow; Agrillo and Nelini).

A Note on Terminology

The terminology used to describe women who choose not to parent has been much discussed. Terms like (chosen or voluntary) "childlessness" and "non-mother" have been criticized by feminist researchers because they imply a lack or an absence and that women's lives are in some way deficient if they do not have children (Blackstone; Doyle, Pooley, and Breen; Gillespie, "Voluntary Childlessness"; Kelly). At the same time, the term "childfree" has been rejected by many women because it is perceived to glorify non-motherhood (Moore). Feminist research has found that often women do not use a particular term (e.g., childless, childfree, and nonparent) to describe themselves but instead simply state that they do not want to have children (Moore). Their framing is one of making a choice about not wanting children rather than embracing being childfree as an aspect of their identities. We also note that all these terms imply that there are no children in these women's lives, whereas many women without biological (or adopted, fostered, or step-) children have professional roles working with children and/or are involved with friends' and families' children.

In acknowledging these tensions as well as the fact that there is no one widely accepted term in feminist research, we use both "chosen" or "voluntary childlessness" and "childfree" throughout this chapter. (We only use the term "childless" when reporting research that uses this term or to refer to the broader category of women who do not have children, including both the voluntary and involuntary childless.)

We are: a white, middle-class, disabled and nonheterosexual woman in her late-forties, who is childless through circumstance (VC); a white, working/middle-class, nondisabled bisexual woman in her early forties, who by her mid-twenties had gradually come to the conclusion that she did not want to have children (NH); a white, middle-class, nondisabled and heterosexual woman in her early fifties, who was planning to have children since childhood and now has three teenagers (NM); and a middle-class, Pākehā (white), disabled, and heterosexual woman in her late-forties, who never wanted children and sought tubal ligation in her mid-thirties (VB).

Problematic Assumption One: Childfree People Can Be Easily Categorized

As noted, voluntary childlessness researchers have been preoccupied with classifying and categorising childfree people, and a common distinction is between early deciders and perpetual postponers. These and other categories have also informed feminist research on women's experiences of childfreedom. For example, U.S. sociologists Braelin Settle and Krista Brumley (see also Gillespie, "Voluntary Child-lessness") divide their participants into active deciders (women who are certain they did not want children, often making this decision early in life) and passive deciders (women who experience no strong push towards or pull away from children; not having children is something that just happened). Leslie Cannold, however, argued that the categories of "early articulators" and "postponers" are too individual-istic and overlook the social context in which childlessness is lived. Furthermore, based on interviews with thirty-five U.S. and Australian women who believed they were fertile but did not currently have children, she concluded that these terms do not appropriately capture the ways in which women come to be childfree. She proposed two alternative categories of "childless by choice" (to describe women who are firmly committed to remaining childless) and "childless by circum-stance." The latter included subcategories of "thwarted mothers" who want children but encounter restraints, such as a partner's lack of desire, and "waiters and watchers," who are ambivalent about parenting and undecided about whether they will have children. However, other research has problematized such fixed categories.

Rachel Shaw's experiential analysis of interviews with three voluntarily childless women in the United Kingdom highlighted a complexity and fluidity in women's journeys to childlessness. She argued that distinguishing between "choice" and "circumstance" was too simplistic to capture her participants' experiences. Similarly, other studies have begun showing that many women, even those who might be classed as early articulators, do not view the choice to be childfree as a one-off decision. Rather the decision is made and remade across the life-course and in relation to changing circumstances (Hayfield et al.; Morell). Most recently, Amy Blackstone and Mahala Stewart interviewed twenty-one women (and ten men) in the U.S. and concluded that their decision-making processes were complex. In contrast to some previous findings, most participants had made a conscious decision not to parent, yet this decision was not a single event but described as a "working decision" and "a progressive one that developed over time" (300). Participants regularly (re)considered their decision; hence, choosing to be childfree was a process rather than a single occurrence (Blackstone and Stewart). Such research blurs the boundaries of fixed categorization of childfree people and suggests that future researchers in this area should think carefully about the definitions they use. Definitions of the childfree population have been strongly influenced by pronatalism, so too has the research, as demonstrated by the tendency of researchers to focus on negative outcomes.

Problematic Assumption Two: Childless Means Negative Outcomes

"A Path Not Taken: A Cultural Analysis of Regrets and Childlessness in the Lives of Older Women" (Alexander et al.)

"Loneliness and Depression in Middle and Old Age: Are the Childless More Vulnerable?" (Koropeckyj-Cox)

"What Childless Older People Give: Is the Generational Link Broken?" (Albertini and Kohli)

"Is Being Childless Detrimental to a Woman's Health and Well-Being across Her Life Course?" (Graham)

These journal article titles—from the voluntary childlessness and broader childlessness literature—clearly show that childlessness (whether chosen or not) is often associated with negative consequences, such as feelings of loneliness, social isolation, depression, regret, and a failure to be a productive and generative citizen who contributes to social reproduction, that is the work required to turn children and young people into productive adults (Blackstone and Greenleaf). Even when researchers seek to challenge these assumptions, they, nonetheless, use them to frame academic discussions of both voluntary and involuntary childlessness. Thus, childlessness is often presented as a (growing) social problem, and much anxiety is expressed about the "far reaching consequences" (Kemkes-Grottenthaler 214) of increases in childlessness and the associated fall in birthrates (Basten) to below replacement level (Boddington and Didham). Since childlessness has been associated with health risks for women (e.g. Marri, Ahn, and Buchman) and a burdensome old age (e.g., Dykstra, "Older Adult Loneliness"), there has been a focus on the costs of childlessness in old age (this body of literature does not typically distinguish between the voluntary and involuntary childless). This research shows that older childless people are more likely than parents to be in institutional care (Koropeckyj-Cox and Call), be reliant on paid care, have smaller social networks—the widowed childless population in particular are vulnerable to social deprivation—have poorer health, and die earlier (Dykstra, "Childless Old Age"). In short, research on childless people has largely painted a gloomy picture of old age and presented a childless old age as one associated with lack and liability (Kohli and Albertini). In contrast to this framing, more recent research has sought to reconceptualize older childless people as a social resource and to explore what they contribute to their families and wider society. For example, research has shown that they are more engaged in volunteering, community work, and civic society than others and often have more diverse social networks (Kelly; Kohli and Albertini).

Problematic Assumption Three: Pronatalism

Arguably, the tendency to paint a gloomy picture of childlessness, particularly in later life, may stem from the pronatalistic understandings that lead to valuing women only to the extent to which they birth and/or raise children. Unsurprisingly, feminist researchers have rejected the social problem framework and instead turned their attention towards pronatalism in the wider society. Such research documents the extent and nature of the stigmatization of women who choose to be childfree (e.g., Jamison, Franzini, and Kaplan; Letherby; Rowlands and Lee; Vinson, Mollen, and Smith) and explores its impact on their everyday lives (Gillespie, "When No Means No"; Turnbull, Graham, and Taket). In one such study, Stephanie Rich et al. conducted a phenomenological analysis of the lived experiences of five childfree women in Australia. These women experienced stigmatization in the form of others' assumptions that they already were, or would inevitably want to be, mothers. Their accounts evidenced how childlessness was perceived as abnormal and unnatural. For example, these women reported that others perceived them as unhappy or as having something wrong with them, and they felt required to justify or excuse their childfree status because it differed from social norms. They also felt discredited in various ways, including being identified as selfish, as lacking compassion, and as being unconcerned about community or the environment.

Feminist researchers have explored how childfree women make sense of their identities as women in a social context in which motherhood and womanhood are equated (Peterson and Engwall) and how they negotiate and manage the stigma associated with being childfree (Addie and Brownlow; Doyle, Pooley, and Breen; Park). Helen Peterson and Kristina Engwall interviewed thirty Swedish childfree women to explore their embodied experiences of being childfree and how they rejected and resisted pronatalist understandings that conflate being a woman with being a mother. Participants positioned themselves as having a lack of biological urge to reproduce, having what the authors termed "silent bodies" (376). Some participants did not rule out that these "silent bodies" may one day "speak" to them; hence, only a few had made permanent contraceptive choices. The women's accounts of their childfree bodies as "'lacking,' 'missing,' 'absence,' 'incorrect' and 'failing'" (382) also evidenced pronatalistic notions of motherhood as an essential requirement of femininity. However, some women reframed childless bodies as more attractive and feminine than those that were, or had been, pregnant. The authors concluded that cultural links between femininity and motherhood remain and argued that these women rejected traditional pronatalistic understandings in order to create their own positive childfree feminine identity.

With regard to negotiating stigma, feminist psychologists analysed email interviews with, and posts to researcher-generated online forums made by, ninety-eight childfree women and men to explore their responses to childlessness stigma (Morison et al). They found that participants both emphasized and disavowed choice. Similar to the women in Peterson and Engwall's research, some participants positioned themselves as "naturally childfree," describing their childlessness as innate and immutable. These researchers argue that this positioning can be understood as a strategy for managing the stigma of voluntary childlessness through disavowing choice and minimizing responsibility for childfreedom. The participants' childlessness just is. Thus, arguably the stigma of chosen childlessness is such that it shapes even how people explain their decision to be childfree. In 1987, Houseknecht argued that women and men rationalize their decision by drawing on "an acceptable vocabulary of motives previously established by the historical epoch and the social structure in which one lives" (316). The notion that one is naturally or essentially childfree, thus, appears to be a currently acceptable framing of childfreedom.

Problematic Assumption Four: That Women Are Socially Responsible for Reproduction

A key assumption underpinning voluntary childlessness research is that women are socially responsible for reproduction (Almeling and Waggoner). The overwhelming majority of research on childlessness has focused on women—particularly on white, middle-class, and nondisabled women in relationships with men or who identify as heterosexual. Researchers have interrogated their decision making, motives, and pathways to childfreedom (Settle and Brumley), their attitudes towards motherhood and children (Kemkes-Grottenthaler), their personality and sex role orientation (Bram), their socio-demographic characteristics (Houseknecht, "Timing of the Decision"), their psychological and physical health and wellbeing (Callan, "The Personal and Marital"; Graham), and their feelings of regret (DeLyser). Although women's reproductive decision making and experiences of childfreedom should be of interest, particularly to feminist researchers with a long-standing tradition of 'giving voice' to women's experiences (Wilkinson), the relentless focus on women in isolation from their male partners and relationships can potentially serve to reinforce social presumptions of women's responsibility for reproduction and related notions that men are sexually driven and uninterested in reproduction (Terry and Braun). Original empirical research on pathways to childfreedom that include (Park; Blackstone and Stewart), or focus specifically on, single or partnered men (Lunneborg) or heterosexual couples (Callan, "Voluntary Childlessness"; Gold; Lee and Zvonkovic) are rare.

More common is secondary analysis of existing data to draw conclusions about childfree men (Dykstra and Hagestad; Dykstra and Keizer; Waren and Pals), or childfree couples, and their life course. In one such publication, Pearl Dykstra and Gunhild Hagestad drew on surveys (not specifically conducted with a focus on childlessness) to compare parents and nonparents, and men and women, in such areas as socioeconomic status, social embeddedness, and health. Their key conclusions included that childlessness "makes more of a difference in men's than in women's lives" (1518), yet there is little primary data to confirm or contest this notion. Sara Pelton and Katherine Hertlein analyzed census data and published studies to examine how "voluntarily childless couples fit and do not fit into a traditional family life cycle" (40) and concluded that they may have different experiences from parents in defining their adult identities.

Empirical studies based on primary data clearly demonstrate that men make and take responsibility for reproductive choices. For example, in Gareth Terry and Virginia Braun's research with twelve men who had voluntarily sought a preemptive vasectomy, men made reproductive choices within the wider context of a pronatalistic society. They often positioned themselves as selfish—a criticism often made of childfree people—and framed this selfishness as an explanation for why they did not want to engage in the difficulties of parenting. At the same time, participants condemned the condemners by positioning parents as equally selfish, thus indicating a belief that all fertility decisions stem from a common motivation (see Park).

Empirical research based on primary data also shows that couples make reproductive decisions together. Kyung-Hee Lee and Anisa Zvonkovic conducted joint interviews with twenty voluntarily childless heterosexual couples in the U.S.. They identify three phases of couple's decision-making process, beginning with "agreement," which is difficult for "nonmutual" couples, where one partner has a "strong childless conviction" (542). "Acceptance" followed, in which couples become more certain about their decision, and, finally, they enter a phase of "closing of the door."

Problematic Assumption Five: Heteronormativity (and Pronatalism in LGBTQ Research)

Neither the voluntary childlessness literature nor the lesbian, gay, bisexual, trans, and queer (LGBTQ) literature has much to say about childfree members of LGBTQ communities. It has often been (implicitly) assumed in the voluntary childlessness literature that lesbian women do not make reproductive choices and are childfree by default. However, although evidence suggests that most lesbians do not have children (Benkov), it also shows that lesbians do make reproductive decisions (Bergstrom-Lynch; Baiocco and Laghi; Mezey, "How Many Lesbians"; Riskind and Patterson); thus, their childfreedom may be chosen. At the same time, in lesbian communities, there has been a historical association of lesbianism and childlessness (Clarke, "Feminist Perspectives"). In the feminist voluntary childlessness literature, a handful of studies of women's lived experiences have included small numbers of lesbian and bisexual women (e.g. one in Carmichael and Whittaker, two in Gillespie, and four in Mollen). However, the commentary on the specific features of these women's experiences is usually confined to a few brief observations.

In LGBTQ social science research, the focus has predominantly been on lesbian parenting rather than the more common experience of childlessness, and until about a decade ago, research was dominated by a concern with developmental outcomes for children (Clarke et al., *Lesbian*). This focus on parenting had a good reason—lesbians were losing custody of children from former heterosexual marriages/ relationships, and they needed to demonstrate to judges, lawyers and others that the "kids are alright" (Clarke, "From Outsiders"). Moreover, even research on families of choice in queer communities (kinlike networks of relationships based on friendship and commitments beyond blood that are emblematic of new ways of doing family) has focused on parenting rather than childlessness. Two landmark texts—*Families We Choose* and *Families of Choice*—dedicate an entire chapter to parenting but do not have a single index entry for childlessness (Weeks, Heaphy, and Donovan; Weston).

Furthermore, research on LGBTQ people's reproductive decision making is oriented to what motivates people to choose to parent and barriers to parenthood, such as internalized homophobia (Robinson and Brewster), rather than what motivates them to choose childfreedom. For example, a chapter in Mezey (*New Choices*), exploring the reproductive decision-making of lesbians with and without children, is entitled "Developing Mothering Desires." Furthermore, in some studies, the definition of childlessness is so general that it does not allow for meaningful conclusions about the decision making of voluntarily childfree individuals and couples (e.g. Bergstrom-Lynch; Mezey, *New Choices*). Thus, pronatalism or a "parental imperative" (Wilson) underpins the LGBTQ literature on kinship, arguably reflecting a growth of pronatalism in queer communities (Morell). In 1987, Nancy Polikoff asked, "Who is talking about the women who do not ever want to be mothers?" and answered "No one." Thirty years later, this is still the case. We know virtually nothing about the meaning and experience of childfreedom for a population the majority of which remains childfree (Mezey, "How Many Lesbians"). There is, however, reason to believe that the meaning of childlessness may be changing for lesbians, as a British study of the experiences of white, middle-class, and childfree lesbians highlighted the ways in which the lesbian baby boom and gay marriage have affected their lives (Clarke et al., "Lived Experiences"). Victoria Clarke et al. argued that legal recognition raises interesting questions about the impact of relational and familial equality on the meaning of childfreedom for nonheterosexuals that should be explored (see also Shaw).

Research on reproductive decision making by same-sex couples and LGB individuals is one of the few sources of data about childfree lesbians. However, this literature is not specifically focused on childfree people but on those who are currently childless. In U.S. research on lesbians' mothering decisions and desires, many participants who were currently childfree had developed a strong desire early in their lives to remain childfree (Mezey, *New Choices*; see also Bergstrom-Lynch). Nancy Mezey argued that early desires are more salient for lesbian women than heterosexual women because lesbians have more control over their reproductive choices and are more able to actively pursue their desires. In this study, reasons for remaining childfree commonly focused on individual biographies, feelings, and desires. These included a negative interpretation of motherhood (influenced by perceptions of their own mothers' self-sacrifice and gender oppression), early experiences with childcare (understood as a burden), a desire for personal and economic freedom (especially for working-class lesbians), the constraints and rewards of work, and internalized homophobia and racial discrimination (for Black lesbians). Motivations for childfreedom also included critiques of lesbian motherhood that echo earlier debates in lesbian communities about the politics of parenting; for example, some of the women thought that lesbians were entering into motherhood to gain heterosexual privilege, without fully considering the consequences and responsibilities. Others held the belief that the world is too harsh a place for children. For some women, there was also the influence of their intimate partnership; for others, their partner was not an influence.

Bisexual women have only occasionally been included in childfree research (e.g. Mollen). In quantitative studies, bisexual people's responses have sometimes been merged with those of other nonheterosexual sexualities. For example, Christina Lee and Helen Gramotnev asked currently childless participants to complete a seven-point scale of sexuality that included "bisexual," but then they split the questionnaire data into "exclusively heterosexual" and "all others." Similarly, in their study of heterosexism and gender role conflict in childless men, Robinson and Brewster merged bisexual men's results with those of gay men due to low numbers of bisexual participants.

Discussion of trans people's experiences of being childfree is even more limited, and, again, the focus in the literature on trans families has been on parenting rather than childlessness. One of the few studies to address childlessness in trans families is Carla Pfeffer's research with the cisgender women partners of trans men. She found that nearly half of the women had no plans to become parents or were not interested in having children, and, for some, this represented an active resistance to normative ideals. Reasons for not wanting or planning to have children included infertility (theirs or their partner's), physical and mental health problems, economic barriers, prioritizing education and/or career, advancing age, citizenship status, and conflict over parenting options.

Problematic Assumption Six: Coercive Pronatalism

Historically, only some groups have been expected to reproduce—the most socially privileged. By contrast, those less privileged (poor, young, old, Black, or disabled) have been actively discouraged from procreation (Morison et al.; Shapiro). This coercive pronatalism potentially explains the previously noted research preoccupation with the sociodemographic characteristics of people who are voluntarily childless. For example, a recent paper examining the sociodemographic characteristics of intelligence sought to explain, from an evolutionary perspective, why some individuals choose not to have children "despite their biological design" (Kanzawa 158). Satoshi Kanzawa argued that more intelligent women are more likely to choose to remain childless; consequently, he predicted, "a decline in the average intelligence of the population in advanced industrial nations" (159). He did not present any value statement about this outcome, but it is difficult not to read into the study a concern about procreation by those who are less privileged.

If coercive pronatalism leads to concerns about socially privileged people failing to procreate, it follows that there would be a lack of interest in voluntary childlessness in other groups. Thus, this phenomenon may also explain the lack of research on women from socially marginalized groups, such as women of colour and women who are working class and disabled, as well as the failure to examine how the experiences of childfree women are shaped by such factors as race and ethnicity, religion, social class, and disability. However, there has been some focus on these populations in the literature on infertility (e.g., Nachtigal). For example, citing research from Pakistan, southern Africa, northern Vietnam, Cameroon, India, and Israel, Arthur Greil, Kathleen Slauson Blevins, and Julia McQuillan argued that a key variable in the experience of infertility is the degree of pronatalism in women's cultural setting: "In developing societies especially, having children may be the key to women achieving adult status and gaining acceptance in the community" (145). Thus, being childless has heavy negative social consequences. Philip Tabong and Philip Adongo's qualitative study on the perceptions of childbearing and childlessness in northern Ghana also identified extensive stigma and manifold social consequences resulting from childlessness, in particular for women. In her study of infertile women in Israel, Larissa Remennick similarly identified widespread pronatalism that her participants seldom challenged: "None of the informants believed that childlessness can be voluntary" (827). The stigma around being childfree was indexed by one participant's framing of childfree women as "barren, selfish, unable of love" (828).

There is limited research on the racially and ethnically marginalised, religious, or disabled childfree population in the (geographic and cultural) West. In their U.S. study of childlessness trends in Black and white women, Jennifer Lundquist, Michelle Budig, and Anna Curtis noted the historical lack of empirical attention paid to Black childlessness (with researchers instead focusing on why Black women have higher fertility rates and more births outside marriage) despite the fact that

41

childlessness levels are now equivalent in the two populations. Historically, one argument to explain higher birthrates in racially and ethnically marginalised populations in the West has been the stronger expectations of parenting in these communities; however, recent research has not always supported this notion. Two U.S. studies focused on perceptions of childfree people among student populations have examined how race intersects with perceptions of childfree people (Koropeckyj-Cox, Romano, and Moras; Vinson, Mollen, and Smith). Tanya Koropeckyj-Cox, Victor Romano, and Amanda Moras found little evidence that race influenced perceptions of childless/childfree couples. In contrast, Candice Vinson, Debra Mollen, and Nathan Smith found that African American women were rated more positively when they had children. The authors explained these findings in terms of more rigidly prescribed gender roles for women of colour.

Research on the experiences of the racially and ethnically marginalised childfree populations is rare. One qualitative study with 143 British South Asian people experiencing infertility provided some suggestions about the potential experience of childfree people of colour, as it found a strong orientation to pronatalist assumptions and, consequently, a rejection of voluntary childlessness in this population (Culley et al.). A handful of feminist studies of the experiences of childfree women have also included one woman of colour each (DeLyser; Mollen; Addie and Brownlow). However, Settle and Brumley's study of twenty childfree women's decision-making pathways is one of the few studies to include several (six) women of colour and to comment on the differences in the experiences of white women and women of colour. They found that the decision to be childfree was partly shaped by race; only white women were always certain that they did not want to have children, whereas women of colour drifted into being childfree but then actively maintained this choice. Settle and Brumley argued that white privilege possibly enables the rejection of cultural expectations of motherhood; white women perhaps have more choice and women of colour feel more community pressure to become mothers. At the same time, life-constraints may be a barrier to motherhood for women of colour, whereas the costs of motherhood are more salient for white women. More commonly, feminist research focuses exclusively on white women (Gillespie, "Voluntary Childlessness"; Peterson), the racial and ethnic membership of the participants is not identified (Doyle, Pooley, and

Breen; Peterson and Engwall), or demographic data on race are not collected. (Rich et al. only documented race through observation and all "appeared of Anglo-European background" [230].) The focus on white, middle-class women is often justified with reference to the claimed typical demographic profile of voluntary childless women—white, educated, and employed (DeLyser); however, it is not clear if this is empirically supported.

Religion is another demographic variable that has been shown to have an impact on rates of voluntary childlessness. For example, a U.S. study showed that since 1982, voluntarily childless women have consistently been much less likely to be religious than women who have children or are involuntarily childless (Abma and Martinez). Similarly, a Canadian study indicated that intended childlessness is linked to religiosity, with identifying as religious and church attendance reducing the likelihood of intended childlessness (Edmonston, Lee, and Wu). A study in the Netherlands, which charted a rise in the public acceptance of voluntary childlessness from 20 per cent to 90 per cent in thirty years, also showed that attending church is related to less acceptance of voluntary childless (Noordhuizen, de Graaf, and Sieben). However, it is important not to equate the attitudes and experiences of those from different religions— for example, Barry Edmonston, Sharon Lee, and Zheng Wu found differences in attitudes to voluntary childlessness depending on religion, and Frank Mott and Joyce Abma found differences within one religion (e.g. between Orthodox and other types of Jews).

With regard to the experience of voluntary childlessness from a religious perspective, Dawn Llewellyn's qualitative interview study with Christian women in the United Kingdom with and without children noted the lack of attention given to the voluntary childless population in faith studies and suggested that this academic silence is echoed in women's experience of their lives. Specifically, participants felt they had to hide their intentional childlessness for fear of negative reactions from their religious community.

Similarly, there is little focus in the literature on voluntary child-lessness among people with disabilities, perhaps due to the fact that an inability to have children is often framed in the broader literature as itself a "reproductive disability" (Webb and Holman 376) or "physical disability" (Herman and Miall 251). Another reason for this lack of a focus is, perhaps, the assumption that disabled people should be childless.

For example, the mothers with disabilities in Carol Thomas's study talked about the concern that they and those around them felt about the risk of their passing on their disabilities to children. For a number of them, this concern dictated their reproductive choices. Participants also referenced the negative social attention they got when they were pregnant: "I do think sometimes they [strangers she encountered] thought that I shouldn't be pregnant.... They'd probably think that whatever I'd got the child has got a chance of being the same" (631).

Engwall offers one of the few examinations of voluntary childlessness for disabled people, drawing on interviews with four women and men with intellectual disabilities (IDs) from a wider study of voluntary childlessness in Sweden. She found that these participants' motives for remaining childfree were different from those of participants without IDs and reflected the very different social context for reproductive decision making for people with IDs. Their motives centred on the concrete and practical difficulties of parenting and relationships with children (a lack of confidence in their abilities to parent), the risk of passing on diseases and disorders, and discomfort caused by children's mockery. Engwall concluded that their reasons for not parenting "may be seen in the light of a societal discourse where they are discouraged from becoming parents" (341).

An Inclusive, Intersectional Framework for Research on Voluntary Childlessness

The contradictions and sizeable gaps in our current understanding of women who choose to be childfree, and childfreedom more broadly, suggest the need for a different approach that avoids the problematic definitions, assumptions, and frameworks that have hampered voluntary childlessness research to date (Shapiro). By proposing an inclusive, intersectional framework and ethos for future feminist research on voluntary childlessness (Dill and Kohlman), we encourage feminist researchers to focus on the full diversity of the childfree population, without losing sight of the importance of giving voice to women's experience. In addition, rather than treating childfree women (and men) as one homogenous group, we urge researchers to examine the distinctive reproductive pressures on different groups of women (and men) (Mott and Abma) and the ways in which race, ethnicity, religion, class, sexuality, and disability shape pathways to childfreedom and living out the childfree choice. Furthermore, we encourage researchers to avoid implicitly reinforcing the assumption that certain groups do not make, or take responsibility for, reproductive choices by examining the experiences of all sexes and genders as well as different-sex and same-sex couples and people who are not in couples. In addition, by shifting our focus away from pathways to childfreedom and the characteristics and personality traits of childfree people to a more holistic focus on their everyday lives and how the choice to be childfree is lived out across the life course, we can avoid the presumption that people make a one-off decision to be childfree. In listening to the voices of the childfree, we can also avoid imposing our categories onto them (e.g., early articulator/perpetual postponer, choice/circumstance, and childfree/childless) and understand how they make sense of, and label, their choices.

Although we have problematized her framing of lesbians' reproductive decision making, Mezey's (*New Choices*) research, nonetheless, provides a useful example of an intersectional approach to research (in part) focused on women's pathways to childlessness, drawing on the principles of multiracial feminism (see also Settle and Brumley). Mezey recruited women with and without racial and class privilege, and, crucially, she explored how race and class shaped the women's narratives. One of the weaknesses of existing research that does include, for example, lesbian and bisexual women as well as women of colour, is that their experiences are not always analyzed as lesbian, bisexual, and women of colour and that the similarities and differences in the experiences of different groups are not explored. Therefore, their sexual and racial identities are not treated as particularly relevant to their experience of childfreedom; instead, they are treated as one homogenous group.

We end this chapter with a checklist of nine recommendations for future research.

Checklist for Inclusive, Intersectional Research

1. Recognize that reproductive choices are not just the province of white, middle-class heterosexuals.
2. Adopt an inclusive, intersectional ethos that acknowledges the range and diversity of childfree populations, including and focusing on LGBTQ people, people of colour, people in nontraditional living arrangements, and disabled people.
3. Examine the similarities and differences in the experiences of different groups and the ways in which experiences of childfreedom are shaped by race, ethnicity, religion, social class, disability, gender, sexuality, and age.
4. Avoid fixed (researcher defined) categories and embrace fluidity and participant-centred definitions and acknowledge that reproductive decisions are contextual and fluid and may have different meanings across the lifespan.
5. Do not assume women's responsibility for reproductive choices (in different-sex relationships).
6. Focus on childfree people as distinct from those who are involuntarily childless.
7. Stop asking questions that assume childfree people are depressed, lonely, and regretful, without disavowing how difficult it is to be childfree in a pronatalist society.
8. Recognize that some childfree people may affiliate with childfree communities and groups and others do not; and do not limit recruitment to childfree communities and groups unless research is specifically focused on those populations.
9. Return research to participants and to the wider childfree population, disseminate research using both academic and nonacademic pathways, and help to reduce feelings of isolation and marginalization among people who are childfree.

Works Cited

Abma, Joyce C., and Gladys M. Martinez. "Childlessness among Older Women in the U.S.: Trends and Profiles." *Journal of Marriage and Family*, vol. 68, no. 4, 2006, pp. 1045-56.

Addie, Elizabeth, and Charlotte Brownlow. "Deficit and Asset Identity Constructions of Single Women without Children Living in Australia: An Analysis of Discourse." *Feminism and Psychology*, vol. 24, no. 4, 2014, pp. 423-39.

Agrillo, Christian, and Cristian Nelini. "Childfree by Choice: A Review." *Journal of Cultural Geography*, vol. 25, no. 3, 2008, pp. 347-63.

Albertini, Marco, and Martin Kohli. "What Childless Older People Give: Is the Generational Link Broken?" *Ageing and Society*, vol. 29, no. 8, 2009, pp. 1261-74.

Alexander, Baine B., et al. "A Path Not Taken: A Cultural Analysis of Regrets and Childlessness in the Lives of Older Women." *The Gerontologist*, vol. 32, no. 5, 1992, pp. 618-26.

Almeling, Rene, and Miranda R. Waggoner. "More and Less Than Equal: How Men Factor in the Reproductive Equation." *Gender and Society*, vol. 27, no. 6, 2013, pp. 821-42.

Baiocco, Roberto, and Fiorenzo Laghi. "Sexual Orientation and the Desires and Intentions to Become Parents." *Journal of Family Studies*, vol. 19, no. 1, 2013, pp. 90-98.

Basten, Stuart. "Voluntary Childlessness and Being Childfree." *The Future of Human Reproduction: Working Paper* 5, 2009, pp. 1-23.

Benkov, Laura. *Reinventing the family. The Emerging Story of Lesbian and Gay Parents*. Crown Publishers, Inc., 1994.

Bergstrom-Lynch, Cara. *Lesbians, Gays, and Bisexuals Becoming Parents or Remaining Childfree: Confronting Social Inequalities*. Lexington, 2015.

Blackstone, Amy. "Doing Family without Having Kids." *Sociology Compass* 8.1 (2014): 52-62.

Blackstone, Amy, and Amy Greenleaf. "Childfree Families." *Families as They Really Are*, edited by Barbara J. Risman and Virginia E. Rutter, Norton, 2015, pp. 137-144.

Blackstone, Amy, and Mahala D. Stewart. "'There's More Thinking to Decide': How the Childfree Decide Not to Parent." *The Family Journal*, vol. 24, no. 3, 2016, pp. 296-303.

Boddington, Bill, and Robert Didham. "Increases in Childlessness in New Zealand." *Journal of Population Research*, vol. 26, no. 2, 2009, pp. 131-51.

Bram, Susan. "Voluntarily Childless Women: Traditional or Non-traditional?" *Sex Roles*, vol. 10, no. 3-4, 1984, pp. 195-206.

Callan, Victor. J. "Voluntary Childlessness: Early Articulator and Postponing Couples." *Journal of Biosocial Science*, vol. 16, no. 4, 1984, pp. 501-9.

Callan, Victor J. "The Personal and Marital Adjustment of Mothers and of Voluntarily and Involuntarily Childless Wives." *Journal of Marriage and the Family*, vol. 49, no. 4, 1987, pp. 847-56.

Cannold, Leslie. "Declining Marriage Rates and Gender Inequity in Social Institutions: Towards an Adequately Complex Explanation for Childlessness." *People and Place*, vol. 12, no. 4, 2004, pp. 1-11.

Carmichael, Gordon A., and Andrea Whittaker. "Choice and Circumstance: Qualitative Insights into Contemporary Child-lessness in Australia." *European Journal of Population*, vol. 23, no. 2, 2007, pp. 111-43.

Clarke, Victoria. "Feminist Perspectives on Lesbian Parenting: A Review of the Literature 1972-2002." *Psychology of Women Section Review*, vol. 7, no. 2, 2005, pp. 11-23.

Clarke, Victoria. "From Outsiders to Motherhood to Reinventing the Family: Constructions of Lesbians as Parents in the Psychological Literature—1886–2006." *Women's Studies International Forum*, vol. 31, 2008, pp. 118-28.

Clarke, Victoria, et al. *Lesbian, Gay, Bisexual, Trans, and Queer Psychology: An Introduction.* Cambridge University Press, 2010.

Clarke, Victoria, et al. "Lived Experiences of Childfree Lesbians in the UK: A Qualitative Exploration." *Journal of Family Issues*, vol. 39, 2018, pp. 4133-55.

Culley, Lorraine A., et al. "British South Asian Communities and Infertility Services." *Human Fertility*, vol. 9, no. 1, 2006, pp. 37-45.

DeLyser, Gail. "At midlife, Intentionally Childfree Women and Their Experiences of Regret." *Clinical Social Work Journal*, vol. 40, no. 1, 2012, pp. 66-74.

Dill, Bonnie T., and Marla H. Kohlman. "Intersectionality: A Transformative Paradigm in Feminist Theory and Social Justice." *Handbook of Feminist Research: Theory and Praxis*, edited by Sharlene N. Hesse-Biber, Sage, 2012, pp. 154-74.

Doyle, Joanne, Julie A. Pooley, and Lauren Breen. "A Phenomenological Exploration of the Childfree Choice in a Sample of Australian Women." *Journal of Health Psychology* 18.3 (2012, pp. 397-407.

Dykstra, Pearl A. "Childless Old Age." *International Handbook of Population Aging*, edited by Peter Uhlenberg, Springer, 2008, pp. 671-90.

Dykstra, Pearl. A. "Older Adult Loneliness: Myths and Realities." *European Journal of Ageing*, vol. 6, no. 2, 2009, pp. 91-100.

Dykstra, Pearl. A., and Gunhild O. Hagestad. "Childlessness and Parenthood in Two Centuries: Different Roads—Different Maps?" *Journal of Family Issues*, vol. 28, no. 11, 2007, pp. 1518-32.

Dykstra, Pearl. A., and Renske Keizer. "The Wellbeing of Childless Men and Fathers in Mid-Life." *Ageing and Society*, vol. 29, no. 8, 2009, pp. 1227-42.

Edmonston, Barry, Sharon M. Lee, and Zheng Wu. "Childless Canadian Couples." *Meetings of the Population Work and Family Policy Research Collaboration*, Gatineau, December 2008.

Engwall, Kristina. "Childfreeness, Parenthood and Adulthood." *Scandinavian Journal of Disability Research*, vol. 16, no. 4, 2014, pp. 333-47.

Giles, David, Rachel L. Shaw, and William Morgan. "Representations of voluntary childlessness in the UK Press, 1990-2008." *Journal of Health Psychology*, vol. 14, no. 8, 2009, pp. 1218-28.

Gillespie, Rosemary. "Voluntary Childlessness in the United Kingdom." *Reproductive Health Matters*, vol. 7, no. 13, 1999, pp. 43-53.

Gillespie, Rosemary. "When No Means No: Disbelief, Disregard and Deviance as Discourses of Voluntary Childlessness." *Women's Studies International Forum*, vol. 23, no. 2, 2000, pp. 223-34.

Gold, Joshua M. "The Experiences of Childfree and Childless Couples in a Pronatalistic Society: Implications for Family Counselors." *The Family Journal*, vol. 21, no. 2, 2013, pp. 223-29.

Graham, Melissa. "Is Being Childless Detrimental to a Woman's Health and Well-Being across Her Life Course?" *Women's Health Issues*, vol. 25, no. 2, 2015, pp. 176-84.

Greil, Arthur L., Kathleen Slauson Blevins, and Julia McQuillan. "The Experience of Infertility: A Review of Recent Literature." *Sociology of Health and Illness*, vol. 32, no. 1, 2010, pp. 140-62.

Hayfield, Nikki, et al. "Women's Experiences of Being Childfree by Choice: Negotiating Identity, Stigma and the Life-Course." *British Psychological Society Psychology of Women Section Annual Conference*, Windsor, July 2015.

Herman, N. J., and C. E. Miall. "The Positive Consequences of Stigma: Two Case studies in Mental and Physical Disability." *Qualitative Sociology*, vol. 13, no. 3, 1990, pp. 251-69.

Houseknecht, Sharon K. "Timing of the Decision to Remain Voluntarily Childless: Evidence for Continuous Socialisation." *Psychology of Women Quarterly*, vol. 4, no. 1, 1979, pp. 81-96.

Houseknecht, Sharon K. "Voluntary Childlessness." *Handbook of Marriage and the Family*, edited by Suzanne K. Steinmetz and Marvin B. Sussman, Plenum Press, 1987, pp. 369-95.

Jamison, Pollyann H., Louis R. Franzini, and Robert M. Kaplan. "Some assumed characteristics of voluntarily childfree women and men." *Psychology of Women Quarterly* 4.2 (1979): 266-273.

Kanzawa, Satoshi. "Intelligence and Childlessness." *Social Science Research*, vol. 48, 2014, pp. 157-70.

Kelly, Maura. "Women's Voluntary Childlessness: A Radical Rejection of Motherhood?" *Women's Studies Quarterly*, vol. 37, no. 2, 2009, pp. 157-72.

Kemkes-Grottenthaler, Ariane. "Postponing or Rejecting Parenthood? Results of a Survey among Female Academic Professionals." *Journal of Biosocial Science*, vol. 35, no. 2, 2003, pp. 213-26.

Koropeckyj-Cox, Tanya, and Vaughn R. A. Call. "Characteristics of Older Childless Persons and Parents: Cross-National Comparisons." *Journal of Family Issues*, vol. 28, no. 10, 2007, pp. 1362-1414.

Koropeckyj-Cox, Tanya, Victor Romano, and Amanda Moras. "Through the Lenses of Gender, Race, and Class: Students' Perceptions of Childless/Childfree Individuals and Couples." *Sex Roles*, vol. 56, no. 7, 2007, pp. 415-28.

Lee, Christina, and Helen Gramotnev. "Predictors and Outcomes of Early Motherhood in the Australian Longitudinal Study on Women's Health." *Psychology, Health and Medicine*, vol. 11, no. 1, 2006, pp. 29-47.

Lee, Kyung-Hee, and Anisa M. Zvonkovic. "Journeys to Remain Childless: A Grounded Theory Examination of Decision-Making processes among Voluntarily Childless Couples." *Journal of Social and Personal Relationships*, vol. 31, no. 4, 2014, pp. 535-53.

Letherby, Gayle. "Childless and Bereft? Stereotypes and Realities in Relation to 'Voluntary' and 'Involuntary' Childlessness and Womanhood." *Sociological Inquiry*, vol. 72, no. 1, 2002, pp. 7-20.

Llewellyn, Dawn. "Maternal Silences: Motherhood and Voluntary Childlessness in Contemporary Christianity." *Religion and Gender*, vol. 6, no. 1, 2016, pp. 64-79.

Lundquist, Jennifer H., Michelle J. Budig, and Anna Curtis. "Race and Childlessness in America, 1988–2002." *Journal of Marriage and Family*, vol. 71, no. 3, 2009, pp. 741-55.

Lunneborg, Patricia W. *The Chosen Lives of Childfree Men*. Bergin and Garvey, 1999.

Marri, Sheetal. R., Chul Ahn and Alan L. Buchman. "Voluntary childlessness is increased in women with inflammatory bowel disease." *Inflammatory Bowel Diseases* 13.5 (2007): 591-599.

Mezey, Nancy J. *New Choices, New Families: How Lesbians Decide about Motherhood*. John Hopkins University Press, 2008.

Mezey, Nancy J. "How Lesbians and Gay Men Decide to Become Parents or Remain Childfree." *LGBT-Parent Families*, edited by Abbie E. Goldberg and Katherine R. Allen, Springer, 2012, pp. 59-70.

Mollen, Debra. "Voluntarily Childfree Women: Experiences and Counseling Considerations." *Journal of Mental Health Counseling*, vol. 28, no. 3, 2006, pp. 269-82.

Moller, Naomi, and Victoria Clarke. "New Frontiers of Family." *The Psychologist*, vol. 29, 2016, pp. 204-08.

Moore, Julia. "Reconsidering Childfreedom: A Feminist Exploration of Discursive Identity Construction in Childfree LiveJournal Communities." *Women's Studies in Communication*, vol. 37, no. 2, 2014, pp. 159-80.

Morell, Carolyn. "Saying No: Women's Experiences with Reproductive Refusal." *Feminism and Psychology*, vol. 10, no. 3, 2000, pp. 313-22.

Morison, Tracy, et al. "Stigma Resistance in Online Childfree Communities: The Limitations of Choice Rhetoric." *Psychology of Women Quarterly*, vol. 40, no. 2, 2016, pp. 184-98.

Mott, Frank L., and Joyce C. Abma. "Contemporary Jewish Fertility: Does Religion Make a Difference?" *Contemporary Jewry*, vol. 13, no. 1, 1992, pp. 74-94.

Nachtigal, Robert D. "International Disparities in Access to Infertility Services." *Fertility and Sterility*, vol. 85, no. 4, 2006, pp. 871-75.

Noordhuizen, Suzanne, Paul de Graaf, and Inge Sieben. "The Public Acceptance of Voluntary Childlessness in the Netherlands: From 20 to 90 Per cent in 30 years." *Social Indicators Research*, vol. 99, no. 1, 2010, pp. 163-81.

Park, Kristin. "Stigma Management among the Voluntarily Childless." *Sociological Perspectives*, vol. 45, no. 1, 2002, pp. 21-45.

Pelton, Sara L., and Katherine M. Hertlein. "A Proposed Life Cycle for Voluntary Childfree Couples." *Journal of Feminist Family Therapy*, vol. 23, no. 1, 2011, pp. 39-53.

Peterson, Helen. "Fifty Shades of Freedom: Voluntary Childlessness as Women's Ultimate Liberation." *Women's Studies International Forum*, vol. 53, 2014, pp. 182-91.

Peterson, Helen, and Kristina Engwall. "Silent Bodies: Childfree Women's Gendered and Embodied Experiences." *European Journal of Women's Studies*, vol. 20, no. 4, 2013, pp. 376-89.

Pfeffer, Carla. "Normative Resistance and Invention Pragmatism: Negotiating Structure and Agency in Transgender Families." *Gender and Society*, vol. 26, no. 4, 2012, pp. 574-602.

Polikoff, Nancy D. "Lesbians Choosing Children: The Personal Is Political." *Politics of the Heart: A Lesbian Parenting Anthology*, edited by Sandra Pollack and Jeanne Vaughn, Firebrand Books, 1987, pp. 48-54.

Remennick, Larissa. "Childless in the Land of Imperative Motherhood: Stigma and Coping among Infertile Israeli Women." *Sex Roles*, vol. 43, no. 11, 2000, pp. 821-41.

Rich, Stephanie, et al. "'Unnatural,' 'Unwomanly,' 'Uncreditable' and 'Undervalued': The Significance of Being a Childless Woman in Australian Society." *Gender Issues*, vol. 28, no. 4 2011, pp. 226-47.

Riskind, Rachel G., and Charlotte Patterson. "Parenting Intentions and Desires among Childless Lesbian, Gay, and Heterosexual Individuals." *Journal of Family Psychology*, vol. 24, no. 1, 2010, pp. 78-81.

Robinson, Matthew. A., and Melanie E. Brewster. "Motivations for Fatherhood: Examining Internalized Heterosexism and Gender-Role Conflict with Childless Gay and Bisexual Men." *Psychology of Men and Masculinity*, vol. 15, no. 1, 2014, pp. 49-59.

Rowlands, Ingrid, and Christina Lee. "Choosing to Have Children or Choosing to Be Childfree: Australian Students' Attitudes towards the Decisions of Heterosexual and Lesbian Women." *Australian Psychologist*, vol. 41, no. 1, 2006, pp. 55-59.

Russo, Nancy F. "The Motherhood Mandate." *Journal of Social Issues*, vol. 32, no. 3, 1976, pp. 143-53.

Settle, Braelin, and Krista Brumley. "'It's the Choices You Make That Get You There': Decision-Making Pathways of Childfree Women." *Michigan Family Review*, vol. 18, no. 1, 2014, pp. 1-22.

Shapiro, Gilla. "Voluntary Childlessness: A Critical Review of the Literature." *Studies in the Maternal*, vol. 6, no. 1, 2014, pp. 1-15.

Shaw, Rachel L. "Women's Experiential Journey toward Voluntary Childlessness: An Interpretative Phenomenological Analysis." *Journal of Community and Applied Social Psychology*, vol. 21, no. 2, 2011, pp. 151-63.

Tabong, Philip T-N, and Philip B. Adongo. "Understanding the Social Meaning of Infertility and Childbearing: A Qualitative Study of the Perception of Childbearing and Childlessness in Northern Ghana." *PLoS ONE*, vol. 8, no. 1, 2013, p. e54429.

Terry, Gareth, and Virginia Braun. "'Sticking My Finger Up at Evolution': Unconventionality, Selfishness, Resistance and Choice in the Talk of Men Who Have Had 'Pre-emptive' Vasectomies." *Men and Masculinities*, vol. 15, no. 3, 2012, pp. 207-29.

Thomas, Carol. "The Baby and the Bath Water: Disabled Women and Motherhood in Social Context." *Sociology of Health and Illness*, vol. 19, no. 5, 1997, pp. 622-43.

Turnbull, Beth, Melissa L. Graham, and Ann R. Taket. "Social Exclusion of Australian Childless Women in Their Reproductive Years." *Social Inclusion*, vol. 4, no. 1, 2016, pp. 102-15.

Vinson, Candice, Debra Mollen, and Nathan G. Smith. "Perceptions of Childfree Women: The Role of Perceivers' and Targets' Ethnicity." *Journal of Community and Applied Social Psychology*, vol. 20, no. 5, 2010, pp. 426-32.

Waren, Warren, and Heili Pals. "Comparing Characteristics of Voluntarily Childless Men and Women." *Journal of Population Research*, vol. 30, no. 2, 2013, pp. 151-70.

Webb, Sandra, and D'Arcy Holman. "A Survey of Infertility, Surgical Sterility and Associated Reproductive Disability in Perth, Western Australia." *Australian and New Zealand Journal of Public Health*, vol. 16, no. 4, 1992, pp. 376-81.

Weeks, Jeffrey, Brian Heaphy, and Catherine Donovan. *Same Sex Intimacies: Families of Choice and Other Life Experiments*. Routledge, 2001.

Weston, Kath. *Families We Choose: Lesbians, Gays, Kinship*. Columbia University Press, 1991.

Wilkinson, Sue. "Theoretical Perspectives on Women and Gender." *Handbook of the Psychology of Women and Gender*, edited by Rhoda K. Unger, Wiley, 2001, pp. 17-28.

Wilson, Blair. "Disciplining Gay and Lesbian Family Life." *Gay and Lesbian Issues and Psychology Review*, vol. 9, no. 1, 2013, pp. 34-45.

Chapter Two

The WINKS: Unravelling the Meaning of (M)Otherhood through a Sociological Lens

Helene A. Cummins

As a result of feminism, women around the world have to a certain extent been advantaged by changing societies. They have gained greater access to higher education, have more employment opportunities and greater social mobility, and have more freedoms around their reproductive choices, including access to contraceptives as well as abortion. These changes have created a more equitable field of options within their work and family lives. Within these parameters, however, sociostructural barriers and social ideologies still limit women's life choices and, to some extent, limit their freedom and lived experiences.

This paper examines women whom I will call the "WINKS," or single women with an income and no kids. I have decided to coin my own term rather than to use the more generic term coined by Eric Klinenberg—"SINKS," or single income, no kids—which relates to both women and men. I argue that single women experience a different trajectory of being childfree than do single men; hence, they are deserving of their own classification, as their experience of being without children is both socially and culturally different than that of men (Rijken and Merz 472). To this end, the WINKS are single incomed women who are childfree.

Women may be childfree by choice, circumstances, or a combination of the two. To help understand how and where childfree women are located in society and what social and cultural factors make up their lives, this chapter will begin by first noting the demographic profile of this group of women. It will examine how educated women are challenged by the structure of the mating gradient, the marriage squeeze, and the processes of both hypergamy and hypogamy. This chapter will also highlight why some women choose and are motivated by the childfree option and give reasons to enhancements found in this way of life. Finally, it will argue that the childfree woman can be a happy, free, and self-confident woman; she has commitments and responsibilities to others; a childfree existence is a way of life that some women are consciously choosing, desiring, and finding, as it provides them full lives of contentment and opportunity, embedded within a culture that continues to favour marriage and motherhood for women. Women who are the "other" are often harshly labelled, devalued, denigrated, and seen to be selfish and self-absorbed social and sociocultural rejected misfits and deviants.

Social Demographics of Global Childfree Women

Although this chapter focuses on Canadian women, it will also examine the demographic patterns of women around the globe as a backdrop to explain the heightened rates of childfree women in the world. In Canada, there was a 10.5 per cent increase of women who lived alone between 2001 and 2006 (Milan, Keown, and Robles Urquijo 6). In 2006, again there was an increasingly high incidence of women who lived alone in Canada, totalling 14.1 per cent (Milan, Keown, and Robles Urquijo 6). Although this number does not necessarily reflect whether those women had children who had grown and left, it does reflect that the single lifestyle is on the rise in Canada. Many of those singles are women, and many are choosing the childfree option. For example, 7 per cent of Canadian women between the ages of twenty and thirty-nine reported that they had no interest in bearing children (Vanier Institute, "Fertility"). Although not all may choose to be childfree, some individuals and couples face infertility, which affects one in six Canadian couples (Government of Canada).

The U.S. presents a similar demographic picture whereby approximately one out of ten women was childfree in the mid-1970s (Livingston 1). In 2014, women between the ages of 40-44 experienced child freedom at a rate of 15 per cent (Livingston 2). One in five women over the age of forty-five are without children in the high income nations of the U.S., Canada, Ireland, the United Kingdom, and Australia. In industrialized countries, estimates place women that are childfree to represent anywhere between 4 to 9 per cent of the population (DeLyser 46). For some countries, such as Germany and Japan, that number can increase to one in three as Gunter Burkart identifies this childfree pattern in Germany as a culture of childlessness. As such, women who embrace this lifestyle choice are not identified as socially defective. The culture and lifestyle are seen as attractive to individual women and are embraced by couples in that nation. The Scandinavian countries of Sweden, Norway, Finland, and Denmark have the highest rate of solo living in the world. Similarly, Suzanne Noordhuizen, Paul de Graaf, and Inge Sieben note that in the Netherlands, those couples that cohabited in the 1960s and remained childless were socially accepted at a rate of 20 per cent; however, by the 1990s, the rate of social acceptance increased to 90 per cent (163). Meanwhile, in the 1990s, Spain and Italy had the lowest fertility rates in the world (Kohler, Billari, and Ortega 643).

In some countries, such as Romania, the topic of childfree women is taboo. It remains a silent social issue, which further clouds its meaning and stigmatizes its entity, rendering childfree women as social outcasts. Communist Russia and Poland, for example, taxed households that did not have children; thus, those who were voluntarily, or involuntarily childfree, were economically penalized by the state for choosing, or not, to be without children.

In low-income countries, the incidence of childlessness is less, given women's lack of access to educational resources as well as contraceptives. When race and ethnicity are factored into the social demographic picture in the U.S., Hispanics are more likely to have children between the ages of forty and forty-four in comparison with white women (17 per cent), Black women (15 per cent), and Asian women (13 per cent) (Livingston 3). Some exceptions can be found in such countries as China, India, and Brazil, which have the fastest growing rates of one-person households in the world. Less is known in the research, however, about "the experiences of childless women and especially poor childless women of color have not been investigated" (Kelly 163).

Some of the explanations of these increases in childfree outcomes may be the high financial costs associated with raising and socializing children from birth to young adulthood and the recent economy downturns. This is an important factor, since raising and socializing children involve significant financial costs to those who care for them.

The Financial Cost of Raising Children in North America

The financial costs of raising children in Canada are significant. The cost estimates vary for raising children until the age of eighteen. For example, in 2004 in Winnipeg, Manitoba, it was estimated to cost approximately $167,000.00 (Manitoba Agriculture). Boys, it was suggested, cost more than girls, as they consume more food, but the costs associated with personal care are higher for girls. A U.S. figure was pegged at a total cost of $243,660.00 (Cornell). If estimates include loss time in waged work of a family member and sending the child to university/college, more realistic monetary figures are set at a range of $700,000.00 to 900,000.00 in the U.S. and approximately $670,000.00 in Canada (McMahon 3).

These figures are indexed according to income; thus, those with fewer socioeconomic resources are less able to spend a lot of money on raising their children. Their financial costs are estimated at 27 per cent less than that of middle-income parents in the U.S. Additionally, there are the financial costs to society that must also be considered, such as healthcare and education costs (Vanier Institute, *The Cost*).

There are also costs associated with getting pregnant. A couple in Kitchener, Ontario, for example, paid $15,000.00 for fertility treatments in order to have their two children (Vallis 2). Childcare costs are also high; in a large city such as Calgary, Alberta, childcare is estimated to cost $1,440.00 per month for two young children (Vallis 1).

These financial costs may dissuade some from wanting to have children at all.

Social Patterns Associated with Educated Women and Partnering

Gloria Steinem remained unmarried for most of her adult life, only marrying at the age of sixty-six to David Bale. She was entirely happy not to have children and valued her freedom and independent lifestyle. Her marriage lasted only three years, as Bale was diagnosed with a brain tumor, was institutionalized in a nursing home, and eventually died at a relatively young age.

The pattern of women who marry and who are potential marriage partners is based upon the marriage gradient, which tends to show that women marry up in social stature and men tend to marry down. This gradient is structured along socioeconomic lines and is influenced by education and income. Men with more education have a greater likelihood to accrue more income and have many partner choices among women who are lower on the gradient (Veevers 176). This creates a universal norm of hypergamy, which solidifies stiff structural competition for mates from the potential pool of eligible partners, especially for women (Veevers 176).

The mating pattern for women with education, and on the top scale of the income gradient, allows them fewer partner choices overall. If there is no one to marry up to, they may find themselves alone. This pattern of mate selection is based on hypergamy (Veevers 175). These women may find that they have fewer choices of probable partners, as their high income earnings and education may make some men feel emasculated; they may also choose not to partner down in social status or follow the hypogamy pattern (Veevers 175). This finding also highlights why older women have higher rates of childlessness. In the U.S., for example, "more education is associated with higher rates of childlessness for women ages 40 to 44" (Livingston 2).

These patterns of eligibility for marriage are based upon what is culturally seen as the ideal marriage in a heterosexual, patriarchal, and capitalistic society. The male is older, taller, and successful and makes the major decisions in the household, whereas the female is typically younger, smaller, and less educated; she stays home to clean and procreate (Baker 74). In more equal intimate relationships, be they heterosexual or homosexual, women typically desire more egalitarian partner relationships. This is not to suggest that men do not desire this as well. Equitable relationships tend to be based on the pattern of social homogamy, whereby, we tend to live, associate, and partner with individuals who are more similar to ourselves in terms of education and who are raised in similar neighbourhoods, undertake similar types of work, and follow the same religion.

Concerning the availability of options open to men, Eric Klinenberg talks about the 1960s culture that pushed the Playboy lifestyle for men to sidestep marriage, children, and stability in order to pursue the world of open options with women. Hugh Heffner's vision, as publicized in his magazine, precluded commitment and morality, let alone partnering for life with dependents in the form of women and children (Klinenberg 44). The focus for men was on individuality, on playfulness, and on having a flying urban lifestyle based on consumerism, which allowed their more favourable access to women. Women were, conversely, to know and to keep their place in the home as wives, and mothers (Fratterigo 751). There was no accompanying positive media forum, nor was there a realistic image for women who were single and without children. Such an image in that era would amount to a derogatory one.

Hence, women were not considered equal partners in relationships. They were encumbered by the lifestyle of marriage and raising and socializing children. They were dissuaded from accessing higher education, which, in turn, allowed for higher income status. Even when women did climb the occupational ladder of opportunity and success, going at it alone and without children, it was considered culturally nonnormative and put one at social risk.

The Workplace and Women

If women were excluded from the images portrayed in the single lifestyle in the 1960s, childfree women continue to be excluded in workplace policy agenda. Elizabeth Hamilton, Judith Gordon, and Karen Whelan-Berry suggest how single women are absent from the work-life academic literature (394). Instead, women who are married with children proliferate in this social policy formulation. Larger cohorts of single women are grouped together in workplace policies such that those who are widowed, separated, and/or divorced are placed on equal footing (Lewis and Borders). Large variations exist between these various cohorts of single women, versus those women with dependents, married women, and those that are childfree women, such as the WINKS.

Women without partners and who are childfree are seen as steady committed workers to the employer, since they will not require long maternity leaves (Hamilton, Gordon, and Whelan-Berry 397). The childfree woman is also often called upon to do extra work on the weekends or stay longer after hours on the job, whereas married employees are often occupied during these times (Hamilton Gordon and Whelan-Berry 397). A stereotypical image of childfree women also exists in which they are seen as largely career driven and highly competitive among their workplace peers and associates (Hamilton, Gordon, and Whelan-Berry 398). Most of the benefits seen to be important to married working women with children are less important to childfree working women. Benefits that may not be required by childfree working women include flextime, maternity leaves, childcare programs for their children after school hours and on holidays, as well as time off when a child is sick (406). These workplace patterns, policies, trends, and ideological discourses based in pronatalism are suggestive of "an ideology that implicitly or explicitly, supports parenthood and encourages fertility" (Rich et al. 228).

The Culture of Childfree Women

Stephanie Rich et al.'s research in Australia shows that certain women are seen as less likely to be good mothers, such as lesbians, teenagers, and single mothers, because of certain prejudices, including homophobia, ageism, and sexism. If mothers are to be seen as givers, caretakers, and patient, selfless beings, childfree women are envisioned as sad, empty, desperate, suffering, selfish, materialistic, and unfeminine beings (Gillespie 50; Kelly 167; Letherby 7; Rich et al. 236). They are representations of the antithesis of what is seen and understood to be normal womanhood and mothering. Hence, not only does the culture hold prejudices against women it also stigmatizes them.

In some countries, such as India, a woman who cannot provide children for her husband suffers profusely (Dandekar 124). Not having children in certain rural areas in India, such as Maharashtra, means a woman can become an outsider in the eyes of her family (Dandekar 124). Their patriarchal culture only supports motherhood and children through the institution of marriage, and this forms the basis for property inheritance: "The entire process of reproduction for women is an 'othering' experience that connects their reproductive body and their children's physical safety to the institution of marriage, which forms the backbone of a governance ideology, regulating ownership and inheritance of private property" (Dandekar 130). To be without child is to be impure and afflicted. Only mothers with children are given power and have positions of respect (Dandekar 133). Sons have more social and cultural worth, and daughters are to be providers of services in their adult years (Dandekar 135).

In Bangladesh, another patriarchal country, a childfree woman is considered to be a social failure; her body is without purpose, and she is seen to be a social deviant (Nahar and van der Geest 382) If the childless woman has little income, she remains at the bottom of the class hierarchy and cannot attend social events and functions (385). Rural childfree women are thwarted publicly, and urban childfree women experience a more hidden form of childlessness (Nahar and van der Geest 385). A woman's inability to have children will often negatively frame her entire identity (Nahar and van der Geest 388).

Similarly, in China, women who are aged twenty-seven or older and have not yet married are negatively labelled as too "free willed" and are called the "leftover women." In search of postsecondary education, these urban women may seek to marry later or not at all. They are socially incomplete and viewed as outsiders in their traditional culture (Reynolds). The negative labels are assumed to incentivize these young women to marry. If they do not, they are seen as government burdens, whereby they will be assumed to be too busy to care for their aging parents, involved as they are in their own life and work (Reynolds). Politically, these unmarried women, and perhaps eventually childfree women, are seen as shameful to the country, to their elders, and to their family.

Amanda Ee Hui Lee, Caroline Pluss, and Chan Kwok-bun's research of sixteen married Chinese-Singaporean voluntary childfree women shows that most often their decisions were motivated by their finances, career pursuits, and concerns that their husbands would be absent in the childrearing; moreover, there was insufficient help in Singapore to assist them in their childcaring pursuits (231). They were also unlikely to tell in-laws and their own parents of their childfree decision (239) and were fearful of the extended commitments of having children. They also felt they would be inadequate as mothers (244) and that they were not attractive enough to find a partner (243). These mothers could not foresee how they could mesh their careers with children, as the added responsibilities would curtail their time and freedom (245).

Childfree women are more likely to have advanced education and to be older and unmarried. They seem to have limited religious affiliation or are atheists; they are also highly committed to their career, have greater work experience, have higher income status, and live in the urban sphere (Abma and Martinez 1052; Avison and Furnham 60; DeLyser 47; Doyle, Pooley, and Breen 399; Hird and Abshoff 351; Jones and Brayfield 1261, Krishnan 89; Rovi 350). For example, in 2015, U.S. women who are medical doctors or hold a PhD were childfree at a rate of 20 per cent; the rate was 25 per cent for those who had a bachelor's degree (Livingston, 2). Social nonacceptance of voluntary childlessness in the Netherlands, meanwhile, is based on more conservative viewpoints by way of religiousity, and those who are more open to a childfree lifestyle again usually have higher levels of income and education (Noordhuizen, de Graaf, and Sieben 163).

Motivations and Outcomes of Being a Childfree Woman

Concerning voluntary childlessness in Australia, Elizabeth Addie and Charlotte Brownlow show that single childfree women have more flexibility in their chosen lifestyle. For these women, this life choice provides them with more educational opportunities as well as chances for career advancement (429), providing them with great personal fulfillment, purpose, and freedom in their lives. They did not worry about marriage, nor did they worry about the fact that they are unpartnered (431). In contrast, Helen Peterson's research in Sweden, where the welfare state allows for women to combine children with success in career, childfree women rarely mentioned freedom to access better careers (189). Palladino Schultheiss notes, however, that "changes in social policy are critically needed so women no longer have to mother or matter" (42). Globally, the workplace does not afford all women equal opportunity structured in workplace policy; hence, the diverse roles and lives of working women need to be politically addressed.

Some scholars have found that due to some type of psychopathology experienced in childhood, or through poor parental role modelling and challenging, or disruptive socialization processes as children, some women, as a result, choose not to have children (Hird and Aschoff 348; Settle and Brumley 7; Reading and Amatea 259). Others have highlighted other factors leading to voluntary childlessness, including concerns about overpopulation and the environment, a dislike of children, the inability to parent, as well as fears associated with childbirth (Hird and Aschoff 353-354).

Gail DeLyser's research of fifteen intentionally childfree midlife women in the U.S. found them to have no regrets and to lead full and interesting lives. Similarly, Braelin Settle and Krista Brumley suggest that child freedom allows for more personal travel time and increased time for one's partner as well as other relationships (12). Peterson found that the majority of the voluntary childless in her sample of Swedish women cited their need for personal freedom. That is, they did not feel controlled, and they experienced both independence and autonomy in their childfree existence (186). This finding supports the notion of the immense power of social structure that works against women as "the only class of women who can be comfortably understood as being ambitious or publicly powerful are those who are unmarried and childfree" (Traister 157).

For some women, who are more "passive deciders," Settle and Brumley found that the childfree choice evolved as a result of aging, the lack of a partner, issues with financial security, or career focus (8). Many thought that children would be part of their life; however, as time marched on, this was not what occurred (9). Having children for many was seen as problematic, possibly resulting in the loss of their career and identity (14). So, remaining childfree allows one more financial opportunities (12). Power may come earlier to women when they are neither married nor have children, and power may translate into wage parity when one delays the events of marriage and children (Traister 159). The single and childfree who live alone and who are over the age of twenty seven have more money to spend on eating out, purchasing more expensive housing and clothes, and enjoying fun, leisurely activities ("Indie Women").

Moving beyond (M)Otherhood

The global stereotype associated with single childfree women as unhappy, lonely, and demoralized is tied into "a mythology, a gloss" (DePaulo 3). It is more mythical than real and locks women into old and outmoded ways of being, precluding health, happiness, freedom, and financial stability with upward mobility. The myths place burdens on the shoulders of childfree women who may often have no burdens and no time to think of loneliness in their full and bright freedom. Women of the otherhood do not typically see the world through "momopia" glasses (Notkin xvi). Instead, they can be seen to be "childfull" (Notkin xxiii) in the numerous roles that they may occupy as aunts and godmothers to their nieces and nephews. And should they be godmothers to godchildren whom they love and adore and with whom they have time to cultivate solid relationships.

Women of the otherhood do and can have it all within their immediate choices and sense of agency. Once women move beyond the myths, stereotypes, and generalizations and fight against the social and structural barriers, they can both individually and collectively live and push back against outmoded ways of being and knowing. They can be their authentic selves and explore life, work, love, and new relationships. Rebecca Traister calls the childfree lifestyle one of "excitement, purpose, reward, recognition" (166). Women can work to become their best selves. Women may nurture their spirit, soul, heart, and way of life in the absence of children. Women can be what they want to be. The WINKS are unsinkable and choosing transformative purposeful lives. They need not be socially or culturally impoverished and desolate.

Lastly, women's lives in the workplace require a reframing and restructuring of policy to meet the needs of the WINKS. Elder care as well as leaves required to aid sick or disabled siblings or relatives should be added to the collective bargaining rights of childfree women. Equal footing with workplace peers is required so that they are not required to stay longer at the job, work overtime, or work weekends to offset the responsibilities associated with one's married peers and their child responsibilities. Flextime may be required by childfree women in the workplace should they have to attend to aging parents or friends and relatives in need or to advance their education. As Traister says, "[There is a] growth of a massive population of women who are living outside those dependent circumstances [which] puts new pressures on the government: to remake conditions in a way that will be more hospitable to female independence, to a citizenry now made up of women living economically, professionally, sexually and socially liberated lives" (298).

The independence and the freedom of the WINKS should not be presumed to be egotistical or selfish. Many of these women have worked hard to achieve academic and career success, which allows them a childfree lifestyle, whether chosen or not. As the world evolves and changes, the WINKS may become the new normal or "the normal life story of women closer to that of men" (Beck and Beck-Gernsheim 54), which can allow them to determine who they are and where they want to go. Instead of asking why women do not have children in the otherhood, the new question could be why men are without children or why there are "famous geezer Dads" (Menon). This would allow women to show their diverse selves and grow into their "other" world.

Works Cited

Abma, Joyce C., and Gladys M. Marinez. "Childlessness among Older Women in the United States: Trends and Profiles." *Journal of Marriage and Family*, vol. 68, no. 4, 2006, pp. 1045-56.

Addie, Elizabeth, and Charlotte Brownlow. "Deficit and Asset Identity Constructions of Single Women without Children Living in Australia: An Analysis of Discourse." *Feminism and Psychology*, vol. 24, no. 4, 2014, pp. 423-39.

Avison, Margaret, and Adrian Furnham. "Personality and Voluntary Childlessness." *Journal of Population Research*, vol. 32, 2015, pp. 45-67.

Baker, Maureen. *Choices and Constraints in Family Life*: Oxford University Press, 2014.

Beck, Ulrich, and Elizabeth Beck-Gernsheim. *Individualization*. Sage Publications, 2002.

Blackstone, Amy, and Mahala Dyer Stewart. "Choosing to Be Childfree: Research on the Decision Not to Parent." *Sociology Compass*, vol. 6, no. 9, 2012, pp. 718-27.

Burkart, Gunter. "Eine Kulture des Zweifels: Kinderlosigkeit und die Zukunft der Familie." *Ein Leben Ohne Kinder Kinderlosigkeit in Deutschland*, edited by Dirk Konietzka and Michaela Kreyenfeld, VS-Verlag fur Sozialwissenschaften, 2007, pp. 401-23.

Cornell, Camilla. "The Real Cost of Raising Kids." *Money Sense*, 10 Aug. 2011.

Dandekar, Deepra. "Childlessness and Empathetic Relationships." *The Oriental Anthropologist*, vol. 14, no. 1, 2014, pp. 123-39.

DeLyser, Gail. "At Midlife, Intentionally Childfree Women and Their Experiences of Regret." *Clinical Social Work*, vol. 40, 2012, pp. 66-74.

DePaulo, Bella. *Singled Out.* St. Martin's Press, 2007.

Doyle, Joanne, Julie Ann Pooley, and Lauren Breen. "A Phenomenological Exploration of the Childfree Choice in a Sample of Australian Women." *Journal of Health Psychology*, vol. 18, no. 3, 2012, pp. 397-407.

Fratterigo, Elizabeth. "The Answer to Suburbia: Playboy's Urban Lifestyle." *Journal of Urban History*, vol. 34, no. 5, 2008, pp. 747-74.

Gillespie, Rosemary. "When No Means No: Disbelief, Disregard and Deviance as Discourses of Voluntary Childless Women." *Gender and Society*, vol. 17, 2000, pp. 122-36.

Government of Canada. *Fertility. Healthy Canadians*, 201, healthy canadians.gc.ca/healthy-living-vie-saine/pregnancy-grossesse/fertility-fertilite/fert-eng.php. Accessed 9 Dec. 2020.

Hamilton, Elizabeth A., Judith R. Gordon, and Karen S. Whelan-Berry. "Understanding the Work-Life Conflict of Never-Married Women Without Children." *Women in Management Review*, vol. 21, no. 5, 2006, pp. 393-415.

Hird, Myra J., and Kimberly Abshoff. "Women Without Children : A Contradiction in Terms?" *Journal of Comparative Family Studies*, vol. 31, no. 3, 2000, pp. 347-66.

Hui Li, Amanda Ee, Caroline Pluss, and Chan Kwok-bun, "To Be or Not to Be: Chinese-Singaporean Women Deliberating on Voluntary Childlessness." *International Handbook of Chinese Families*, edited by Chan Kwok-bun, Springer, 2013, pp. 231-48.

"Indie Women." *The Curve Report*. NBC Universal, 2012, thecurve report.com/category/films/indie-women/. Accessed 9 Dec. 2020.

Jacobson, Cardell K., and Tim B. Heaton. "Voluntary Childlessness among American Men Women in the Late 1980s." *Social Biology*, vol. 38, 1991, pp. 79-93.

Jones, Rachel K., and April Brayfield. "Life's Greatest Joy? European Attitudes towards the Centrality of Children." *Social Forces*, vol. 75, 1997, pp. 1239-70.

Kelly, Maura. "Women's Voluntary Childlessness: A Radical Rejection of Motherhood?" *Women's Studies Quarterly*, vol. 37, no. 3-4, 2009, pp. 157-72.

Klinenberg, Eric. *Going Solo: The Extraordinary Rise and Surprising Appeal of Living Alone.* The Penguin Press, 2012.

Kohler, Hans Peter, Francesco C. Billari, and Jose Antonio Ortega. "The Emergence of Lowest-Low Fertility in Europe During the 1990s." *Population and Development Review,* vol. 28, no. 4, 2002, pp. 641-80.

Krishna, Vijaya. "Religious Homogamy and Voluntary Childlessness in Canada." *Sociological Perspectives* 36.1 (1993): 83-93.

Letherby, Gayle. "Childless and Bereft? Stereotypes and Realities in Relation to 'Voluntary' and 'Involuntary' Childlessness and Womanhood." *Sociological Inquiry,* vol. 72, no. 1, 2002, pp. 7-20.

Lewis, Virginia, G., and L. DiAnne, Borders. "Life Satisfaction of Single Middle-Aged Professional Women." *Journal of Counselling and Development,* vol. 74, no. 1, 1995, pp. 94-100.

Livingston, Gretchen. "Childlessness Falls, Family Size Grows Among Highly Educated Women". Pew Research Centre, May 7, 2015.

Manitoba Agriculture. *The Costs of Raising Children.* Government of Manitoba, 2004. home.gicable.com/jqgregg/Cost%20of%20 raising%children.pdf. Accessed 9 Dec. 2020.

McMahon, Tamsin. "Million-dollar Babies." *Macleans,* 30 Sept. 2013, www.macleans.ca/society/life/million-dollar-babies/. Accessed 9 Dec. 2020.

Menon, Vinay. "Let's Pick on Mick, Not Jen: Celebrity Wombs Like Aniston's Need Less Attention. Famous Geezer Dads Need More." *The Toronto Star,* 17 July 2016, pp. E1 and E4.

Milan, Anne, Leslie-Anne Keown, and Covadonga Robles Urquijo. "Women in Canada: A Gender-Based Statistical Report: Families, Living Arrangements, and Unpaid Work." Statistics Canada Catalogue no. 89-503-X, December 2011.

Nahar, Papreen, and Sjaak van der Geest. "How Women in Bangladesh Confront the Stigma of Childlessness: Agency, Resilience, and Resistance." *Medical Anthropology Quarterly,* vol. 28, no. 3, 2014, pp. 381-98.

Noordhuizen, Suzanne, Paul de Graaf, and Inge Sieben. "The Public Acceptance of Voluntary Childlessness in the Netherlands: From 20 to 90 Percent in 30 Years." *Social Indicators Research,* vol. 99, 2010, pp. 163-81.

Notkin, Melanie. *Otherhood: Modern Women Finding a New Kind of Happiness.* Seal Press, 2014.

Palladino Schultheiss, Donna E. "To Mother or Matter—Can Women do Both?" *Journal of Career Development*, vol. 36, no. 1, 2009, pp. 25-48.

Peterson, Helen. "Fifty Shades of Freedom. Voluntary Childlessness as Women's Ultimate Liberation." *Women's Studies International Forum*, vol. 53, 2015, pp. 182-91.

Reading, Janet, and Ellen S. Amatea. "Role Deviance or Role Diversification: Reassessing the Psychological Factors Affecting the Parenthood Choice of Career-Oriented Women." *Journal of Marriage and the Family*, vol. 48, no. 2, 1986, pp. 255-60.

Reynolds, Christopher. "Viral Video Inspires China's 'Leftover Women'" *The Toronto Star*, 18 Apr. 2016, www.thestar.com/news/world/2016/04/18/viral-video-inspires-chinas-leftover-women.html. Accessed 9 Dec. 2020.

Rich, Stephanie, et al. "'Unnatural.' 'Unwomanly,' 'Uncreditable' and 'Undervalued'" The Significance of Being a Childless Woman in Australian Society." *Gender Issues*, vol. 28, no. 4, 2011, pp. 226-47.

Rijken, Arieke J., and Eva-Maria Merz. "Double Standards: Differences in Norms on Voluntary Childlessness for Men and Women." *European Sociological Review*, vol. 30, no. 4, 2014, pp. 470-82.

Rovi, Susan. "Taking 'No' for an Answer: Using Negative Reproductive Intentions to Study the Childless/Childfree." *Population Research and Policy Review*, vol. 13, no. 4, 1994, pp. 343-65.

Sarlo, Christopher A. "The Cost of Raising Children." The Fraser Institute, 2013.

Settle, Braelin., and Krista Brumley. "It's the Choices You Make That Get You There: Decision-Making Pathways of Childfree Women." *Michigan Family Review*, vol. 18, no. 1, 2014, pp. 1-22.

Szalma, Ivett, and Judit Takacs. "Who Remains Childless? Unrealised Fertility Plans in Hungary." *Czech Sociological Review*, vol. 51, no. 6, 2015, pp. 1047-75.

Traister, Rebecca. *All the Single Ladies.* Simon and Schuster, 2016.

United States Census Bureau. *2006-2008 American Community Three Year Estimates.* United States Government, 2015.

Vallis, Mary. "How Much Does it Cost to Raise a Family?" *Today's Parent*, vol. 24, no. 3 2007, pp. 1-7.

Vanier Institute of the Family. "Fertility Intentions: If, When and How Many?" *Fascinating Families.* Vanier, 2008.

Vanier Institute of the Family. *The Cost of Raising Children, Families Count: Profiling Canada's Families.* IV. Vanier, 2010.

Veevers, Jean. "The 'Real' Marriage Squeeze: Mate Selection, Mortality, and the Mating Gradient." *Sociological Perspectives*, vol. 31, no. 2, 1988, pp. 169-89.

Chapter Three

Childless or Free of Children? Self-Definition and Being Childfree

Stuart Gietel-Basten, Jasmijn Obispo, Clare Ridd,
and Sonia Yuhui Zhang

An Issue of Definition

Within demography and sociology, the concept of "childlessness" is used and implemented almost without thought. When we think of childlessness rates, for example, in formal demographic terms, we would generally consider the population involved to be women aged forty-five or above. The reason for this rather arbitrary upper age limit is based upon the biological (and, to a degree, social) challenges of bearing children after this age. Apart from the arbitrariness of the age, this definition, of course, ignores the potential pathways to children through surrogacy and adoption. For men, the definition is arguably much harder, given the potential to father children at ages seemingly without an upper age bound, although the biological limitations are certainly present.

More importantly, however, is the definitional cleavage between voluntary and involuntary childlessness. These two definitions are useful within demography inasmuch as they suggest alternative pathways to childlessness. These multiple pathways have been explored in numerous studies (e.g., Tanturri and Mencarini for Italy). The term "involuntary childlessness" tends to imply that women and men have been unable to have children, usually for biological reasons. This definition is set up in contrast to those who have chosen to not bear children. For example, the U.S. National Survey distinctly compares the "voluntarily childless" and the "not voluntarily childless" (Waren). Numerous studies have sought to identify the predictors of voluntary childlessness among women and men and have uncovered the following ones: being less traditional and conventional in their gender roles (Bram; Baber and Dreyer; Callan); lower levels of religious observance (Mosher et al., "The Importance"; Heaton, et al.; Mosher et al., "New Patterns"); urban residency (DeOllos and Kapinus); greater financial stability and professional employment (Crispell; Bachu; Cwikel et al.); and higher levels of education (Abma et al.; Bachu; Biddlecom and Martin; Keizer et al.; Kneale and Joshi).

Numerous studies have, however, identified a clear inadequacy in considering childlessness as a binary. What about the so-called perpetual postponers (Kneale and Joshi) who find themselves to be voluntarily— and then, perhaps, involuntarily—childless as a consequence? What of those whom Carolyn Morell refers to as the "wavering noes," who despite moments of wanting, sometimes desperately, to bear children never, in fact, do?

Part of this debate over the definition of childlessness and the pathways thereto concern the very name itself. Within the literature, there is a clear distinction between childless and childfree. This goes beyond syntax. The former term implies that a couple or person is explicitly without something that is, perhaps, naturally expected (Paul)—bereft, in other words (Rovi; Letherby). Say, for example, being homeless or friendless. Being free of something, however, is far more positive and implies a kind of emancipation from something either by choice or by good fortune, such as carefree or disease-free. For Morell, this dichotomy of concepts can be translated into the female physiology as comparing the status of the womb as either a space of "vacant emptiness" or a space or "radical openness" (318). Rosemary Gillespie has identified two distinct yet interrelated motivational factors toward choosing to be childfree—the "attraction or pull of being childfree" (126) and the "rejection or the push away from motherhood" (129). The attraction of being childfree is characterized by increased freedom and better relationships with partners and others, while the push from motherhood involves a loss of identity and a rejection of the activities associated with motherhood.

In this sense, then, being childfree is an explicit rejection of childbearing; it is something beyond being voluntarily childless. I have argued elsewhere that there has been a significant decline in stigma towards childless women and men in a variety of cultural settings (Basten), although this is far from complete (Ashburn-Nardo; Koropeckyj-Cox et al.). This change is both imposed from others and is projected outwards in terms of a sense of confidence and self-worth. Part of this change clearly involves changes in social referencing. Although Sharon K. Houseknecht observed the importance of normative approval for childlessness within limited social contexts as a counterbalance to the negative stereotyping of others in the 1970s and even though Lise Motherwell and Suze Prudent advocated the use of psychotherapeutic techniques as recently as 1998, the ability to communicate and create social networks is entirely different today. On Facebook alone, there are a wide variety of groups for the childfree, each with hundreds of members, and a number of dedicated internet message boards and forums exist to provide support and shared experiences.

As well as internet-based discussion forums, however, a large number of social groups for the childfree are increasingly coming into existence, facilitated by the power of the internet to identify and communicate with like-minded people. Not only do these groups serve as spaces where members' decisions are regarded as normative and advice and social support can be given, but they also diminish the so-called social capital argument made by some anthropologists, which suggest that child bearers interact with more people as a result of the contacts and networks associated with their offspring. Both of these virtual and real groups display a large degree of heterogeneity in their outlook. G.N. Ramu's study of voluntarily childless couples in Winnipeg, for example, found that they did not comprise anything remotely resembling a "hedonistic, spontaneous, proselytizing, subculture" (130). In contrast, a number of views expressed on internet forums may be perceived as acutely self-assertive. For example, the mailing list for *www.childfree.net* states: "WARNING: Anti-child or anti-parent sentiments are sometimes expressed on this list; if this offends you, please don't subscribe" ("Childfree Mailing List."

One website that explicitly utilizes the connectedness afforded by the internet to create physical contact between like-minded people is *meetup.*

com. On this website, users can search for an interest and look for local groups local who hold real-life meetings. In the United States (U.S.) and the United Kingdom (U.K.) in particular, there are a large number of childfree meetup groups, especially in larger urban areas. In many cases, these meetup groups have their own websites that outline their activities as well as their objectives. A cursory examination of just a few of the websites of these childfree groups shows, to no surprise, a wide range of activities, memberships, and objectives. Some are pragmatic and straightforward. For example, the group Childfree by Choice Women in Austin says the following: "This group is for Austin area women who are childfree by choice and in their late twenties to early forties who would like to meet other like-minded women for happy hour, dinner, drinks, shows, movies, etc" ("Childfree by Choice"). In the same city, the group Austin No Kidding has a rather more extended introduction:

> Welcome to Austin No Kidding! (ANK!), the social group for adult couples and singles who never have had children. If you are not a parent, and would like to socialize with other adults who are also childfree, please join us. We sponsor several activities a month and a variety of special events. There are no membership dues or fees; we are all volunteers. In ANK!, we have fun, make friends, and create a community for Austin-area adults who are childfree. It is that simple. Our members, for whatever reason, are not parents. In ANK!, we recognize that it can be difficult for adults who are not parents to find friendship with others who are similarly childfree. Our many events celebrate the freedom and spontaneity of being an adult without children. We are always ready for new ideas. ("Austin No Kidding")

Again, echoing Ramu's study of the childless in Winnipeg, rather than a "hedonistic, spontaneous, proselytizing, subculture," the activities of these meetup groups are more likely to involve trips to the bowling alley. However, this is not to say that explicitly identifying with a childfree group is not, in itself, a political or expressive act. Exploring this motivation in greater depth is the goal of this chapter.

Self-Definition in Childfree Meetup Groups

Although numerous studies have differentiated between voluntary childlessness, involuntary childlessness, and childfree at a conceptual level in numerous studies, scholars have given less attention to how individual men and women self-define and how they rationalize this self-definition. Given the definitional fluidity outlined in the previous section, this study sets out to explore in greater depth how the childless define themselves and how this definition is justified. More particularly, we wanted to examine the extent to which being childfree really is the radical alternative to childless in the minds of ordinary men and women as well as in the minds of sociologists.

To do this, we approached the main listed contact points for all of the childfree meetup groups in the U.K., the U.S., and Australia as listed on *meetup.com* in March 2009. We asked these contact persons to circulate an outline of the broader project on being childfree to group members and asked interested parties to contact the research team to take part. Participants were then sent a short questionnaire covering a wide variety of aspects relating to being childfree, of which the questions regarding definitions were just one part.

Within the survey, participants were asked "Which of the following (childfree/voluntary childless/childfree by choice/childless/other) would you use to identify yourself?" and "What do you understand to be the difference between these terms?" In the findings section below, we report the quantitative responses to the question regarding self-definition and the results of a thematic analysis of the justification of the choice of term. Given that the textual responses to the justification question were generally rather short—averaging around 59 words—it was not possible to perform an especially in-depth qualitative analysis.

In order to maintain anonymity, the particular group to which respondents belong is not linked to the responses here. The sample consisted of forty people, thirty-six of whom were female and four male. The majority of respondents hailed from groups based in the U.S. and Canada, with just one respondent from Australia. There was no geographical association to responses. Ages ranged from twenty-three to sixty-five, with a mean age of forty; 64.1 per cent defined themselves as having no religious affiliation or being atheist or agnostic. Of those who declared a religious belief, 35.7 per cent attended a religious service once a month or more; 71.8 per cent were either married or living with a partner, the remainder being single, divorced, or separated. All had completed high school, and 76.9 per cent possessed bachelor's degrees or higher. The median personal income was $65 000 compared to the U.S. average household income of $52,029; 85 per cent of the sample were heterosexual, 5% homosexual, and 10% bisexual. By far the largest ethnic group represented was white, non-Hispanic/non-Latino, accounting for 77.5% of the sample.

The study was approved by the Central University Research Ethics Committee of the University of Oxford (Ref: SSD/CUREC1/09-128).

Findings

As can be seen in Table 1, one survey respondent chose to refer to herself as "childless," whereas the majority of respondents either preferred referring to themselves as "childfree" or "childfree by choice." For the males specifically, however, no clear preference can be seen. No males identified themselves as childless. As such, this finding implies that there is a qualitative difference in self-definition between being viewed as childless and some other definitions. In terms of the objective of this study, then, it appears that the question of how those without children self-define is not a purely academic issue in the minds of sociologists. This analysis considers the reasons for these preferences or lack of preference concerning the labels for not having children. The demographic characteristics of the respondents are set out in Appendix 1.

Table 1: Responses to the Question "Which of the Following (Childfree/Voluntary Childless/Childfree by Choice/ Childless/Other) Would You Use to Identify Yourself?"

	Female	Male	Not Specified	Total
Childless	1	0	0	1
Childfree	12	1	1	14
Voluntarily Childless	4	1	0	5
Childfree by Choice	14	1	0	15
Voluntarily Childless/ Childfree by Choice	2	0	0	2
Other/Not specified	4	1	0	5
Total	**37**	**4**	**1**	**42**

There are recurring themes in the survey responses, both concerning specific terms and in the comments in general, as similar ideas arise in the explanations of different terms. The results show diverse interpretations of the discussed terms, descriptions that are contradictory at points. For example, some respondents' understanding of what it means to be "voluntarily childless" are the same as their own and other definitions of the term "childfree by choice"; they view both labels as implying one has chosen not to have any children. In contrast, two definitions of "childfree" appear to be partially in opposition to each other ; some respondents view the term as implying that one has made a choice not to have children and does not perceive this as a loss but as liberating. Other respondents do not find that an initial choice to not have children defines being "childfree"; rather, one can be childfree after initially attempting to have children.

One essential point seems to have led to most of the divergence in the responses—that is, whether having a child is always essentially a matter of choice. Having a child entirely as a matter of choice is related to an understanding of what having a child means, whether, for example, the limits are drawn at the ability to conceive personally or not. Other people see the limits to freedom in having a child, taking note of possible circumstances that circumvent having children. These factors influence how respondents decide to refer to themselves. For some, it was not important whether or not their nonparenting status was initially born out of a choice regarding how they would like to be called, yet several of these people placed significance on expressing their attitude towards not having children through the label they selected. For others, making evident their fundamental freedom in this decision was essential in determining how they referred to themselves.

This analysis establishes several themes based on the survey responses in order to gain a better understanding of how the respondents choose to refer to themselves and why. Most significantly, this study notes that the name many of the participants picked is related to their desire to claim agency in their not having any children. In this sense, choosing a name for themselves is a way of expressing a state of mind. As a consequence, the sole notion of not having children as the absence of something to be sympathized with—which is how many understand the term "childlessness"—is being uprooted.

The analysis will first consider understandings of being childless, noting the repeated interpretation of this term as suggestive of lack, the absence of choice, unfulfillment, and so on. Subsequently, the analysis considers the desire to accentuate not having children as a personal choice rather than an "accident or circumstance" (respondent A) (see Appendix). The study will then focus on the desire to subvert the conventional notion of not having children as something negative. It notes several ways in which the respondents do this—first, by expressing their not having children as something positive. The survey reveals that there is a perceived sense of liberation associated with not having children for numerous reasons. For example, several participants see it as a way of claiming agency in their lives, not feeling the need to conform to societal expectations or other normative pressures. Furthermore, five respondents chose not to refer to themselves by any of the given possible labels. Notably, in these respondents, we see a desire to remain apolitical and strive for something more neutral—thus, not referring to not having children as something that is per se positive but nonetheless freeing themselves from the negative associations related to the term "childless." Respondents also mention their choosing not to have children as a kind of lifestyle, one around which a community can potentially be established. Several respondents, however, speak of the unnecessarily explicit nature of some of the labels, such as "childfree by choice," and the vocal character of people they associate with them.

A recurring understanding of the term "childless" highlights a sense of unfulfillment or incompleteness due to an inability to have children. Most of these responses note the personal desire of these individuals to have children, thus leading to a sense of dissatisfaction. One female describes a childless person as follows: "A person who does not have children for whatever reason, usually because they are sterile, single, or got married at a late age. These people usually want children but could not have them for whatever reason." (B). Similarly, another female sees "childless" as referring to a person who "doesn't have children due to circumstances rather than choice" (C). Some, however, note that this individual may not personally feel the desire to have children but experiences external normative pressures that make them feel a sense of lack, for example: "Childless ... has more of a negative connotation and usually refers to either a situation in which a person/couple would like to have children but can't for various reasons or doesn't want to and is feeling the social stigma of not having procreated, or also is on the fence between these two situations" (D). Likewise, another respondent perceives the term as "used by those who regret or belittle the status of nonparenting," implying an "incomplete state, or a lesser place in society, for example being homeless" (E).

We see that the term is often associated with an inferior or negative state of mind; the word is recurrently perceived as being associated with negative perceptions or sentiments related to nonparenting. Interestingly, a female who abstains from defining herself with one of the terms in the survey does not consider the term "childless" in a negative sense; she describes the "childless" as "those who do not have children, regardless of the reason" (F). Perhaps, her disinclination to define her status as nonparent has influenced her understanding of the term, for she does not accentuate the factor of choice in her not having any children.

The survey results show a strong desire to emphasize not having children as a personal choice one is free to make rather than an accident or circumstance. Most commonly, the respondents refer to themselves as "voluntarily childless," "childfree," or "childfree by choice" to underline their agency in not becoming parents. A thirty-year-old female understands being "childfree" and "childless" as simply not having children, but she adds: "It could mean that she wants to have/adopt children in the future or cannot have children but doesn't necessarily mean she has chosen not to have children" (G). She, therefore, chose "voluntarily childless/childfree by choice" because she feels they both signify consciously the decision to abstain from having children. In this response, we see that "childfree" and "childless" are not understood as permanent states and are not considered as fixed states of mind, whereas "voluntarily childless" and "childfree by choice" are actual positions that one decides to enter. We see similar responses elsewhere. The comments of a thirty-two-year-old female participant, who uses "voluntarily childless" to define herself, conceptualizes "childfree or childless" as those who are not able to conceive, thus viewing these states more permanently.

One sixty-five-year-old female's response clearly expresses her desire to emphasize the freedom she has exercised in her decision not to have children. The respondent selected "childfree by choice" because she chose not to have children, not because she could not: "I never tried. I had no miscarriage. No one else had any control over my decision, not even any input" (H). This respondent is stressing a clear sense of independence Moreover, she wants to make clear that she is not without children because of circumstance or anything other than her personal will. Some participants do not see a substantial difference between "childfree" and "childfree by choice," considering both labels as indicative of something positive. One of the respondents, who does not note much variance in the terms, prefers "childfree by choice" because she likes "the emphasis on choice" (I).

Although respondents often emphasis their decision not to have children, this decision was not necessarily straightforward or indicative of the individual's initial lack of desire procreate. One respondent explains: "My interpretation of 'childless by choice' or 'voluntarily childless is that of a person/couple who can't have children but chooses not to go ahead with fertility treatments or adoption, and is still in the process of reaching resolution on this matter, so this person/couple hasn't reached complete peace of mind" (J). In contrast to some of the examples above, in which an absence of desire to have children is evident, regardless of the ability to conceive or not, this case reveals a different choice concerning nonparenting. The respondent does not equate the decision with immediate personal gratification but, nonetheless, chooses a label to reflect her decision to remain childless, thus also claiming agency yet in a distinct manner. Such individuals claim agency in the sense that they determine how they respond to their inability to conceive also on an emotional level. Another recurring definition of voluntarily childless in the survey is a person "with a spouse/partner who cannot or does not want kids or has no kids because of sexual orientation" (K). Once again, we see that although the individual may not have decided not to have children initially, they have still decided not to become parents, making a choice over how they view themselves.

The responses also reveal participants' aspirations to free themselves from the notion of nonparenting as something negative. Recurrently, the respondents refer to ideas of "lack" and "loss" when speaking of the term "childless," whereas many of them feel that terms such as "childfree" and "childfree by choice" imply freedom, something positive. A fifty-six-year-old male who defined himself as childfree by choice explains: "Childfree, voluntary childless and childfree by choice are all pretty much the same and view not having kids as a good thing. Childless is don't have kids but wanted them or regret not having them" (L). Like several other respondents, he distinguishes the first three terms from childless. He is, therefore, able to express his satisfaction with not having children and to distinguish himself from the term "childless." Many of the survey participants with similar responses also mention the notion of freedom in their definitions of the terms. A twenty-nine-year-old female states that "childfree insinuates a positive emotion attributed to being 'free of children'" (M). She describes her personal view of not having children as positive, since she is free from what she considers to be a burden; the term "childfree" allows her to express this alternative state of mind. Furthermore, she chooses "childfree by choice to emphasize that it was a conscious decision." She desires to accentuate further that her not having any children was a matter of choice rather than a defect. In these responses, the individuals are claiming agency by stating how they view themselves and nonparenting.

Similarly, another female chose "childfree" to express her agency: "'Childless' and 'voluntarily childless' imply a lack of something, and I'm not voluntarily choosing not to lack anything! So those terms are objectionable to me. Childfree by choice is just a mouthful" (N).

This female, however, believes that "voluntarily childless" still connotes a lack, something she strongly does not sense. For this respondent, being able to express that she is not incomplete appears essential. In contrast to the twenty-nine-year-old female, she finds the qualifier "by choice" unnecessary.

Likewise, the respondents accentuate the absence of a sense of lack by presenting not having children from the perspective of being free. As another female respondent explains, "'Childless' implies the absence of something. Freedom is a choice not to be encumbered either by children or society's expectations" (O). She chooses "childfree" in order to display her experienced freedom. Her understanding of being childfree expresses a sense of liberation due to not having children to look after, but she also feels liberated from a perceived normative role women are subjected to. These respondents have chosen terms expressing that having children does not intrinsically define one's sense of fulfillment or completeness. They are claiming agency over their freedom in general, as they show their ability to feel fulfilled or achieve a sense of completeness on their grounds as opposed to having the conditions defined by societal expectations. Viewing nonparenting as "immunity from obligation" (P), as one respondent phrases it, enables these respondents to clarify their positive state of mind concerning not having children.

It should be noted, however, that being childfree does not result from a choice in all responses, and, consequently, it is not always viewed as something innately good. One respondent writes the following: "The term 'childfree' refers to a similar situation as [being childless], with the difference that this particular situation isn't necessarily the result of an initial choice (for instance, the couple can't have children), but it still leads to a positive resolution (the couple decides that they can live happily without children) rather than a negative/stagnant situation (the couple becomes childless)" (Q). She describes "childfree by choice" as being without children by choice and leading a fulfilled and content life despite not becoming a parent. In her understanding of "childfree," the individual initially does not have children due to circumstance rather than choice. Nonetheless, she suggests that this does not necessarily need to lead to a negative state of mind, greater feelings of loss or absence. Instead, the couple can still exercise their freedom in determining how they respond to their situation. They also have agency in achieving a sense of fulfilment through their choices to be childfree.

In contrast, numerous respondents chose not to refer to themselves by any particular name, for example, preferring to state they have no kids. One forty-one-year-old male writes: "They are all labels that people want to assign themselves so they can be different. My wife and I just don't have an urge for children and only recently discovered people call themselves all of these things" (R). He has no need to define himself as a nonparent. He expresses why he and his wife do not have children— they do not wish to have any—but he does not believe that they need a label to express this. This fifty-eight-year-old female respondent further explains this idea:

> I have not heard of any of these terms before this survey. If people ask, I just say I don't have any kids. "Childfree" and "childfree by choice" sound like someone who thinks people shouldn't'have a child as a political statement (which I don't think it is). "Childless" and "voluntarily childless" sound pretty clinical but less hostile than the others. But then I think all of these are politically weighted terms that overstate a very personal decision. (S)

This response is reflective of the respondents who feel that not having children is a personal choice that does not need to be labelled. Additionally, she further explains that such labels are not adequate, as they conceptualize nonparenting as something political; presenting not having a child as a political act would the decision less of a personal choice. As another respondent puts it, "We rarely ever explain because it's no one's business but ours" (T). These individuals do not desire to be vocal about their decision not to have children, in contrast to those participants who seek to be explicit about their decision. Several participants seem to want to establish a lifestyle around their status as no-parents, something they feel the title they assign themselves would allow for. One female chooses "voluntarily childless/childfree by choice" because she feels these "terms make it seem more like a lifestyle choice" around which one can more straightforwardly "develop a community" (U).

Conclusions

Definitions are often applied as shorthand; they are easy ways to determine typologies or groups of people. If nothing else, the postmodern turn has taught us to be far more sensitive towards the construction of these definitions and groupings. Defining the childless as a group is clearly problematic, both demographically and sociologically. A wide literature has taken this definitional homogeneity to task and outlined not only the various pathways to childlessness but also the tremendous heterogeneity in form. However, in common with most journeys into the postmodern, there is the dual danger that one analyzes everything out of existence, being left with no meaningful grouping upon which one can perform any useful analysis, that this intellectual wrangling over the social construction of a given term is simply that—an intellectual concern rather than one which is reflective of the lived experience of the subjects of our research.

In this chapter, we have sought to explore and unpack the notion of being childfree but in a person-centered manner. Rather than imposing our theoretical views on the population, we have tried to find out how people define themselves and what these definitions mean to them. Overall, the survey results give some insight into the potential reasons why people without children may choose to label themselves in a certain way. Importantly, they reveal varying understandings of the meaning of not having children or the lack thereof. These understandings appear to be intertwined with the reasons of these individuals for not having children. For some, it appears to be highly significant and empowering to have a name for themselves that defines their status with respect to not having children, most importantly because it enables them to have agency, in various respects, over how the define themselves. For others, not having children is a personal matter that does not require definition.

This study's findings, thus, present an (expectedly) inconsistent view of what it means to be childfree. For some, it is a radical statement of a particular lifestyle, one that rejects parenthood. For others, frankly, it was just a nonissue; it was just the way they were. Thinking more along the terms of a person-centered study of definitions could potentially serve both the more imperially minded demographer and the more introspective sociologist as well.

Appendix: Demographic Characteristics of Respondents; the Letter Indicates Relevant Quotations

Quote	Gender	Age
A	Female	57
B	Female	45
C	Female	45
D	Female	42
E	Not specified	Not specified
F	Female	28
G	Female	30
H	Female	65
I	Female	37
J	Female	35
K	Female	42
L	Male	56
M	Female	29
N	Female	42
O	Female	57
P	Female	35
Q	Female	42

R	Male	41
S	Female	58
T	Female	38
U	Female	23

Works Cited

Abma, J. C., et al. "Fertility, Family Planning, and Women's Health: New Data from the 1995 National Survey of Family Growth." *Vital and Health Statistics. Series 23, Data from the National Survey of Family Growth*, vol 19, 1997, pp. 1-114.

Ashburn-Nardo, L. "Parenthood as a Moral Imperative? Moral Outrage and the Stigmatization of Voluntarily Childfree Women and Men." *Sex Roles*, vol. 76, no. 5-6, 2016, pp. 393-401, link.springer.com/article/10.1007/s11199-016-0606-1. Accessed 11 Dec. 2020.

"Austin No Kidding." *Meetup*, 2016, www.meetup.com/austin nokidding/. Accessed 1 Sept. 2016.

Baber, K. M., and A. S. Dreyer. "Gender-Role Orientations in Older Child-Free and Expectant Couples." *Sex Roles*, vol. 14, no. 9-10, 1986, pp. 501-12, link.springer.com/article/10.1007/BF00287450. Accessed 11 Dec. 2020.

Bachu, A. "Is Childlessness among American Women on the Rise." *US Census Bureau. Population Division Working Paper* POP-WP037, 1999, www.census.gov/population/www/documentation/twps0037/twps0037.html. Accessed 11 Dec. 2020.

Basten, S. A. "Voluntary Childlessness and Being Childfree." The Future of Human Reproduction: Working Paper #5, University of Oxford, citeseerx.ist.psu.edu/viewdoc/download?doi=10.1.1.701.9495&rep=repl&type=pdf. Accessed 11 Dec. 2020.

Biddlecom, A., and S. Martin. "Childless in America." *Contexts*, vol. 5, no. 4, 2006, p. 54.

Bram, S. "Voluntarily Childless Women: Traditional or Non-traditional?" *Sex Roles*, vol. 10, no. 3-4, 1984, pp. 195-206, link.springer.com/article/10.1007/BF00287774. Accessed 11 Dec. 2020.

Callan, V. J. "Single Women, Voluntary Childlessness and Perceptions about Life and Marriage." *Journal of Biosocial Science*, vol. 18, no. 4, 1986, pp. 479-87, www.ncbi.nlm.nih.gov/pubmed/3782198. Accessed 11 Dec. 2020.

"Childfree by Choice Women in Austin." *Meetup*, 2016, www.meetup. com/Childfree-Women-of-Austin-late-20s-to-early-40s/. Accessed 1 Sept. 2016.

"Childfree Mailing List." *Childfree.net*, 2016, www.childfree.net/list. html/. Accessed 1 Sept. 2016.

Crispell, D. "Planning No Family, Now or Ever.: *American Demographics*, vol. 15, no. 10, 1993, pp. 23-24.

Cwikel, J., et al. "Never-Married Childless Women in Australia: Health and Social Circumstances in Older Age." *Social Science and Medicine*, vol. 62, no. 8, 2006, pp. 1991-2001. www.ncbi.nlm.nih. gov/pubmed/16225976. Accessed 11 Dec. 2020.

DeOllos, I. Y., and C. A. Kapinus. "Aging Childless Individuals and Couples: Suggestions for New Directions in Research." *Sociological Inquiry*, vol. 72, no. 1, 2002, pp. 72-80, onlinelibrary.wiley.com/doi/ abs/10.1111/1475-682X.00006. Accessed 11 Dec. 2020.

Gillespie, R. "Childfree and Feminine: Understanding the Gender Identity of Voluntarily Childless Women." *Gender and Society*, vol. 17, no. 1, 2003, pp. 122-36, www.jstor.org/stable/3081818? seq=1#metadata_info_tab_contents. Accessed 11 Dec. 2020.

Heaton, T. B., et al. "Religiosity of Married Couples and Childlessness." *Review of Religious Research*, vol. 33, no. 3, 1992, pp. 244-55, www. jstor.org/stable/3511089?seq=1#metadata_info_tab_contents. Accessed 11 Dec. 2020.

Houseknecht, S. K. "Reference Group Support for Voluntary Childlessness: Evidence for Conformity." *Journal of Marriage and Family*, vol. 39, no. 2, 1977, pp. 285-92, www.jstor.org/ stable/351124#metadata_info_tab_contents. Accessed 11 Dec. 2020.

Keizer, R., et al. "Pathways into Childlessness: Evidence of Gendered Life Course Dynamics." *Journal of Biosocial Science*, vol. 40, no. 6, 2008, pp. 863-78, www.ncbi.nlm.nih.gov/pubmed/18093349. Accessed 11 Dec. 2020.

Koropeckyj-Cox, T. et al. "University Students' Perceptions of Parents and Childless or Childfree Couples." *Journal of Family Issues* vol., 39, no. 1, 2018, pp. 155-79 journals.sagepub.com/doi/abs/10.1177/0192513X15618993?journalCode=jfia. Accessed 11 Dec. 2020.

Kneale, D., and H. Joshi. "Postponement and Childlessness: Evidence from two British Cohorts." *Demographic Research*, vol. 19, no. 58, vol. 2008, pp. 1935-64. www.demographic-research.org/Volumes/Vol19/58/. Accessed 11 Dec. 2020.

Letherby, G. "Childless and Bereft?: Stereotypes and Realities in Relation to 'Voluntary' and 'Involuntary' Childlessness and Womanhood." *Sociological Inquiry*, vol. 72, no.1, 2002, pp. 7-20, psycnet.apa.org/record/2003-01722-001. Accessed 11 Dec. 2020.

Morell, C. "Saying No: Women's Experiences with Reproductive Refusal." *Feminism and Psychology*, vol. 10, no. 3, 2000, pp. 313-22, journals.sagepub.com/doi/abs/10.1177/0959353500010003002?journalCode=fapa. Accessed 11 Dec. 2020.

Mosher, W. D., et al. "Religion and Fertility in the United States: The Importance of Marriage Patterns and Hispanic Origin." *Demography*, vol. 23, no. 3, 1986, pp. 367-79, link.springer.com/article/10.2307/2061436. Accessed 11 Dec. 2020.

Mosher, W. D., et al. "Religion and Fertility in the United States: New Patterns." *Demography*, vol. 29, no. 2, 1992, 199-214, www.jstor.org/stable/2061727?seq=1#metadata_info_tab_contents. Accessed 11 Dec. 2020.

Motherwell, L., and S. Prudent. "Childlessness and Group Psychotherapy: Psychological and Sociological Perspectives." *Group*, vol. 22, no. 3, 1998, pp. 145-57, www.jstor.org/stable/41718889. Accessed 11 Dec. 2020.

Paul, P. "Childless by Choice." *American Demographics*, vol. 23, 2001, pp. 45-50.

Ramu, G. N. "Voluntarily Childless and Parental Couples: A Comparison of Their Lifestyle Characteristics.: *Lifestyles*, vol. 7, no.3, 1985, pp. 130-45, link.springer.com/article/10.1007%2FBF00986582. Accessed 11 Dec. 2020.

Rovi, S. L. D. "Taking 'NO' for an Answer: Using Negative Reproductive Intentions to Study the Childless/Childfree."

Population Research and Policy Review, vol. 13, no. 4, 1994, pp. 343-65, www.jstor.org/stable/40229717?seq=1#page_scan_tab_contents. Accessed 11 Dec. 2020.

Tanturri, M. L., and L. Mencarini. "Childless or Childfree? Paths to Voluntary Childlessness in Italy." *Population and Development Review*, vol. 34, no. 1, 2008, pp. 51-77, www.jstor.org/stable/25434658?seq=1#metadata_info_tab_contents. Accessed 11 Dec. 2020.

Waren, W. "Characteristics of Voluntary Childless Men." Paper presented at Population Association of America Annual Meeting. New Orleans, LA., 2008, paa2008.princeton.edu/papers/81767. Accessed 11 Dec. 2020.

Section II

Gender/Race
Transgressions and
Conventional Views of
Otherhood

Chapter Four

"Am I Less of a Woman Because I Don't Have Kids?" Gender Resistance and Reification among Childfree Women

Amy Blackstone

For many, opting out of parenthood in the cultural context of pronatalism comes with a host of social pressures and stigmas. These challenges are particularly salient for women because their identities as women may be called into question as a result of their choice not to become mothers. As childfree women face social responses regarding their choice, some push back and challenge the gendered norms and institutions that frame them as deviant. Others, perhaps not considering how the pressure to parent is linked to gender, wind up reifying the very norms and beliefs that cast their choice as deviant. In this chapter, I examine what role gender plays in women's decisions not to have or rear children.

Scholarly inquiry into the stigma faced by childfree women took off in the 1970s, and the literature has grown substantially since. In the following sections, I review childbearing trends in the United States (U.S.) to provide the context for my research findings, which are based on a sample of women in the U.S. I then briefly disentangle the concepts of "childless" and "childfree" and go on to consider prior scholarly work on the childfree choice as a deviant path, framing the discussion within broader examinations of heteronormativity. Analyzing data from interviews with thirty-one childfree women, I explore how these women talk about gender, how they resist gender, and how they reify gender in their descriptions of their childfree choice.

Who Are Childfree People?

Initially, studies of nonparents used the term "childless" to refer to all such individuals, whether they were nonparents by choice or by circumstance (Houseknecht, "Reference Group Support"; Mosher and Bachrach). As the choice not to rear children became more common and entered the public consciousness, new terminology emerged to distinguish individuals who were nonparents by choice from those who did not have children but wished to have them (Bartlett; Blackstone and Stewart; Defago; Gillespie, "Childfree and Feminine"). Some use the terms "voluntarily childless" and "involuntarily childless" to distinguish between these two groups. Others prefer the term "childfree"—a more positive descriptor that emphasizes choice rather than the lack of something, in reference to the voluntarily childless. Here, I use the term "childfree", as my focus is on those who have made the explicit and intentional choice not to have or rear children.

In the U.S., fertility rates have been below the population replacement level of 2.1 children per woman for almost all periods since the 1970s (Mather). Today, around 15 per cent of women in the U.S. reach their fortieth birthday without having had a child (Livingston). Research indicates that about half of these women have chosen not to have children, whereas the other half are involuntarily childless (Abma and Martinez; Graham et al.). Although these figures may seem striking, they are part of a larger trend across Western societies. Across the globe, the U.S. has the eighty-third lowest fertility rate of the 224 countries listed in *The World Factbook*. Demographers interested in what drives fertility rates to vary find that urbanization, higher age at first marriage, and better access for women to healthcare, education, and employment are all correlated with lower fertility rates (Bachu; Chandra et al.; Crispell; DeOllos and Kapinus; Hagestad and Call; Keizer et al.; Mosher et al.).

Much prior research on childfree people explains the choice as the result of key social movements, such as the zero population growth movement of the 1960s, the feminist movement of the 1970s, and the resultant increase in reproductive choice and labour force participation among women (Bartlett; Campbell; Gillespie, "When No Means No"; Ireland; McAllister and Clarke). Another line of research examines the micro-level processes that explain individuals' motives for remaining childfree (Gillespie, "Childfree and Feminine"; Houseknecht, "Voluntary Childlessness"; Park, "Choosing Childlessness"). Other studies focus on the stigma associated with remaining childfree (Park, "Stigma Management") and attitudes about childlessness (Caron and Wynn; Koropeckyi-Cox and Pendell). This work frames the childfree choice as a deviant life course path and considers where, how, and why perceptions of childfree people develop.

A Deviant Choice?

One line of inquiry in the literature on stigma and deviance as related to the childfree choice examines childfree women's own feelings about gender and relationships. For example, in 1986 Victor Callan found that when compared to women who desired having children, women wanting no children had less traditional expectations of male partners ("Single Women"484). They also valued personal, social, and financial independence and stimulating intellectual interactions with their partner more than women who wanted children (485). Callan concludes that for childfree women who wish to remain so, "a less traditionally sex-typed male partner will allow the development of this adult-centered lifestyle" (485). Other studies from this same period found similar results (Baber and Dyer).

In a more recent study, Nicky Newton and Abigail Stewart found that compared to mothers, women without children rated significantly lower on personality traits associated with conventional femininity and higher on traits associated with masculinity (312). For example, the non-mothers in Newton and Stewart's study rated relatively lower on nurturance and warmth but higher on independence and autonomy (312). Margaret Avison and Adrian Furnham, too, found that childfree people rate significantly higher on the trait of independence than do parents (56). And Rosemary Gillespie found that some women opt out of parenthood as a "radical rejection of motherhood" ("Childfree and Feminine" 123).

Not all studies reach the same conclusion about childfree women's views on gender. Susan Bram, for example, concludes that although women without children hold fewer traditional sex-role orientations than mothers, they do hold some traditional gender beliefs. Fiona McAllister and Lynda Clarke go further, suggesting those without kids are, in fact, conventional in their thinking about gender. More recently, Sara Holton and colleagues found no significant difference between mothers and women without children with respect to their attitudes towards women and motherhood (684). In other words, non-mothers were no more or less likely to hold traditional beliefs about women and motherhood than were mothers. Likewise, Melissa Graham and colleagues found no significant differences between mothers and non-mothers in their beliefs about whether children are significant burdens (10). They also found that belief in the notion that children are one of life's greatest joys does not predict whether a woman will ultimately become a mother. Taken together, these findings suggest that despite the dominant narrative about childfree women's rejection of traditional views of gender, the reality is more complex.

Whatever attitudes they report themselves, childfree women are often cast by others as transgressive deviants, rejecting their true nature (Gillespie, "When No Means No"). Studies examining cultural perceptions of childfree women find that they are believed to be selfish, emotionally troubled, maladjusted, unfeminine, too involved with work, and less warm than mothers (Blackstone and Stewart; Callan, "Perceptions of Parenthood"; Copur and Koropeckyj-Cox; Kelly; Koropeckyj-Cox et al.; Mueller and Yoder; Veevers). It is clear from these findings that the predominant ideology of pronatalism shapes the context in which to understand the choice not to have children (Gillespie, "When No Means No"). Indeed, as Myra Hird argues, insofar as studies attempt to explain childlessness, "the association between femininity and sexual reproduction remains implicit" (6). But to understand the choice, we must make our cultural assumptions visible.

Childfree women are cast as deviant because they do not fit predominant, and rather narrow, views of how women and men interact and form bonds (Blackstone, "Childfree by Choice"). These views are shaped by a heteronormative ideology, which posits that women should bear and care for children (or should at least want to do so) and that men should aspire to procreate and rear children with women. Heteronormative ideology also prescribes that women should conduct and present themselves in a way that is sexually desirable to men. Even those who meet some of the requirements of heteronormative self-presentation and behavior, perhaps by participating in heterosexual relationships, may not be fully honouring heteronormative ideals if they do not desire having children or starting a family.

Cultural norms centred on heteronormative binaries of sex (male-female), sexuality (heterosexual-homosexual), and family (biological-chosen) prescribe not only that adults must couple with and marry individuals of the other sex but also that they must then go on to rear children together (Oswald, Blume, and Marks). Because such norms exist, it makes sense that the choice to remain childfree is most typically understood as a form of gender transgression. Even women who adhere to the binaries of sex, gender, and sexuality, with feminine self-presentations and marriages to men, are suspect unless they go on to have children. Indeed, marriage has traditionally been considered the first step towards creating a normal family, with childrearing considered the next logical step (May; Russo; Veevers). As Gilla Shapiro has said, women's voluntary childlessness "offers an opportunity to transgress the cultural image that womanhood equates to motherhood" (11).

Data and Methods

The data come from qualitative interviews with thirty-one women who have chosen not to parent. Snowball sampling techniques, in which research participants aid in recruiting other participants for the study, were used to recruit participants from an initial purposive sample, selected based on characteristics of the population of interest: women whom I knew to be childfree. The sample is not diverse in terms of social class, race, or sexuality; most of the women I interviewed are in middle- or upper-middle class professions. All participants are white except for one (two declined to provide their race), and most participants are heterosexual (two are lesbian women and five chose not to share sexual identity). The women I interviewed ranged in ages from twenty-one to fifty at the time of the interview; most participants were in their mid- to late thirties.

Using a general interview guide (Warren and Karner), I asked participants to describe their experiences in their own words. The interview guide contained three broad categories of questions: 1) your decision; 2) responses from others; and 3) reflections. All interviews covered the three areas but the extent to which women focused on specific topics varied. One advantage of this particular methodological approach is that participants are empowered to share factors that are most important to them rather than those that I guessed may be most important. The interviews, lasting between sixty and ninety minutes each, took place at a time and location of participants' choosing. All interviews were audio recorded and later transcribed.

The process of analyzing, or coding, qualitative data is dynamic and ongoing (Lofland et al.) and analysis is generally conducted using an inductive approach (Esterberg; Lofland et al.). For this chapter, I analyzed the data inductively, and multiple iterations of coding were conducted. Using the qualitative solutions and research (QSR) data management and analysis software program NVivo, I first coded each transcript according to the themes outlined in the interview guide (your decision, responses from others, and reflections). I then went through the transcripts once more to identify common themes across the interviews and pulled out like categories of data, which were coded together. I and a research assistant then independently read the passages for gender-related themes and references and linked those that seemed to reflect similar themes. Once the data had been coded independently, the results were reviewed and discussed. The groups of passages having something to do with gender were then labelled using a name intended to succinctly portray the themes present in each particular grouping of coded passages. To protect participants' confidentiality, all names in the following sections are pseudonyms, and I have removed or slightly altered other potentially identifying details.

Findings

When examining the role that gender plays in childfree women's decisions and experiences, three themes emerged from the data. First, there was a notable absence of gender in respondents' reflections on their decision and experience as childfree; gender quickly became salient, however, once respondents were asked about its role. Second, some respondents seem to reify gender norms and differences as they described their decision not to have children. Finally, in reflecting how they came to the decision and what responses they had faced as a result, many childfree women also resisted heteronormative understandings of gender.

Gender's Invisibility

Judith Lorber once said: "Talking about gender for most people is the equivalent of fish talking about water. Gender is so much the routine ground of everyday activities that questioning its taken-for-granted assumptions and presuppositions is like wondering about whether the sun will come up" (13). This sentiment reflects the pattern revealed in my analysis of interviews with childfree women.

In general, gender did not seem to immediately come to mind when women talked about not having kids. In fact, only one respondent, Emily, mentioned gender without my asking what role, if any, it may play in her decision. A married woman in her mid-thirties at the time of my interview with her, Emily shared the following at the outset of her interview:

> I think I'm probably a little more evangelical [about being childfree] because of my gender and, and you know, all of the ramifications that go along with that. I think it's in a sense easier for men, and I feel like women have to be more strident in their decision and more solid because of the stuff you get from society and people. I just feel like I've got to be more clear and definitive in what I say when people ask me about my child status.

Although Emily was the only respondent to mention gender without being prompted, I gave all participants the chance to discuss gender when I asked them what role they think their gender plays in their decision to not have kids. When prompted, respondents had quite a lot to say on the subject. Allison, a partnered woman in her mid-thirties who works full time in nonprofit fundraising, responded quickly with the loud proclamation "HUGE!" and went on to explain, "I think I am realistic enough to know that no matter what arrangement I have in any relationship, the women are the primary caregivers." Julie, a social worker in her mid-forties, responded similarly: "For the mother, it's even more consuming, that role as a parent. You lose a lot of yourself for a while." And Janet, a partnered woman in her early thirties who works in real estate, noted, "If I were a man, no one would give me a hard time about not having kids."

Participants' comments about gender, whether prompted during the interview or not, tell us something about how they understand the concept and how and whether they believe gender is linked to parenting decisions. In some ways, not talking about gender (at least not until prompted) could be understood as a way of reifying gender norms. Keeping gender out of the conversation prevents discussion about the heteronormative ideals that are at the centre of mainstream conceptions of women's roles and of what counts as family. At the same time, once they are asked about the role of gender, participants seem to resist these ideals.

Reifying Gender

Although some childfree women may reify gender simply by not considering it, other participants reinforced heteronormative ideals in the comments they made about their choice to remain childfree. In these comments, participants cited heteronormative ideals by reinforcing gender and family stereotypes and by claiming that they have no motherhood material within them.

Reinforcing stereotypical definitions of gender and family is one of the primary ways that respondents reify gender. For example, while reflecting on what family means to her, Robin, a married woman in her late thirties who works in the tech industry, noted the following: "The woman is more involved with taking care of the child. [As a woman] I'd be the one waking up more often to feed the baby and more involved in the personal care of the child, much more involved. I would have more responsibilities than my partner. I know I would feel that burden more than if I were a man." Similarly, Kim, a married teacher in her early forties said, "I don't have to clean the house, do laundry and dishes and all that stuff. Those are things that I like about not having kids." It is notable that neither woman seems to challenge traditional gendered divisions of labour in the household. Although it was clear from their interviews that they would be dissatisfied with such an arrangement, their solution was to avoid having to face the possibility by not having children.

Janet recalled that in her young adult years, she intended to have children. As she put it, "I thought I would probably have kids because I was married; I got married young and that was the next logical step." Janet's plan to have children was based on what she saw those around her doing. Other participants also described the normative path of marrying and having children as being something they learned from a young age. As Robin put it, her choice not to have kids is, "kind of weird, especially if you look at the toys that girls have, you think, how come I wasn't programmed to be a little parent? What went wrong?"

Other women, too, suggested that by not following the path they were socialized to believe was normal, they felt something must be wrong them rather than considering that something may be wrong with the path presented to them. For example, when faced with the reality that her choice differed from that of her peers, Jill, a partnered social worker in her early thirties, questioned herself rather than questioning her peers: "I look at all my high school friends on Facebook, and I'm the only one who isn't married and doesn't have kids. I question myself, like if there's something wrong with me that I don't have that." Rather than question whether there is something wrong with the institution of marriage or with the assumption that she should want to have children, Jill questioned herself.

Jessica, a partnered nonprofit employee in her mid-twenties, also questioned if there was something wrong with her. What began as a reflection on her negative feelings about women who do not embrace getting their periods, since it is a "natural part" of being a woman, quickly turned to a focus on how she too must be "unnatural," since she does not want children. As Jessica put it:

> I'm very saddened by the fact that there are all these drugs out there now that can allow women to menstruate like once a year. That to me seems so unnatural. I love how natural that part of the female body is. I feel very connected to that. I'm not the person that is like angry when I'm menstruating or something. But it's interesting because then I look at my choice to not to have kids, and I just wonder if that's almost like someone choosing to have their period just once a year. I think that feeling I have about kids is an unnatural path for a woman.

Beliefs about what is natural for women came up in many of the interviews. Women invoked the idea of maternal instinct, claiming to have none while suggesting that a lack of it was somehow unnatural. In no case did an interviewee question the origins or legitimacy of the concept itself. As Janet put it, "Women are supposed to have this nurturing, caring, maternal instinct. Supposed to, but I don't have it. And when I tell people I don't have it they say 'yes you do.'" Annie said simply, "I just don't have that maternal instinct" and Brittany said, "I know that I'm not mother material." Emily said, "I just never felt that maternal instinct at all." Participants seemed to think the desire to bear children is felt by nearly all women and that they are the exception. As Kim said, "I just never felt that urge to have that real maternal instinct, which I think a lot of women do especially as you get older in your thirties." Allison said, "I've wondered what will happen if the biological clock kicks in. Especially in the last couple years, I have kind of thought, 'Shouldn't mine be kicking in about now?' But it doesn't."

What is striking about how much the idea of maternal instinct saturated the interviews is that the concept itself has almost no support in the scientific literature. Although it is true that scientists have discovered a possible genetic link to nurturing traits in female mice once they have pups (Ribeiro et al.), the genetic drive in mice to nurture pups once born does not equate to a genetic drive in humans to become pregnant. Indeed, the drive to have children is far more social than it is innate. By describing most women as having a maternal drive, participants reify heteronormative notions of what it means to be a woman in our culture. And by claiming that they are unusual because they lack such a drive, participants affirm the misconception that all real women are mothers. Of course, a number of participants also expressed annoyance and even anger over social pressures to bear and rear children, and it was in these moments that their resistance to gender norms was most clear.

Resisting Gender

Two subthemes emerged from the theme of resisting gender. First, participants resist gender when they challenge negative social responses to their choice and the pressure to have kids. They also resist gender by redefining family and challenging the notion that their own families of choice are not real.

For the women I interviewed, the pressure they felt to have kids, and their responses to it, were very clearly about gender. For example, Kim, in reflecting on how others respond to her choice, posed the following question and statement during her interview: "Am I less of a woman because I don't have kids? I don't think so." While speaking about her family and friends who sometimes questioned her choice not to have children, Janet said the following: "I think if they're gonna put their thoughts on me, I'm putting it back on them. When they tell me 'Oh, Janet, you won't have lived until you've had children. It's the most fulfilling thing a woman can do!' then I just name off the ten fulfilling things I did in the past week that they didn't get to do because they have kids."

Women also resist gender by pushing back against pressure from healthcare professionals to bear children and by broaching the subject of sterilization with resistant doctors. Julie, who had a tubal ligation at age thirty-six, was "forced to watch a film" in her doctor's office about the permanence of the procedure. It also took several visits to convince him to approve the procedure. When she first asked for it, Julie's doctor said, "Oh you really don't want to do that." To which, she replied: "Yes, I do." She continued: "I was very honest with him and told him, 'If I get pregnant, I'm gonna abort it.'" Her doctor then acquiesced but not before making her watch the film.

Mandy, who was in her late twenties when she first asked about tubal ligation at a regular annual exam, reported:

Every time I asked my nurse practitioner about sterilization, she'd dismiss it and say, "Oh, you're too young." ... She would talk about, "Is your husband ok with this?" And that doesn't really matter, you know? I would say, "Yes, you know we've talked about this but really this isn't his decision. This is me and my body but yes you know I have talked to my husband about this. It's not about him."

Mandy said she stopped asking for a while but became interested again a few years later when a friend of hers became unintentionally pregnant and, subsequently, had a tubal ligation. Mandy's friend told her she wished she had pushed to have the tubal ligation years earlier. This time Mandy avoided her nurse practitioner and went straight to her friend's doctor, finally receiving the surgery she had been requesting for years. At her next appointment with the nurse practitioner, Mandy shared what she had done: "The very interesting thing about it is that

AMY BLACKSTONE

when I went back to my nurse practitioner and told her what I did she said, 'Well good for you for taking control of your body.' ... It was odd. Sort of like a reactionary thing and not genuine. I didn't really feel comfortable seeing her anymore after that."

Emily, too, faced medical professionals who doubted her ability to make the decision for herself: "I was twenty six when I had my tubes tied. And I had several physicians come up to me and say, you know, 'Are you sure? Are you sure? Are you sure?' And, in fact, the day of the surgery, the doctor went into the waiting room without my knowledge or permission and asked my parents, 'Are you sure she's really sure?'" The inappropriateness of her doctor going behind her back to her parents without her consent aside, luckily for Emily, her parents were supportive of her decision and assured the doctor that this was what she wanted. Not all women receive such support from their families.

Janet said the pressure from her mother and grandmother is overwhelming sometimes, but that she had learned not to be affected by it:

I literally got a phone call from my mom at seven o'clock in the morning on a Monday morning, when she knows I do not get up until eight, and it was like, "Hi sweetheart, how are you, how was your weekend, I want a kitten and a puppy and a grandbaby. [Increasing her volume, she yells,] When are you going to give me grandbabies?!" ... And my grandmother would be ok if I had a bunch of one night stands and got knocked up. She wants me to have kids that badly.... It's like she doesn't care if I'm married first or happy.... So, I just live my life. I'm very adamant about it. Ultimately this is who I am. I'm a happily nonmarried woman without children, and I'm hot to trot!

April's response to her mother, after years of incessant pressuring, was more direct: "Oh screw you. Don't try to force me to live the life you want for me."

In Jessica's family, her aunt was the biggest source of pressure to have children. She eventually lost touch with her aunt's family as a result. Jessica explained how the pressure from her aunt caused her to reflect on the choices available to women:

We don't really have a connection with them anymore.... There was definitely a pressure from her to be a certain way. I just wonder if we had grown up in an environment where it was like here are all the choices, choose what you want to do as opposed to here's the choice... [trails off]. I feel like once you have access to choices, once you know they exist, you can make your decision. I just think that if people did have access to other choices and it wasn't stigmatized, it would be different.... I just think there are so many reasons why people with kids have them that aren't really their own reasons.

In the face of unsupportive family members, some women resisted gender by redefining family in a way that did not depend upon their fertility (Blackstone, "Doing Family Without Having Kids"). Many talked about the fact that family for them is not defined by biological or sociolegal connections, such as marriage. Instead, participants defined partners, pets, friends, and neighbours as their families. As Mandy said, "Family is me and Tim and our little kids [nodding towards her two Weimaraner lounging on the floor]." For Brittany, "Family is comfort. It is a feeling of belonging." And for Sara, "Family is a group of people who are linked to one another by a commitment to each other. They are united despite any kind of differences; it's a togetherness." Tonya, a divorced heterosexual teacher in her early forties, expressed that family does not have to mean blood but instead, "Family is loving and supportive relationships."

Jan, a married research scientist in her early forties, took on heteronormative notions of marriage and family more directly:

On the whole, the institution of marriage as a transfer of property from one family to another, where the whole purpose in life is to create babies, is pretty ugly. My definition of family has nothing to do with that. It's about making a better life for ourselves, together. I guess I feel like the expectation that every woman is gonna have children is some kind of way to control women's bodies. Women have a lack of control over their own reproduction. And I feel like we're going backwards in that. I mean, with regulatory language in the law and reducing access to abortion. It's pretty scary. I think this is kind of a way to control women's sexuality.

By emphasizing that they choose their families, participants raised questions about the utility of definitions that are overly reliant on biology or traditionally heteronormative connections, such as marriage. And in doing so, participants resisted gender.

Conclusion

Although women's choice not to have children is often, and sometimes accurately, described as a challenge to gendered norms and institutions, childfree women themselves do not always cast their choice in this light. Those who opt out of parenthood do so within the cultural context of pronatalism, and this context very much shapes how they think and talk about their choice. In the end, the choice is both resistant and reifying of gender. Childfree women, at times, push back against heteronormative ideals designed to limit their options at the same time that they feel and sometimes reify those ideals. When it comes to the question of gender resistance or reification, the choice not to have kids is at once neither and both.

Many women do not consciously think of their choice not to have kids as being about gender, but they do call up gendered norms and ideals in their descriptions of their choice and responses to that choice. In some ways, by not considering how their choice to be childfree may be linked to gender, participants allow the heteronormative dichotomies of and connections between gender, family, and parenting to go unquestioned. At the same time, many participants do resist gender and gendered ideals. By questioning and pushing back against the social pressure participants feel to have children, they invariably wind up questioning the gendered expectations that go hand in hand with that pressure. Furthermore, by creating their own, new forms of family, participants highlight the ways that family is not something that is necessarily linked to heteronormative ideals.

What these women's reflections teach us is that the choice not to have kids is one that is made in the context of competing and sometimes contradictory ideas and ideals. In the end, as with most all of life's major choices, it is complicated.

Works Cited

Abma, Joyce C., and Gladys M. Martinez. "Childlessness Among Older Women in the United States: Trends and Profiles." *Journal of Marriage and Family*, vol. 68, no. 4, 2006, pp. 1045-56.

Avison, Margaret, and Adrian Furnham. "Personality and Voluntary Childlessness." *Journal of Population Research*, vol. 32, no. 1, 2015, pp. 45-67.

Baber, Kristine M., and Albert S. Dreyer. "Gender-Role Orientations in Older Child-Free and Expectant Couples." *Sex Roles*, vol. 14, no. 9, 1986, pp. 501-12.

Bachu, Amara, and Martin O'Connell. *Fertility of American Women.* U.S. Census Bureau, 1998.

Bartlett, Jane. *Will You be Mother: Women Who Choose to Say No.* London: Virago Press, 1996.

Blackstone, Amy. *Childfree by Choice: The Movement Redefining Family and Creating a New Age of Independence.* Dutton, 2019.

Blackstone, Amy. "Doing Family Without Having Kids." *Sociology Compass*, vol. 8, no. 1, 2014, pp. 52-62.

Blackstone, Amy, and Mahala Dyer Stewart. "Choosing to be Childfree: Research on the Decision Not to Parent." *Sociology Compass*, vol. 6, no. 9, 2012, pp. 718-27.

Bram, Susan. "Voluntarily Childless Women: Traditional or Non-traditional?" *Sex Roles*, vol. 6, nos. 3/4, 1984, pp. 195-206.

Callan, Victor J. "Single Women, Voluntary Childlessness and Perceptions about Life and Marriage." *Journal of Biosocial Science*, vol. 18, no. 4, 1986, pp. 479-87.

Callan, Victor J. "Perceptions of Parenthood and Childlessness: A Comparison of Mothers and Voluntarily Childless Wives." *Population and Environment*, vol. 6, no. 3, 1983, pp. 179-89.

Campbell, Elaine. *The Childless Marriage: An Exploratory Study of Couples Who do Not Want Children.* Tavistock, 1985.

Caron, Sandra L., and Ruth L. Wynn. "The Intent to Parent among Young, Unmarried College Graduates." *Families in Society: The Journal of Contemporary Human Services*, vol. 73, no. 8, 1992, pp. 480-87.

Chandra A, et al. "Fertility, Family Planning, and Reproductive Health of U.S. Women: Data from the 2002 National Survey of Family Growth. National Center for Health Statistics." *Vital Health Stat*, vol. 23, no. 25, 2005, pp. 1-174.

Copur, Zeynep and Tanya Koropeckyj-Cox. "University Students' Perceptions of Childless Couples and Parents in Ankara, Turkey." *Journal of Family Issues*, vol. 31, no. 11, 2010, pp. 1481-1506.

Crispell, Diane. "Planning No Family, Now or Ever." *American Demographics*, vol. 15, no. 10. 1993, pp. 23-24.

Defago, Nicki. *Childfree and Loving It!* Fusion Press, 2005.

DeOllos, Ione Y. and Carolyn A. Kapinus. "Aging Childless Individuals and Couples: Suggestions for New Directions in Research." *Sociological Inquiry*, vol. 72, no. 1, 2002, pp. 72-80.

Esterberg, Kristen G. *Qualitative Methods in Social Research.* McGraw-Hill, 2002.

Gillespie, Rosemary. "Childfree and Feminine: Understanding the Gender Identity of Voluntarily Childless Women." *Gender & Society*, vol. 17, no. 1, 2003, pp. 122-36.

Gillespie, Rosemary. "When No Means No: Belief, Disregard, and Deviance as Discourses of Voluntary Childlessness." *Women's Studies International Forum*, vol. 23, no. 2, 2000, pp. 223-34.

Graham, Melissa, et al. "Why are Childless Women Childless? Findings From an Exploratory Study in Victoria, Australia." *Journal of Social Exclusion*, vol. 4, no. 1, 2013, pp. 70-89.

Hagestad, Gunhild O., and Vaughn R. Call. "Pathways to Childlessness: A Life Course Perspective." *Journal of Family Issues*, vol. 28, no. 10, 2007, pp. 1338-61.

Hird, Myra J. "Vacant Wombs: Feminist Challenges to Psychoanalytic Theories of Childless Women." *Feminist Review*, vol. 75, no. 1, 2003, pp. 5-19.

Holton, Sara, Jane Fisher, and Heather Rowe. "Attitudes Toward Women and Motherhood: Their Role in Australian Women's Childbearing Behaviour." *Sex Roles*, vol. 61, nos. 9-10, 2009, pp. 677-687.

Houseknecht, Sharon K "Reference Group Support for Voluntary Childlessness: Evidence for Conformity." *Journal of Marriage and the Family*, vol. 39, no. 2, 1977, pp. 285-92

Houseknecht, Sharon K. "Voluntary Childlessness." *Handbook of Marriage and the Family*, edited by Marvin B. Sussman and Suzanne K. Steinmetz, Plenum Press, 1987, pp. 369-95.

Ireland, Mary S. *Reconceiving Women: Separating Motherhood from Female Identity.* Guilford, 1993.

Keizer, Renske, Pearl A. Dykstra, and Miranda D. Jansen. "Pathways Into Childlessness: Evidence of Gendered Life Course Dynamics." *Journal of Biosocial Science*, vol. 40, no. 6, 2008, pp. 863-78.

Kelly, Maura. "Women's Voluntary Childlessness: A Radical Rejection of Motherhood?" *Women's Studies Quarterly*, vol. 37, no. 3-4, 2009, pp. 157-72.

Koropeckyj-Cox, Tanya and Gretchen Pendell. "Attitudes about Childlessness in the United States: Correlates of Positive, Neutral, and Negative Responses." *Journal of Family Issues*, vol. 28, no. 8, 2007, pp. 1054-82.

Koropeckyj-Cox, Tanya, et al. "University Students' Perceptions of Parents and Childless or Childfree Couples." *Journal of Family Issues*, vol. 39, no. 1, 2018, doi: 10.1177/0192513X15618993.

Livingston, Gretchen. *Childlessness*. Pew Research Center, 2015.

Lofland, John, et al. *Analyzing Social Settings: A Guide to Qualitative Observation and Analysis*. Wadsworth, 2006.

Lorber, Judith. *Paradoxes of Gender*. Yale University Press, 1994.

Mather, Mark. "The Decline in U.S. Fertility." Population Reference Bureau, 2014.

May, Elaine Tyler. *Barren in the Promised Land: Childless Americans and the Pursuit of Happiness*. Harvard University Press, 1997.

McAllister, Fiona (with Lynda Clarke). *Choosing Childlessness*. Family Policy Studies Centre, 1998.

Mosher, William D. and Christine A. Bachrach. "Childlessness in the United States: Estimates from the National Survey of Family Growth." *Journal of Family Issues*, vol. 3, no. 4, 1982, pp. 517-42.

Mosher, William D., Linda B. Williams, and David P. Johnson. "Religion and Fertility in the United States: New Patterns." *Demography*, vol. 29, no. 2, 1992, pp. 199-214.

Mueller, Karla A., and Janice D. Yoder. "Stigmatization of Non-Normative Family Size Status." *Sex Roles*, vol. 41, no. 11-12, 1999, pp. 901-19.

Newton, Nicky J., and Abigail J. Stewart. "The Road Not Taken: Women's Life Paths and Gender-Linked Personality Traits." *Journal of Research in Personality*, vol. 47, no. 4, 2013, pp. 306-16.

Oswald, Ramona Faith, Libby Balter Blume, and Stephen R. Marks. "Decentering Heteronormativity: A Model for Family Studies." *Sourcebook of Family Theory and Research*, edited by Vern L. Bengtson et al., Sage, 2005, pp. 143-54.

Park, Kristin. "Choosing Childlessness: Weber's Typology of Action and Motives of the Voluntary Childless." *Sociological Inquiry*, vol. 75, no. 3, 2005, pp. 372-402.

Park, Kristin. "Stigma Management Among the Voluntarily Childless." *Sociological Perspectives*, vol. 45, no. 1, 2002, pp. 21-45.

Ribeiro, Ana C., et al. "siRNA Silencing of Estrogen Receptor-Expression Specifically in Medial Preoptic Area Neurons Abolishes Maternal Care in Female Mice." *PNAS*, vol. 109, no. 40, 2012, pp. 16324-29.

Russo, Nancy Felipe. "Overview: Sex Roles, Fertility and the Motherhood Mandate." *Psychology of Women Quarterly*, vol. 4, no. 1, 1979, pp. 7-15.

Shapiro, Gilla. "Voluntary Childlessness: A Critical Review of the Literature." *Studies in the Maternal*, vol. 6, no. 1, 2014, pp. 1-15.

The World Factbook 2013-14. Central Intelligence Agency, 2013.

Veevers, Jean E. "Voluntary Childlessness and Social Policy: An Alternative View." *The Family Coordinator*, vol. 23, no. 4, 1974, pp. 397-406.

Warren, Carol A. B., and Tracy Xavia Karner. *Discovering Qualitative Methods: Field Research, Interviews and Analysis*, Roxbury, 2005.

Chapter Five

(M)Otherhood: An Autoethnographic Exploration of Being Empowered and Childfree

Cassandra D. Chaney

"Sick and selfish."
—Veggie Mama on May 4, 2016

"Shouldn't that ship have sailed already?"
—Kb on May 4, 2016

"You're never too old to make mistakes."
—Anonymous on May 5, 2016

"Congratulations!!! A baby at any age is such a blessing. It makes me so sad to see women criticizing her age. Every woman walks her own path, let us not throw stones. A mature mother can offer so much, please stop the judgment."
—Cynthia on May 4, 2016

When Janet Damita Jo Jackson (born May 16, 1966)—the American singer, songwriter, dancer, and actress—made the public announcement she would postpone her scheduled Unbreakable Tour to concentrate on planning her family in October 2016 with her then-husband Wissam Al Mana, this news caused a lot of controversial commentary. Although many individuals like Cynthia congratulated Jackson, others like Veggie Mama, Kb, and

Anonymous, asserted that Ms. Jackson's decision was "sick and selfish," as her window of childbearing had passed; her decision to become pregnant at age forty-nine (and give birth to her child at age fifty) was, thus a mistake. (All comments were from the May 4, 2016 edition of *People* magazine.]

As I discuss my own voluntarily childlessness in this chapter, I purposefully draw attention to the announcement of Ms. Jackson. Although I do not share the fame, wealth, and marital status of her, as a university professor, I have more formal education than she does and, thus, greater knowledge of the historical and contemporary realities of African American women. However, regardless of how many people know us, regardless of how much money we earn, or regardless of how many people we influence through our work, we are both Black women, and people make certain assumptions about us both based on when we choose to become mothers or consciously choose to opt out of motherhood.

The purpose of this chapter is to discuss my voluntary decision to be childfree. As I discuss my life choice, I will use an autoethnographic and oppositional gaze approach to examine comments and discussions that I have had regarding motherhood in my life. Writing about autoethnography, Robin Boylorn says the following: "Autoethnographers look in (at themselves) and out (at the world) connecting the personal to the cultural. Autoethnographic research combines the impulses of self-consciousness with cultural awareness reflecting the larger world against personal lived experiences oftentimes blurring the lines between them" (413). The oppositional gaze, in contrast to the autoethnographic gaze, is critical, interrogational, oppositional; it is consciously aware, seeks to document, and is concerned with issues of race and racism (hooks). The oppositional gaze resists intended and embedded ideologies based on racist and internalized racist views. American author, feminist, and social activist, bell hooks believes that the oppositional gaze leads to agency because "there is power in looking" (115). She continues: "We [Black women] can both interrogate the gaze of the Other but also look back, and at one another, naming what we see" (116). When Black women position themselves as spectators and gazers, they can use their critical eye to resist and, in some situations, recognize stereotypical representations (414). Essentially, in autoethnography, researchers expose their soul to their audience, and through this emotional and psychological nakedness, they had better understand themselves, appreciate their personal values, validate the experiences of others, and create better understanding of the choices made by themselves and others (Ellis 15; Ellis and Bochner 35).

Thus, my goals for this work are threefold. First, it is my sincere desire that those who can relate to my experiences remain empowered in their decision to stay childfree. Second, I desire to build upon the current literature on women who are voluntarily childfree by positioning the discussion of motherhood via the perspective of an African American woman in the professorate. Finally, I also desire to help those who find it difficult to understand why many Black women remain childfree to broaden their definition of what empowerment is and what empowerment means in the lives of many Black women. As I proceed on this internal and external journey, I need to make it clear that I am not the voice for all Black women, within and outside of the professorate. To attempt to do so would be irresponsible and make the lived experiences of these women invalid.

In the section that follows, I present relevant literature on the topic of mothering. I begin by discussing the historicity of the African female slave's mothering during and after slavery. After this, I highlight the four categories of singles identified by Peter Stein. Following this, I discuss the characteristics of those who are voluntarily childfree. Lastly, I discuss reproductive justice and present a novel way of intellectualizing being voluntarily childfree through the lens of consciousness and personal empowerment.

Literature Review

During slavery, motherhood was a tumultuous experience for African women. Some historians conclude that the total loss in persons removed, many of whom were women, including those who died on the arduous march to coastal slave marts and those killed in slave raids, exceeded the sixty-five to seventy-five million inhabitants remaining in Africa at the trade's end (Berlin 10; Genovese 45; Kolchin 8; Levine 15). Over ten million died as a direct consequence of the Atlantic slave trade alone; however, many more died in transport. Once they made it to American soil, the African female slave in America had the dual role of caring for her own children and those of her slave master. Slave masters sought to maximize the productivity of their labour force via their chopping cotton, and washing, ironing, and cooking. To this reality, Jacqueline Jones notes that "Black women's parental obligations, and affective relations more generally, played a key role in their struggle to combat oppression, for their attention to the duties of motherhood deprived whites of full control over them as field laborers, domestic servants, and 'brood sows.'" (10). Indeed, the persistence with which enslaved women sought to define on their own terms "what a woman ought to be and do would ultimately have an impact on American history long after the formal institution of bondage had ceased to exist" (10).

Tragically, after the emancipation of the slaves, the racist residue that permeated society stripped many Black women of their human right to rear their children to adulthood and to enjoy seeing them free in society. According to Elwood Beck and Stewart Tolnay, "Between Emancipation and the Great Depression, about 3,000 Blacks were lynched in the American south" (526). Regardless of whether these unjust murders and lynchings were due to protecting white male homogeny, as a form of social control, or anger over economic loss, one thing was clear: The emotional, mental, and spiritual pain of losing their children (particularly their sons) to an unjust society sustained by unjust laws was an unspeakable loss for many African American mothers (Allen et al. 12; Olzak 402; Phillips 361).

Historical realities have altered the salience of motherhood. Historian Stephanie Coontz acknowledges that many regard the 1950s as a golden period in American history, a time when the nuclear, two-parent family was the norm (12). In particular, this generation gave birth to the baby boomers (those born between 1946 and 1964) and the largest number of people born during a particular year. More babies were born in 1946 than ever before: 3.4 million, which was 20 per cent more than in 1945. This was the beginning of the so-called baby boom. In 1947, another 3.8 million babies were born; 3.9 million were born in 1952; and more than four million were born every year from 1954 until 1964, when the boom finally tapered off. By then, there were 76.4 million baby boomers in the U.S. They made up almost 40 per cent of the nation's population. However, the 1960s saw a great erosion of the nuclear family as the women's liberation movement advanced the belief that women were more than merely wives and mothers. In fact, with the introduction of the birth control pill, women, for the first time in the nation's history, asserted their right to be sexually free and childfree. During this pivotal time in American history, several renowned scholars wrote volumes celebrating the voluntarily childfree woman. Famous early works on nonparenthood and being childfree include *The Baby Trap* (1971) by Ellen Peck and William Granzig, *Mother's Day is Over* (1973) by Shirley Radl, and *Pronatalism: The Myth of Mom and Apple Pie* (1974) by Ellen Peck and Judith Senderowitz. Other prominent works during this time are *A Baby Maybe* (1975) by Elizabeth Whelan and *The Parent Test: How to Measure and Develop Your Talent for Parenthood* (1978) by Ellen Peck and William Granzig. The 1970s were especially notable because this was the first time the nation was advocating the single, childfree lifestyle.

In response to the massive coming out of the single population in the 1970s, due in large part to the preeminent scholars previously mentioned, Stein has identified four categories of singles based on the attitudes of single individuals: voluntary/stable singles, involuntary/stable singles, voluntary/temporary singles, and involuntary/temporary singles. Although single people move between these categories throughout life, a single person's satisfaction and overall wellbeing depends on perception (Stein 50). Voluntary stable singles tend to be single by choice and are generally satisfied with their decision (Stein 50). Involuntary stable singles tend to be dissatisfied with their singlehood, such as single, college-educated women challenged in finding a suitable mate and have trouble adjusting to permanent singlehood (Stein 50). Voluntary temporary singles are not opposed to marriage, but they do not prioritize marriage to the same degree as involuntary singles (Stein 50). Involuntary temporary singles are never-married individuals who are actively seeking a mate or previously married people, such as widows and divorcees (Stein 50). These categories created great diversity within the single population as voluntary and involuntary singles chose their path to independence by making the decision to parent alone or remain childfree (O'Brien 301; Veevers 28).

Characteristics of Individuals Who Are Voluntarily Childfree

There are unique characteristics of individuals who are voluntarily childfree, and two of these traits specifically relate to religion and race. According to Laurie Chauncey and Susan Dumais, Catholics, people in religiously homogamous marriages, and those who attend worship services frequently have lower rates of voluntary childlessness (Krishnan 91; Mosher and Bachrach 532; Poston 259). Yet the childless-by-choice demographic are often characterized by no religious affiliation and/or low-to-no church attendance, with the latter consistently proven to be the strongest religious variable to predict voluntary childlessness (Mosher and Bachrach 532; Rovi 355). Religious norms generally encourage high levels of fertility and traditional values, which can run counter to the values of a family with no children. Race is another defining characteristic of the voluntarily childfree. While the racial and ethnic makeup of the voluntarily childless is difficult to ascertain, recent statistics have revealed that while the number of children born to African American and Latino couples has substantially risen, the number of children born to white parents has seen a marked decrease. According to the most recent statistics from the U.S. Census Bureau, even though non-Hispanic whites are experiencing negative population growth (seeing 61,841 more deaths than births between 2013 and 2014), the number of ethnic minority births has increased from 32.9 to 37.9 per cent during this same time.

Although the number of childfree individuals has increased, in recent years, not having children is lower among Blacks than whites because of higher levels of fertility among Blacks (Mosher and Bachrach 532). Moreover, studies that do include Blacks and whites find a higher proportion of voluntary childlessness among whites (Boyd 183; Veevers 285). Clearly, the fertility rate of most Black (and Latina) women has outpaced that of white women, who are, largely, more educated and socioeconomically stable than Blacks and Latinas.

Contemporary Validation of Childfree Individuals

The decision to remain childfree, largely, does not carry with it the stigma that it once did. In general, political movements of the 1960s and 1970s—including the early years of the second wave of feminism, environmentalism, and the movement for reproductive choice—resulted in a societal shift from pronatalism to a voluntarily childfree status. Most notably, in her well-known tome, *The Baby Trap*, Ellen Peck advocates that women forgo motherhood and focus on marital and sexual satisfaction. Spurred by the success of her book, Ellen Peck and

Shirley Radl created the National Organization for Nonparents (NON) in Palo Alto, California in 1972, which advances the notion that people could choose not to have children—to be childfree. The foundation of NON was revolutionary because it was the first platform to allow women to speak openly regarding their fears or beliefs that mothering could not seamlessly fit with their career ambitions. Although this organization never became a truly viable political movement, it attracted approximately two thousand members in its heyday.

On August 1, 1973, the National Alliance for Optional Parenthood (NAOP, formerly NON) celebrated Nonparents Day by awarding a male and female national nonparent of the year. This organization actively fights pronatalism (attitudes and advertisements promoting or glorifying parenthood) by validating the choice of individuals who consciously choose to be childfree. The condemnation of consciously deciding to be married and childfree was so powerful that *Time* magazine wrote the following in 1972: "The cultural bias against childless couples is so strong that husbands and wives cannot choose non-parenthood freely; they know they will be branded selfish, shallow and neurotic" (Berman). Even though NAOP ended in 1982, it elevated the childfree life choice by making August 1 International Childfree Day, a day of celebration (Beach et al. 97).

After NAOP ceased, another organization began to advance the interests of the voluntarily childfree. Established in 1984, Just Kidding! proudly touts itself as "an international social club for adult couples and singles who have never had children." The organization explains what specifically it is and what it is not: "We are neither a business nor a dating service. We are non-political, non-religious, and do not endorse or oppose any cause. We are a social club for adults without children. No more, no less!" No Kidding! members are between "18 to 80 (and up!)"; it has active chapters in Canada, New Zealand, and the U.S. and encourages individuals who currently do not have a chapter in their local area to start one.

Reproductive Justice

Patriarchy directly affects the notion of womanhood by sustaining the ideology that motherhood defines women. In our published manuscript, my coauthor and I write as follows, "According to Dorothy Roberts, patriarchy specifically affects the notion of motherhood by sustaining the ideology that women are defined by motherhood. She asserted that in this patriarchal society, women are strongly encouraged and pressured to become mothers, and that pronatalism causes many to "define women as mothers or potential mothers" (Chaney and Brown 20). However, not all women accept the pressure to define themselves solely by motherhood. SisterSong, the Black feminist collective, coined the term "reproductive justice" and defines it as the right to have children, the right not to have children, and the right to raise one's children in a healthy environment. The theory of reproductive justice was created because regardless of their parental status, women of colour were looking for a way to clearly articulate the needs of their communities. Since their founding in 1997, SisterSong's three-core reproductive justice principles reflect the theory and practice collectively learned and shared. In particular, these core reproductive justice principles are based on the belief that every woman has the human right to do the following: (1) Decide if and when she will have a baby and the conditions under which she will give birth; (2) Decide if she will not have a baby and her options for preventing or ending a pregnancy; and (3) Parent the children she already has with the necessary social supports in safe environments and healthy communities and without fear of violence from individuals or the government (Ross). However, later in this chapter, I offer the term "reproductive empowerment" to describe Black women who, regardless of social class, are voluntarily childfree and are intrinsically empowered by their decision.

Several realities make the decision to be childfree difficult for many to accept. First, being a mother is a salient experience for many African American women (Barnes 10; Chaney, "The Character" 520; Chaney and Fairfax 31; McAdoo 125). The renowned Black family scholar, Harriett Pipes McAdoo, was one of the first academicians to focus on the extended family support that poor Black mothers frequently rely on (125). Future work drew attention to how family poverty affects Black mothers' parenting, mental health, and social support (Klebanov, Brooks-Gunn, and Duncan 441), welfare stigma among low-income, Black single mothers (Jarrett 370), as well as the various ecological contexts that make motherhood more difficult for low-income, single African American mothers (Reis, Stein, and Bennett 550). My work confirms the salience of motherhood for many Black women as well. During my published qualitative examination of the written responses of fifteen African American women between the ages of eighteen and fifty-five (mean age of 32.6 years), or women of childbearing age, I show how they define womanhood in terms of feminine attitudes (strength, sensitivity, and sensuality) and feminine behaviours (familial care, their own physical appearance, and self-respect). In addition, womanhood demonstrates a woman's ability to care for her home and take the lead in the absence of male leadership.

Second, Black womanhood is most often associated with popular media-driven personas. In her essay, "Mammies, Matriarchs, and Other Controlling Images," Patricia Hill Collins presents five stereotypical personas of the African American woman. She writes, "Portraying African American women as stereotypical mammies, matriarchs, welfare recipients, and hot mommas has been essential to the political economy of domination fostering Black women's oppression" (142). In addition to the aforementioned tropes, Hill Collins notes a fifth trope, the Black Lady, who is another version of the modern Mammy—namely, the hard-working Black professional who works twice as hard as everyone else:

> The image of the Black Lady also resembles aspects of the matriarch thesis: Black ladies have jobs that are so all consuming that they have no time for men or have forgotten how to treat them. Because they so routinely compete with men and are successful at it, they become less feminine. Highly educated Black ladies are deemed to be too assertive—that's why they cannot get men to marry them. (89)

Extending Collins's assessment of The Lady, many regard these Black women as too assertive to secure a marriage mate or, like Ms. Jackson, as too "sick and selfish" when they delay motherhood or voluntarily opt not to become mothers.

Finally, as previously mentioned, the fertility rate of most Black (and Latina) women has outnumbered that of white women. Although white middle-class women and women of other races who choose to be childfree find it difficult to receive personal and social validation, racism is a unique stressor for Black and Latina women because they are more likely to bear children as poor, unmarried/single mothers. Therein lies the unsaid realities of racism and sexism (the greater acceptance of choices made by white women and the dismissal of those made by Black women), socioeconomic status (classism), and the subjugation of women's role as wife and mother (patriarchy). These interlocking social realities align well with Kimberlee Crenshaw's intersectionality theory, which studies how different power structures interact in the lives of minorities, especially Black women. During her interview with Bim Adewunmi on April 2, 2014, Crenshaw said as follows:

> Class is not new and race is not new. And we still continue to contest and talk about it, so what's so unusual about inter-sectionality not being new and therefore that's not a reason to talk about it? Intersectionality draws attention to invisibilities that exist in feminism, in anti-racism, in class politics, so obviously it takes a lot of work to consistently challenge ourselves to be attentive to aspects of power that we don't ourselves experience.

However, she stresses, this has been the project of Black feminism since its very inception: drawing attention to the erasures, to the ways that "women of colour are invisible in plain sight" (qtd. in Adewunmi).

The word "motherhood" elicits a range of complex and varied thoughts, emotions, and experiences. In her tome *The Impossibility of Motherhood: Feminism, Individualism, and the Problem of Mothering*, Patrice DiQuinzio writes:

> Some women do not want to become mothers and never do; some women do not want to become mothers and nonetheless do; some women want to be mothers but are unable to do so for a variety of reasons; some women find great satisfaction and a sense of accomplishment in mothering; some women become mothers in circumstances that prevent their experiencing such satisfaction in mothering and some women regret having become mothers. (viii)

The truth of DiQuinzio's statement is a perfect complement to the statements I have received regarding motherhood from family, friends, and acquaintances as well as assumptions related to these statements [See Table for Comments and Assumptions Made Regarding Motherhood].

- "You should have at least one child. You need someone to take care of you when you get old" (my late maternal grandmother).
- "Being a mother is by far, the most important thing in my life" (my mother).
- "Being a mother is one part of who I am, but not the most important part. I am a daughter, a mother, and a student. But the role of mother is no more important than the other parts of me" (a single, professional, and divorced Black mother of an adult son in his late twenties).
- "You would be an excellent mother" (my maternal aunt that is married and mother of three adult children and five grandchildren).
- "You don't have children because you don't want to mess up your body" (a Black male).
- "Don't have children. The biggest source of pain in my life has been my children" (a professional Black female and mother of two sons in their thirties).
- "I'm telling you this for your own good. I have seen many women like you ... women your age that didn't care about having children because they were so focused on establishing their careers. Then, the day comes when they want children, and they can't have them. They come to me crying, asking me what I can do for them. You better hurry up and get pregnant soon before it is too late" (my obstetrician/gynecologist).
- "Don't worry. You'll get your chance one day" (a single, white female professor who has a three-year-old son).

Table: Comments and Assumptions Made Regarding (M)Otherhood

Comments	Assumptions
"You should have at least one child. You need someone to take care of you when you get old."	My child would have the desire to care for me in my old age. My child would have the ability to care for me in my old age. My ability to care for myself is contingent on my child/children.
"Being a mother is by far, the most important thing in my life."	Motherhood should be the most important thing in a woman's life.
"Being a mother is one part of who I am but not the most important part. I am a daughter, a mother, and a student. But the role of mother is no more important than the other parts of me."	Motherhood should trump all other identities held by a woman.
"You would be an excellent mother!"	I want to be a mother. I am confident that I would be an excellent mother.
"You don't have children because you don't want to mess up your body!"	My choice to be childfree is solely based on physical appearance. Women who were pregnant cannot get back to their prepregnancy weight. Physical appearance is a critical feature of being a woman.
"My advice to you is to never have children. My children have been the biggest source of pain in my life. I regret having them."	Motherhood is the greatest source of joy in a woman's life. Mothers do not regret having children. Mothers are responsible for their children throughout their lives.

"I'm telling you this for your own good. I have seen many women like you … women your age that didn't care about having children because they were so busy focusing on establishing their careers. Then, the day comes when they want children, and they can't have them. They come to me crying, asking me what I can do for them. You better hurry up and get pregnant soon before it is too late!"	I would regret my decision of being childfree. I should view a child as more important than a career. I should place more value on experiencing motherhood than choosing a man that would make a loving and committed father.
"Don't worry. You'll get your chance one day."	I worry about being childfree. My chance for motherhood will come. Assistive technologies/adoption will be available to me should I choose to use them.

My Autoethnographic Stance on Being Empowered and Childfree

I am a highly educated Black woman. I am highly religious and voluntarily make the decision to be childfree. My religion does not actively promote individuals to have children. In fact, my religion advocates sexual abstinence until marriage and that I marry a man who shares my faith, and that any children born within marriage receive biblical principles by both parents. To be clear, I personally value sexual abstinence and experienced relationship difficulties when I dated a man that shared my level of education but did not share my faith. In addition, my religion stresses parents to be keenly aware of the immense responsibility that is set before them. My religion reminds me we currently live in critical times, and it is difficult for parents to rear children in the current world climate. However, at the core of my faith is the belief that happiness is an internal state, has little to do with what is around me, and is rooted to the acknowledgement that God will give me everything that I need when I most need it.

During my lifetime, I have seen many negative changes in the world, and these changes have led me to often wonder why people consciously make the decision to bring children into the world. The first of these concerns is that the world is not a safe place to live. In my life, I have seen AIDS, 911, the Zika virus, an increasing number of parents that physically and sexually abuse or murder their children, and mass shootings in such places as Columbine, Colorado; Blacksburg, Virginia; Aurora, Colorado; Newton, Connecticut; Charleston, South Carolina; and Orlando Florida. Even though many parents claim the world has always been bad, daily local and national news reports provide resounding evidence that the parental responsibility of keeping children safe is substantially more difficult than it was in times past. In addition, I have seen the moral climate increasingly worsen. When I was a child, stores did not sell clothing that sexualized children, nor was I exposed to media content that promoted a pseudo-reality of life (e.g., reality-television programs that promote vanity, materialism, and lack of respect for authority, poor manners, aggressive behaviour, and sexual promiscuity) or was patently sexual and/or violent in nature. In fact, during my childhood and adolescence, I was never directly or indirectly exposed to pornographic images and would snicker when I saw individuals walk into the room with the large black curtain with the cautionary words on the outside, "21 and over" in the video store. Sadly, inappropriate images and content bombard children and adolescents who can easily view pornography on their computer or smartphone. The video games of my childhood (*Pac-Man* and *Lady Pac-Man*) have been replaced with three-dimensional video games like *Grand Theft Auto*, in which the goal is to rise in the underworld community by exploiting, raping, and murdering others. Songs are also a lot more sexually explicit than when I was a child. The sexual innuendo is no longer there and has been replaced with flagrant sexual specificity. For example, Marvin Gaye's sexual anthem "Let's Get It On" or the Starland Vocal Band's "Afternoon Delight" have been replaced with songs like "Slob on my Knob" by the rap group Three3 Six6 Mafia (2009), "Lick the Pussy" by the rap group Beatnuts (1994), or WAP (an acronym for "Wet-Ass Pussy") by Cardi B. and Megan Thee Stallion (2020). Clearly, we are living in an age when many children are force fed the belief that sexual promiscuity is normal.

Furthermore, it saddens me that many children's reliance on connecting with others via Smartphones and social media sites like Facebook, Instagram, and Twitter has created a "me-generation," very unaware of the feelings and needs of others. During many conversations with parents, I have learned that many of them feel as though they are watching their children drift away from them and have no way to close the chasm that exists and is growing between them. I grew up during a time when families were close, at least mine was. When I was a teenager, social media did not exist, and the only bully that one had to worry about was the bully on the school playground. Sadly, the children of today experience bullying in person and on the internet (cyberbullying). In fact, children's reliance on social media has made them less connected to their parents, more self-conscious and depressed, more likely to be targeted by internet predators, and more likely to experience the pain of being bullied by hundreds of people that are known and unknown to them. I cannot bring children into a world that is as chaotic, unstable, and frightening as the current one. The decision to be childfree is a conscious one that empowers me, not one that depresses me.

In my life, I have had many conversations about motherhood. Generally, these discussions were never specifically about motherhood, yet the topic of motherhood subtly weaved its way into the conversation. Some of these discussions are from family members that have known me my entire life and have seen me in several contexts to know that I have qualities that would make me not only a good but also an exceptional mother. In fact, when one of my maternal aunts was observing me with my sister's children, she told me: "You would be an excellent mother!" When I frequently cared for my maternal grandmother when her health declined, one day she told me: "You should have at least one child. You need someone to take care of you when you get old." From her eyes, I could see that my grandmother felt comfort that her oldest granddaughter cared for her, and she wanted me to have the same comfort in my waning years. However, after working six years for an agency that investigated cases of abuse and neglect of elderly individuals, I became keenly aware that children actually abuse and exploit their elderly parents. My mother also valued motherhood. One day when I asked her about the importance of being a mother in her life, she replied, "Being a mother is by far, the most important thing in my life." As I looked in her eyes, I saw that although she had my sisters and me when she was very young (under twenty-two), she truly meant that she had absolutely no regrets giving birth to my sisters and me. In my interactions with the children in my family, I am especially skilled at demonstrating warmth with discipline.

I know how to make children feel safe, even when at the time, they do not understand or fully agree with the decisions that I consistently make in their best interests.

Not every Black woman in the world can be a biological mother or can have the qualities needed to be a good mother; not every Black woman has the desire to be a mother. Once a Black man asked me if I had children, and when I told him that I did not, he immediately said, "You don't have children because you don't want to mess up your body!" In that moment, having just met me, this man made two erroneous assumptions about me: Vanity, not practical empowerment, was the motivation for my choice to be childfree; and pregnant women cannot get back to their prepregnancy weight. How unfair to assume that interest in my physical appearance would trump the long-term decision of not bringing a child into a world that is quickly declining. In that moment, I was angry yet discouraged that a man like him (and people like him) could be so presumptive and ignorant.

During one of the many conversations that I had with a good female friend regarding her sons (who were both ungrateful yet she willingly spent her money to get them out of various legal troubles), this beautiful, articulate, and college-educated woman told me: "My advice is to you is to never have children. My children have been the biggest source of pain in my life. I regret having them." There are two reasons why this comment stuck with me. For one, I had never heard a woman say these words aloud. Up until that time, I erroneously assumed that women never regretted their decision to become mothers. In a strange way, I believe this woman told me this to diminish any regrets that she felt that I might have had about not having any children. It was as if, in that moment, she consciously lifted the shroud of motherhood as the pinnacle of a woman's life and shared the secret that motherhood was a decision that she oftentimes regretted. I could not help but wonder how many other women had the same feelings that she did. Second, it pained me that this woman told me that after two very difficult pregnancies that her children would not be grateful that she did not abort them or give them up for adoption. Instead of being thankful for a mother that worked hard to give them the better things in life, they frequently cursed her and caused her much emotional pain. I could not help but wonder if when she first held both of her sons in her arms for the first time, years later; she would utter the words that she said to me?

Sadly, many women rush to become mothers during their childbearing years. It irritates me when people in society make women feel like they have to become mothers before their biological clock completely stops. When women internalize these assessments, it may force them to make life decisions, such as marriage and motherhood, which they may not want or be ready. In addition, regardless of the intent, it is unethical for a physician to tell me:

> I'm telling you this for your own good. I have seen many women like you ... women your age that didn't care about having children because they were so busy focusing on establishing their careers. Then, the day comes when they want children, and they can't have them. They come to me crying, asking me what I can do for them. You better hurry up and get pregnant soon before it is too late!

It is morally wrong and quite rude for a healthcare professional to advocate that I go against my religious beliefs just because my window of opportunity to have children is closing. These types of comments invalidate my choice as well as the choices made by millions of women who have consciously made the decision not to become mothers, who are willing to postpone what they want for what is in the best interest of their children, or who are willing to adopt children to fulfill that part of their identity. Currently, there are thousands of children in the foster care system who will age out because individuals and couples never saw them as fitting in their preconceived image of what their perfect family looks like. These children need love too.

As a group, white, professional women have more opportunities to rear children in stable two-parent homes than Black, professional women. As a Black family scholar, I know very well the statistics: White couples, Latino couples, and Asian couples are substantially more likely to marry and stay married than African American couples. Related to this, even Black children in cohabitating unions are more likely to have their parents' relationship end before it culminates in a marriage, and many Black children grow up in homes where their father is not present. In fact, the majority of Black children today are born to unmarried Black women, who go on to rear their children in single-mother headed households, a reality that has existed since the 1970s. As I make the decision to remain childfree, please be clear that my decision connects to what is in the best interest of my unborn children. At this point in my life, I have not met a man who shares my religion, values, and life goals, so I do not want to contribute to the growing statistics of single, Black mothers. Even though my socioeconomic status puts me in a different category than my less-educated Black sisters, at the end of the day, I would have the same joys, challenges, and fears of Black women who rear children in America. Although most of the negative rhetoric surrounding Black mothers has been negative, I do not want other women to look at me and assume that fathers have no real value in the lives of children. For me, a potential partner must demonstrate love, honour, respect, and commitment to me before I would ever consider him being a father to my children. Since I have not met such a man (and maybe never will), why should I lower my high standards for a quality life partner merely for the sake of motherhood? I refuse to lower my standards. So, when a white, professional woman who makes the conscious decision to have a child while unmarried tells me "Don't worry. You'll get your chance to be a mother one day," I am perplexed why she or anyone else would feel that my life is less satisfying because I am a childfree Black woman. Since I do not want the chance to become a mother in the world that we live in, I never worry about motherhood. In fact, I frequently worry about the children born to one or more parents who do not love them, care for them, or make them feel secure. I do worry about how children fare when the world that they live in is so chaotic and unsafe. My religious values and faith have assured me that God will give me a full life and that that full life does not predicate on motherhood. I am not less than because of my choice not to become a mother. I am empowered by it.

Reproductive Empowerment

In this work, I discuss my voluntary decision to be childfree via an autoethnographic lens. I position my decision within the scholarly literature as well as such organizations as the NAOP and No Kidding!, which advocate the choice to be voluntarily childfree. In addition, I provide statements that I have received regarding motherhood as well as critically determine assumptions that underlie such statements. At this point, I would like to turn the gaze outwards and question why many in society question, are skeptical of, or oppose my right, as well as the right of other women, to voluntarily refrain from bearing children. Of course, television and film media largely influence the presumptive positionality of motherhood in society and largely tout motherhood as the most important identity women assume (Fischer 22; Kaplan 32). For example, Florida Evans (*Good Times*), Claire Huxtable (*The Cosby Show*), Mother Winslow (Family Matters), and Aunt Vivian (*Fresh Prince of Bel-Air*) are four, prominent African American mothers on television that have become beacons of strength in America's consciousness ("Black TV Moms: Our Favorite Sitcom Mamas").

Reproductive empowerment is an intellectual stance that consciously moves beyond merely thinking of women as biological mothers or motherhood as the ultimate life goal of all women. Most important, this stance is rooted in a keen religious and/or spiritual awareness that God provides everything that one needs and that God provides what one needs when they most need it. Furthermore, this position recognizes historical and contemporary realities that make rearing children difficult and, thus, a valid rationale to opt out of biological motherhood. Fundamentally, this stance recognizes the historical and contemporary challenges of parenthood for African American women, especially as it relates to their limited marital and collaborative parenting options. Returning to the historical entry of Africans to America, the descendants of those individuals lived in a society that created disadvantages for themselves and their children, and, sadly, contemporary African American parents and their children are victims of institutional discrimination (Chaney, "Institutional Racism").

As a Black feminist, I value the multiple roles that women embrace in their lives and object to arguments in which feminists argue which female is superior: the one who finds fulfillment in her life as a wife and mother or the one who finds fulfillment in establishing and solidifying her career. Furthermore, I am keenly aware of the historicity that makes an enjoyable, stress-free experience of motherhood considerably more difficult for African American women. Even though the fertility of Black American women is generally higher than that of white women, the children of women in the former group are more likely to be poor, unemployed (Wulczyn et al. 65), and unmarried. In addition, Black women are more likely than white women to rear their children as single parents (Dixon 43), enter and exit the foster care system (Chaney and

Spell 90), experience incarceration (Alexander 5) and be murdered during their lives (Chaney and Robertson 46). Realistically, since Black families face a variety of internal (e.g., weakened family structures) and external (e.g., racism, discrimination, and prejudice) stressors in their lives, motherhood is more emotionally taxing for Black women than women of other races.

Reproductive empowerment elevates the thoughts, feelings, and experiences of those who are voluntarily childfree. At its core, this intellectual philosophy acknowledges: (1) what voluntarily childfree women think about motherhood (the subjective and objective willingness to be a biological parent (e.g., whether motherhood is a role they want to assume in today's world); (2) how voluntarily childfree women feel about motherhood (e.g., not all Black women desire or will have the opportunity to become biological mothers); (3) voluntarily childfree women's experiences regarding motherhood (e.g., the limited opportunities for Black women to be biological mothers). As I turn the gaze outwards, I clearly recognize that the race, gender, and socioeconomic status of individuals shape their views regarding motherhood as well as their opportunities and experiences. To be clear, even though society has seen fewer stable marriages and more single-mother headed households than in decades past, white men and women and their children are more advantaged than families of colour. Essentially, this means that members of the socially advantaged group are more likely to elevate motherhood as the life goal of all women and be skeptical of professional Black women who are voluntarily childfree.

Key to this intellectual position is recognizing how Black women who are voluntarily childfree are stable social mothers to children that are not biologically their own. *The Medical Dictionary* defines motherhood in three ways: genetic, gestational, and/or social. While the genetic is defined as "a woman whose contribution to the child is the ovum, and hence genes" and the gestational mother is "a woman whose uterus was used for the nurturing and development of an embryo into a baby," the social mother is "a woman who rears the baby after birth." Although a "social mother" may or may not directly relate to women who have the primary responsibility to rear their children, I assert that it can also apply to women who make the decision to be voluntarily childfree yet who are instrumental in helping women rear their children.

Fundamentally, reproductive empowerment acknowledges the

physical, financial, emotional, and spiritual work that voluntarily childfree women engage in when they help rear the children of others. Historically, this form of parentage was common among African female slaves who reared their biological children, the children of their slave masters, and the children separated from their biological parents during the slave trade and found themselves on foreign plantations (Jones 63). Too often, when a child reaches certain developmental milestones in his or her life, many believe the biological parents are the primary source of that child's success, whereas social parents are relegated to a tertiary place in that child's development and progress. The longer that I have been in academe, the more I recognize that I have had a profound effect on my students, many of whom are away from their parents and see me as a social mother that they can trust, confide in, seek advice from, and share their triumphs and disappointments. Although I have made the conscious decision not to become a biological mother, I feel empowered when I contemplate how I directly and indirectly enhance the lives of children and young adults within and outside of my family as they go out into the world.

Conclusion

At this point, I remind everyone who questions, are skeptical of, or oppose my right, as well as the right of other women, to forgo bearing children that the right to bear children is a fundamental right. Although we are committed to our decision to be childfree, there are many ways that we support single-parent households as they rear their children. In addition, I provide various statements and assumptions regarding motherhood, which lend strong support to Patrice DiQuinzio's assessment regarding the various thoughts, feelings, and emotions associated with motherhood. At the onset of this chapter, I mentioned the pregnancy of the forty-nine-year-old and subsequent motherhood of the American singer, songwriter, dancer, and actor Janet Jackson. Although many individuals express the opinion that Ms. Jackson's opportunity to bear children had passed, as a Black feminist, I commend her decision to become pregnant at a time that was best and right for her. However, I desire that all women do what is right and best for them. Although we live in a society that greatly values biological motherhood, it is my desire that all women, regardless of race, are empowered, as they remain voluntarily childfree. In closing, since every woman has the right to feel empowered regardless of whether or not she is a biological mother, in her quest for personal fulfillment, every woman has the right to walk her own path.

Works Cited

Adewunmi, Bim. "Kimberlé Crenshaw on Intersectionality: 'I Wanted to Come Up with an Everyday Metaphor That Anyone Could Use.'" *New Statesman*, 2 Apr. 2014, www.newstatesman.com/lifestyle/2014/04/kimberl-crenshaw-intersectionality-i-wanted-come-everyday-metaphor-anyone-could. Accessed 12 Dec. 2020.

Alexander, Michelle. *The New Jim Crow: Mass Incarceration in the Age of Colorblindness.* The New Press, 2012.

Allen, Daniel C. "Learning Autoethnography: A Review of Autoethnography: Understanding Qualitative Research." *The Qualitative Report*, vol. 20, no. 2, 2015, pp. 33-35.

Allen, James, et al. *Without Sanctuary: Lynching Photography in America.* Twin Palms, 2000.

Barnes, Riché J. Daniel. *Raising the Race: Black Career Women Redefine Marriage, Motherhood, and Community.* Rutgers University Press, 2015.

Beach, Lee Roy, et al. "The Expectation-Threshold Model of Reproductive Decision Making." *Population and Environment*, vol. 5, no. 2, 1982, pp. 95-108.

Beck, Elwood M., and Stewart E. Tolnay. "The Killing Fields of the Deep South: The Market for Cotton and the Lynching of Blacks, 1882–1930." *American Sociological Review*, vol. 55, 1990, pp. 526-39.

Berlin, Ira. *The Making of African America: The Four Great Migrations.* Penguin, 2010.

Berman, Eliza. "'Selfish, Shallow and Neurotic': How the Conversation on Childlessness Got Started." Time, 8 Apr. 2015, time.com/3813535/national-organization-for-non-parents/. Accessed 12 Dec. 2020.

"Black TV Moms: Our Favorite Sitcom Mamas." *Huffington Post*, 12 May 2013, www.huffingtonpost.com/2013/05/12/black-tv-moms-ourfavorit_n_3262723.html. Accessed 12 Dec. 2020.

Boyd, Robert L. "Racial Differences in Childlessness: A Centennial Review." *Sociological Perspectives*, vol. 32, no. 2, 1989, pp. 183-99.

Boylorn, Robin M. "As Seen on TV: An Autoethnographic Reflection on Race and Reality Television." *Critical Studies in Media Communication*, vol. 25, no. 4, 2008, 413-33.

Chauncey, Laurie, and Susan A. Dumais. "Voluntary Childlessness in Marriage and Family Textbooks 1950–2000." *Journal of Family History*, vol. 34, no. 2, 2009, pp. 206-23.

Chaney, Cassandra. "Institutional Racism: Perspectives on the Department of Justice's Investigation of the Ferguson Police Department." *Western Journal of Black Studies*, vol. 39, no. 4, 2016, pp. 312-30.

Chaney, Cassandra. "The Character of Womanhood: How African American Women's Perceptions of Womanhood Influence Marriage and Motherhood." *Ethnicities*, vol. 11, no. 4, 2011, pp. 512-35.

Chaney, Cassandra, and Arielle Brown. "Is Black Motherhood A Marker of Oppression or Empowerment? Hip-Hop and R&B Lessons about" Mama." *The Journal of Hip Hop Studies*, vol. 2, no. 1, 2015, pp. 12-46.

Chaney, Cassandra, and Colita Nichols Fairfax. "The Obamas and the Culture of Black Parenting in America." *Journal of Pan African Studies*, vol. 5, no. 10, 2013, pp. 20-50.

Chaney, Cassandra, and Meghan Spell. "'In the System': A Qualitative Study of African American Women's Foster Care Stories." *Western Journal of Black Studies*, vol. 39, no. 2, 2015, pp. 84-101.

Chaney, Cassandra, and Ray V. Robertson. "Armed and Dangerous? An Examination of Fatal Shootings of Unarmed Black People by Police." *Journal of Pan African Studies*, vol. 8, no. 4, 2015, pp. 45-78.

Collins, Patricia Hill. *Black Feminist Thought: Knowledge, Consciousness, and the Politics of Empowerment*. Routledge, 2002.

Coontz, Stephanie. *The Way We Never Were: American Families and the Nostalgia Trap*. Basic Books, 1992.

Daryanani, Issar, et al. "Single Mother Parenting and Adolescent Psychopathology." *Journal of Abnormal Child Psychology*, vol. 44, no. 7, 2016, pp. 1411-23.

Denzin, Norman K. *Interpretive Autoethnography.* Vol. 17. Sage Publications, 2013.

DiQuinzio, Patrice. *The Impossibility of Motherhood: Feminism, Individualism, and the Problem of Mothering.* Routledge, 2013.

Dixon, Patricia. *African American Relationships, Marriages, and Families: An Introduction.* Routledge, 2013.

Ellis, Carolyn. *The Ethnographic I: A Methodological Novel about Autoethnography.* Rowman Altamira, 2004.

Ellis, Carolyn S., and Arthur Bochner. "Autoethnography, Personal Narrative, Reflexivity: Researcher as Subject." *Handbook of Qualitative Research*, edited by N. K. Denzin and Y. S. Lincoln, Sage Publications, 2000, pp. 733-68.

Fischer, Lucy. *Cinematernity: Film, Motherhood, Genre.* Princeton University Press, 2014.

Genovese, Eugene D. *Roll, Jordan, Roll: The World the Slaves Made.* Vintage, 1976.

hooks, bell. *Black Looks: Race and Representation.* Academic Internet Pub Inc., 2006.

"Is Janet Jackson Pregnant? Singer Expecting First Child, Multiple Reports Claim." *People*, 4 May 2016, celebritybabies.people.com/2016/05/04/janet-jackson-pregnant-expecting-first-child/. Accessed 12 Dec. 2020.

Jarrett, Robin L. "Welfare Stigma among Low-Income, African American Single Mothers." *Family Relations*, vol. 45, no. 4, 1996, pp. 368-374.

Jones, Jacqueline. *Labor of Love, Labor of Sorrow: Black Women, Work, and the Family, From Slavery to the Present.* Basic Books, 2009.

Kaplan, E. Ann. *Motherhood and Representation: The Mother in Popular Culture and Melodrama.* Routledge, 2013.

Klebanov, Pamela Kato, Jeanne Brooks-Gunn, and Greg J. Duncan. "Does Neighborhood and Family Poverty Affect Mothers' Parenting, Mental Health, and Social Support?" *Journal of Marriage and the Family*, vol. 56, no. 2, 1994, pp. 441-55.

Kolchin, Peter. *American Slavery: 1619-1877.* Macmillan, 2003.

Krishnan, Vijaya. "Religious Homogamy and Voluntary Childlessness in Canada." *Sociological Perspectives*, vol. 36, no. 1, 1993, 83-93.

Levine, Lawrence W. *Black Culture and Black Consciousness: Afro-American Folk Thought from Slavery to Freedom*. Vol. 530. Oxford University Press, 1978.

Mattes, Jane. *Single Mothers by Choice: A Guidebook for Single Women Who Are Considering or Have Chosen Motherhood*. Three Rivers Press, 2013.

McAdoo, Harriette Pipes. "Black Mothers and the Extended Family Support Network." *The Black Woman*, vol. 21, 1980, pp. 125-44.

McDermott, Chan. "Single Mothers by Choice: A Guidebook for Single Women Who are Considering or Have Chosen Motherhood." *Journal of Human Lactation*, vol. 12, no. 2, 1996, pp. 162-62.

Mosher, William D., and Christine A. Bachrach. "Childlessness in the United States Estimates from the National Survey of Family Growth." *Journal of Family Issues*, vol. 3, no. 4, 1982, pp. 517-43.

No Kidding (NK!—We're Childfree). The International Social and Networking Club for Childfree Couples and Singles, www.nokidding.net/index.html. Accessed 12 Dec. 2020.

O'Brien, Mary. "Never Married Older Women: The Life Experience." *Social Indicators Research*, vol. 24, no. 3, 1991, pp. 301-15.

Olzak, Susan. "The Political Context of Competition: Lynching and Urban Racial Violence, 1882–1914. » *Social Forces*, vol. 69, no. 2, 1990, pp. 395-421.

Park, Kristin. "Stigma Management among the Voluntarily Childless." *Sociological Perspectives*, vol. 45, no. 1, 2002, pp. 21-45.

Peck, Ellen. *The Baby Trap*. B. Geis Associates, 1971.

Peck, Ellen, and Judith Senderowitz. *Pronatalism: The Myth of Mom and Apple Pie*. Crowell, 1974.

Peck, Ellen and William Granzig. *The Parent Test: How to Measure and Develop Your Talent for Parenthood*. Putnam, 1978.

Phillips, Charles David. "Exploring Relations among Forms of Social Control: The Lynching and Execution of Blacks in North Carolina, 1889–1918." *Law & Soc'y Rev*, vol. 21, 1987, p. 361-74.

Poston Jr, Dudley L. "Voluntary and Involuntary Childlessness among Catholic and Non Catholic Women: Are the Patterns Converging?" *Social Biology*, vol. 37, no. 3-4, 1990, pp. 251-65.

Poston, Jr., Dudley L., and Kathryn Beth Kramer. "Voluntary and Involuntary Childlessness in the United States, 1955–1973." *Social Biology*, vol. 30, no. 3, 1983, pp. 290-306.

Radl, Shirley L. *Mothers Day Is Over*. Charterhouse, 1973.

Reis, Janet, Linda Barbera-Stein, and Susan Bennett. "Ecological Determinants of Parenting." *Family Relations*, vol. 35, no. 4, 1986, pp. 547-54.

Rosenthal, Lisa, and Marci Lobel. "Stereotypes of Black American Women Related to Sexuality and Motherhood." *Psychology of Women Quarterly*, vol. 40, no. 3, 2016, 414-27.

Ross, L. "Understanding Reproductive Justice." *Trust Black Women*, 2011, www.trustblackwomen.org/our-work/what-is-reproductive-justice/9-what-isreproductive-justice. Accessed 12 Dec. 2020.

Rovi, Susan L. D. "Taking 'No' For an Answer: Using Negative Reproductive Intentions to Study The Childless/Childfree." *Population Research and Policy Review*, vol. 13, no. 4, 1994, pp. 343-65.

Stein, Peter J., ed. *Single Life: Unmarried Adults in Social Context*. St. Martin's Press, 1981.

Stein, Peter J. *Single*. Prentice Hall, 1976.

Stein, Peter J. "Singlehood: An Alternative to Marriage." *Family Coordinator*, vol. 24, no. 4, 1975, pp. 489-503.

The Medical Dictionary. "Social Mother." *Medical Dictionary*, 2016, medical-dictionary.thefreedictionary.com/social+mother. Accessed 12 Dec. 2020.

Thompson, S. "Survey Paints Portrait of Black Women in America." *The Washington Post*, 22 Jan. 2013, www.washingtonpost.com/politics/survey-paints-portrait-of-black-women-in-america/2011/12/22/gIQAvxFcJQ_story.html. Accessed 12 Dec. 2020.

Veevers, Jean E. *Childless by Choice*. Butterworth, 1980.

Whelan, Elizabeth M. *A Baby?... Maybe: A Guide to Making the Most Fateful Decision of Your Life*. Bobbs-Merrill, 1980.

Wulczyn, Fred, et al. "Poverty, Social Disadvantage, and the Black/White Placement Gap." *Children and Youth Services Review*, vol. 35, no. 1, 2013, pp. 65-74.

Chapter Six

Voluntary Childfree Women: Abandoning Infants by Domestic Servants and Street Beggars in Ethiopia

Victoria Team

"Can a mother forget the baby at her breast and have no compassion
on the child she has borne? Though she may forget."
—Isaiah 49:15

Introduction

Recent studies have presented the concept of motherhood as an umbrella term. In addition to its traditional meaning, it now encompasses other types of motherhood, including motherhood through adoption, foster motherhood (Dorgan), surrogate motherhood (Pande), IVF motherhood (Inhorn), and angel motherhood (van der Sijpt). Similarly, the concept of childlessness has also broadened in the literature. In one of the earliest descriptions of voluntary childlessness, Jean Veevers states that it "focuses mainly upon married persons who choose not to have children in spite of being licensed and indeed expected to do so" (3). This concept later referred to a woman's decision not to have children for a variety of reasons, including her career and independence as well as a better lifestyle (Shaw). Other reasons include feminism ones, in that motherhood should be a choice rather than a necessity (Basten), as well as environmental ones, in that having children may further deplete the earth's natural resources (Walker).

However, some women may decide to remain childfree by abandoning their children. There is no clear definition of child abandonment as a practice (Panter-Brick); moreover, in some countries, this practice is a criminal offence. However, there are a few types of child abandonment identified in the literature, including open or legal abandonment, when the child is placed in an adoption facility and parental details are taken, as well as secret or illegal abandonment, when the child is left in an unauthorized place for abandonment and the parents cannot be identified (The University of Nottingham). Parents may or may not return to their children and their responsibilities after a period of time, which makes abandonment either temporary or permanent (The University of Nottingham).

Infant abandonment is a common practice across time and cultures. The primary reason for this practice is either the harsh financial circumstances of mothers and their inability to provide basic needs for their child or the women's desire to hide their unsanctioned sexual activities, which resulted in the unwanted pregnancy and child (Fuchs; Boswell; Ransel). Nowadays, illegal infant abandonment in developed countries is uncommon due to improved access to contraceptive technologies and termination services as well as the availability of state organized anonymous adoption services, where the unwanted infant could be left (Pruitt). In some developing countries, illegal infant abandonment still remains a common practice (Tadele).

In this chapter, I discuss the illegal practice of abandoning infants by Ethiopian street beggars and domestic servants who had an unplanned and unwanted pregnancy and childbirth. Wishing to remain childfree and also having no resources for mothering, some women abandoned their newborn babies in hospital maternity departments, under the gate of missionaries' houses, and simply in the market. I present this practice as a different type of voluntary childlessness that I witnessed while practicing in Ethiopia as a general practitioner for over ten years, from 1989 to 1999. In line with the theme of this anthology, I adopt the women's perspective rather than mothers' and infants', although to most people these three perspectives may seem inseparable.

Background

Ethiopia is located in East Africa; it is one of the most populous countries in the Horn of Africa and one of the poorest countries in the world (Alemayehu). Historically, the country has been affected by political instability, war, drought, and famine (Endale). A majority of the general population lives below the poverty line, having limited access to food, water, and shelter (Parker and Woldegiorgis). Women have lower educational rates and poorer employment prospects as compared with men (Molla). Violence against women (Team and Hassen) also includes various traditional practices, including female genital mutilation, early marriage, forced marriage, and marriage by abduction (Assefa et al.). Ethiopia is also characterized by high fertility rates, particularly in 1980s, when the rate was approximately seven births per woman per lifetime (World Bank, "Fertility Rate"). The maternal mortality rate was high in 1990s and is still high, as about 20 per cent of maternal deaths are related to pregnancy termination (Tesema et al).

Unplanned and unwanted pregnancies and births are common among street beggars and domestic servants, who have no access to contraceptives (Belete). Although in Addis-Ababa, the capital of Ethiopia, and some other major cities—including Ambo, Awassa, Desse, Jimma, Mekele, Shashamane, and Sidamo—and also in some rural areas, contraceptives are available and distributed for free in hospitals, health centres, and family planning clinics, it is unlikely that they reached these population groups. Domestic servants were also unable to negotiate their use because they are frequently forced into sex (Erulkar and Ferede). Domestic servants are expected to comply with requests for sexual favours by the men of the house to remain employed; cases of rape, too, are not uncommon (Belete; Kifle). Street beggars were raped and gang raped (Misganaw and Worku; Tadele). They also tend to trade sexual favors to gang leaders for using a particular territory to work on. Many of these women are unaware of contraceptives, as they have no opportunities to attend a family planning clinic.

With a few exceptions, such as when the woman's life is endangered or she has severe health issues, pregnancy termination is not practiced in the country; this procedure has been outlawed and criminalized mainly on religious grounds (Wada). Until the 2004 law reform, the termination of pregnancy that occurred because of rape and/or incest was not permitted (Singh et al.). Prior to 2004, social and financial circumstances were not taken into consideration either; now, extreme poverty is considered as an indication for pregnancy termination (Wada). In Addis Ababa, some international agencies provide abortion; for example, Balcha Hospital, which is run by health professionals from the ex-USSR. However, the fees charged for pregnancy termination in Balcha Hospital are high; thus, this procedure is affordable only for the wealthiest women. Illegal abortions are available (Tadesse et al.), but women are also required to pay large sums of money; and maids and beggars, the most disadvantaged people, cannot pay.

Some women, however, do not want to terminate their unplanned, unintended, and even unwanted pregnancies. According to their religious beliefs, pregnancy termination is seen as killing the child. Married women, even the most financially disadvantaged, who already have many children, usually keep the pregnancy until term and have the child. Some domestic servants, too, prefer to give birth and later take their newborn children to their birthplace village, where their parents or other relatives can look after the child. Because of their religious beliefs and/or lack of access to termination services, some women are forced to give birth and later abandon the unwanted newborn child, which is a common issue, particularly among domestic servants. Cases of extreme methods of abandonment also exist, when women will throw their newborns into toilet pits, sewers, or a river (Tadele).

Some street beggars show their big belly to people to increase their chances of receiving money from passersby. It is not unusual to see postpartum street beggars lying on the roadside together with their newborn babies and yelling for financial support. They will sometimes put a curved knife near the baby as an ultimatum to other people, as if saying, "If you do not support me, I would rather kill my newborn baby than see him die from hunger."

Who Needs This Boy? Who Needs This Girl?

Working in the maternity ward of one of the largest hospitals in Addis-Ababa, I noticed that new mothers had different responses to my announcement: "You've got a baby boy" or "You've got a baby girl." Many women were happy; they praised God, thanked the doctors, and blessed their newborn babies. Some women, who had a large family, were worried, saying that they did not know how they would manage their growing family. Other women, however, responded, "Who needs this baby boy?" or "Who needs this baby girl?" At first, I was not sure about the reasons behind this reply. Later, when I asked my workplace colleagues, they said that these postpartum women were either domestic servants or street beggars who had an unwanted pregnancy and that they may abandon their newborn child. The abandonment of the newborn babies in maternity wards was not uncommon in Ethiopia at that time. Women were not talkative. Sometimes, the information that they were a domestic servant and their pregnancy was unwanted was the only information that we had. At some point in time, they would simply disappear, leaving their baby in the maternity ward. This was a semilegal type of abandonment. Many pregnant women did not have their identity card with them, and they occasionally provided false details.

One day, we admitted a street beggar, a lady in her thirties, who was in labour. She already had a seven-year-old daughter, whom she brought with her to the hospital. While the mother was in a labour room, the staff members from the maternity ward were entertaining the little girl. When the baby was born, we allowed the girl to visit her mother. When she came back, we asked her, if she liked her newborn baby sister, but she said: "Who needs this baby girl? My mum said that all girls are *sharmutoch* [whores], who bring only troubles. We need a baby boy, who will grow up and feed the family. He will become a *kisawlake* [pocket thief]; my mum will teach him how to steal, and we will get rich." The street mother disappeared from the maternity ward that night, taking only her older daughter with her. On the patient card, the doctor on admission had written that the lady had been raped many times and that she did not know who the father of her child was.

Working in the outpatient department of the same hospital, I heard a lot of sad and heart-breaking stories about sexual harassment. Most of these stories were shared by adolescent girls, who were brought to the capital city from a rural area to work in the houses of their wealthier relatives and their friends. Many of them came to the central hospital to seek help for termination-related complications, usually bleeding after an incomplete abortion, which was performed illegally. Illegal abortion usually consisted of the insertion of either a wooden stick or a piece of a plastic tube from an intravenous line system into the cervix. High doses of various medicines, for example Ampicillin capsules for a week-long course, were taken all at once. Chloroquine, an antimalarial medicine, was a commonly used aborticide. Some women said that they were unable to pay at once for these illegal services and would need to pay the cost in smaller sums when they would get better and commence work. A few women said that their female head of the household was a nice lady, who agreed to cover the cost of the illegal abortion when she suspected that her son was involved in a relationship with the servant girl. However, not all heads of the household were good. There were many cases when pregnant girls were requested to leave the house without any pay, particularly if a female head of household suspected that their servant was in a relationship with her husband. Most servant girls said that the reason behind the termination was their inability to provide for the child and to keep working at the same time. They also said that they did not want to place a burden on their families, who lived in poverty and were unable to provide for their own children.

In 1990, I started working in one of the largest children's clinics, Birla Pediatric Clinic, situated on the premises of Yekatit 12 Hospital in Addis-Ababa. This clinic was established and run by the famous Indian industrial proprietor, Shri. Basant Kumar Birla, a fact I did not know at that time. Prior to the first morning meeting, followed by the rounds, one of the doctors was looking for his patient's card. His patient's name was Michael (the baby's name, a pseudonym) Birla. I said that I had had a card reading Alemush (the baby's name, also pseudonym) Birla. I asked if they were brother and sister given they shared the father's name. (In Ethiopia, traditionally, the father's name is used as a surname). The doctor smiled with sadness and said: "They are all brothers and sisters here. This is the ward for abandoned children. Nobody knows their real name. Staff members give them a first name, but all of them have the same father's name, which is Birla, after the name of the person who founded this clinic." Most of the children were left by their mothers, who were domestic servants and were unable to provide for their children.

Infant Abandonment: Whose Deviant Behaviour?

In the past, voluntary childlessness was considered deviant behavior (Gillespie). The deviancy of childlessness lay in its "radical rejection of mothering," as Maura Kelly has argued (157). It continues to be unfavourably viewed by most societies and traditional families (Graham and Rich). In late eighteenth and early nineteenth century, in the Western world, "unlimited child-bearing was the duty of every married woman" (Mercer 27). Not only childlessness, but any "limitations of family size were viewed as extreme selfishness", and contraceptives were viewed as "an unjustifiable intervention in the 'true' course of nature" (Mercer 27). In Africa, motherhood comprises the core of womanhood (Nnaemeka). Reproducing and mothering are two of the most important gender roles that define women in Africa (Nyamongo); women's religious duties are based upon the biblical principle "be fruitful and multiply." Children in Ethiopia are viewed as family assets, and parents expect reciprocal care; militarized state officials, at the same time, expect women to produce soldiers for the nation (Team). Childfree women are viewed unfavorably. The option not to have children is never considered a choice; rather, an inability to produce offspring, which is usually linked with infertility, illness, curses, and a lack of God's blessing (Ombelet et al.).

Social Circumstances and Deviant Behaviour

Abandoning infants, in all societies, is considered deviant behaviour, which is also criminal behaviour. The society and the media endlessly judge this practice, ignoring women's individual situations and existing gender-related violence (Boswell; Ransel). Anne Edwards argues that to understand deviant behaviour, three major questions should be considered:

1. What are the norms or rules which members of a group or a society are expected to observe and how should they be defined?
2. What sorts of people under what kinds of conditions violate these norms?
3. How and on whom are the norms enforced, how are detected rule-breakers treated and what are the consequences of social and societal reaction to deviant behaviour? (294)

Edwards emphasizes the importance of the second question, related to population groups and their social circumstances, which contributes to the violation of societal norms. She believes that answering this question will help social researchers to identify the potential causes of deviant behaviour.

Street beggars and domestic servants as population groups are vulnerable in all aspects. They are financially disadvantaged, socially excluded, and sexually abused (Erulkar and Ferede). Both positions are the lowest in terms of the hierarchy of jobs and the wages that women receive (Erulkar and Ferede). Rape and survival sex (see Wojcicki 268), which is "the trading of sexual favours out of desperation" (Nattrass 27), happen in both positions.

Edwards's third question for understanding of deviant behaviours is "on whom are the norms enforced?" (294), and the answer is obvious: women. The role of men as a group is invisible in infant abandonment; they do not have any responsibility in this practice. Ethiopian society, expecting compliance with the defined gender norms, can provide better services for people who live below the poverty level. However, the politics of militarization adopted by Ethiopian governments since the late 1970s and their involvement in three consecutive wars—the Ethiopian-Somali War (1977–1978, and 1982), the Ethiopian Civil War (1974–1991), and the Ethiopian-Eritrean War (1998–2000)—as well as the structural adjustment program introduced in 1991, has all contributed to extreme poverty in the country (Tadesse et al). When a greater proportion of the general population lives below the poverty line (Parker and Woldegiorgis), the needs of domestic servants and homeless people are rarely prioritized. The needs for special services and programs for these disadvantaged groups are highlighted by researchers on an ongoing basis (Edwards et al.; Kifle; Erulkar and Ferede). If state-organized adoption services are unavailable and/or inaccessible, women may rely on abandoning their newborn child in a hospital, on a busy street, at the market, or under the gates of the homes of wealthy people. Women's practice of infant abandonment in Ethiopia was criminalized, and women were prosecuted according with the law (Tadele). However, the failure of the state to protect women's sexual freedom, to provide contraceptives, to improve access to pregnancy termination services, and to increase the availability of adoption services was rarely taken into consideration when individual criminal cases were discussed. As Catherine Panter-Brick notes, "To say that the parents have abandoned their children here is a smokescreen deflecting attention from society's own neglect" (19). Infant abandonment reflects women's personal and structural vulnerability. The concept of structural violence was defined by James Quesada, and Laurie Kain Hart, and Philippe Bourgois as "a positionality that imposes physical-emotional suffering on specific population groups and individuals in patterned ways"; they view structural violence as "a product of class-based economic exploitation and cultural, gender/sexual, and racialized discrimination, as well as complementary processes of depreciated subjectivity formation" (340). They further write: "Economically exploited and politically subordinated individuals and collectivities often internalize their externally generated depreciated status in a complex and poorly understood process of embodiment that shapes their behaviors, practices, and self-conceptions" (342).

Infant Abandonment: Childless and Childfree by Choice

Stuart Basten highlights the importance of distinguishing the terms "childless" and "childfree" (9). Comparing the terms "childless" and "homeless," he argues that the term "childless" sounds as if a person is lacking something; for example, some women could be childless as a result of infertility (9). Conversely, he views the term "childfree" as more positive, indicating "a kind of emancipation from something either by choice or by good fortune" (9). However, both terms are equally applicable to the situation of street beggars and domestic servants who decide to abandon their unwanted infants. Some beggars and servant girls may already have a child who is looked after by their parents or distant relatives; the abandonment of their newborn could be considered as their will to become childless, that is one child less, as in the case of the street beggar that I have discussed. In abandoning their newborn, they may want to become childfree—that is, they are free from caring for an unwanted child or for the child of the perpetrator who would serve as a constant reminder of an unwanted sexual relationship either survival sex or rape. They will remain free from the burden of care, which they would be unable to provide as a mother but which is expected from mothers by a particular society. Even if they do not have children, they may prefer to remain childfree temporarily, similar to other women who decide to delay childbearing (Mills et al.).

Choice to Have and Not to Have a Child

Prior to discussing the concept of choice to not have a child, I would like to discuss the concept of choosing to have a child, applying Julie Fennel's four-stage model of fertility behaviour. Fennel describes this typical pathway to child acquisition: 1) the person decides to have a child; 2) the person acquires a partner; 3) the person does not use contraceptives; and 4) the person gets pregnant and gives birth to a child (29). The first two stages of the model seem to be inapplicable to the situation of domestic servants and street beggars in Ethiopia. They were forced to become mothers with a partner whom they do not want to become the father of their child. In regard to stage three, the couple wants to have a child, so they do not use contraceptives. In the case of vulnerable women, they do not use contraceptives because they wish to have a child, but because they are unaware of them, are unable to access them, or are unable to negotiate their use. Stage four refers to the pregnancy of the person who wishes to have a child, which is not the case for unwanted sex and rape. Being incapable of saying "no" to unwanted sex and unplanned pregnancy, these women were forced into motherhood against their choice. The concept of "forced motherhood" is described as "coercion into motherhood" due to the societal normalization of sexual violence, the lack of services for pregnancy termination, and the lack of women's awareness of their reproductive rights (Colom 37). Forced motherhood indicates women's lack of choice in all aspects of the reproductive pathway: unwanted sex, unwanted pregnancy, unwanted motherhood, and unwanted children. Orna Donath notes the following: "Though most women become mothers, this shared outcome should not obscure the diverse meanings of the process. Central to this complexity is the construction and reconstruction of a mother's biography and her negotiation of the circumstances in which she became a mother" (203). Infant abandonment is the only option available for domestic servants and street beggars in Ethiopia if they want to exercise their choice to remain childfree.

Alien Abandonment

In "Child Free," an episode of *Insight*—the leading Australian forum for debates and sharing personal experiences—some women said that they prefer to remain childless because they view pregnancy as possession by an alien and do not want their body to be invaded by an alien. This metaphorical comparison has also appeared in classic feminist writings. Adrienne Rich was the first feminist author who compared a fetus with an alien: "Without doubt, in certain situations the child in one's body can only feel like a foreign body introduced from without: an alien" (64). Sheila Kitzinger has also compared women's experience of pregnancy with "possession" (78). In the case of pregnancy because of rape, women's feeling of possession could be heightened. Women who become pregnant because of rape may perceive their unborn baby as an offspring of their perpetrator, which becomes unwanted from conception. Some cases could be complicated—for example, when women domestic servants who have a regular partner have an unwanted sexual relationship with the household owner and do not know who the father of their child is.

Studies on women's experiences of war-time sexual violence indicate that many children born out of rape are rejected by their mothers and by society and may be subjected to neglect, abandonment, and even infanticide (Seto; Hamel). In a study conducted by Marie-Eve Hamel with Rwandan and Bosnian women victims of war-related rape, some women said that they saw their child as a "son/daughter of a killer" (298). In general, there are a few options available to women pregnant after rape, which are pregnancy termination, placing the child in an orphanage or giving the child up for adoption, and keeping the child in a family or in an extended family (Stevens). Lacking the elementary right for sex free from coercion, lacking access to contraceptives, lacking access to termination services, and lacking access to state-organized adoption services, female domestic workers and street beggars in Ethiopia are left with the only viable option being to give birth and to abandon the unwanted child. Although infant abandonment is an extreme method, there are even more extreme methods, such as killing the newborn child. Some women may resort to this option if they have an unwanted child when they become pregnant as a result of rape or have nothing to provide for their child (Tadele).

Infant Abandonment: Prioritizing Career over Parenting

Western women who decide to be childfree frequently mention that they prioritize their career over motherhood (Settle and Brumley). Although it is difficult to compare the situation of Ethiopian street beggars and servant girls with career-oriented Western women, there is a similarity in their choice to be childfree, which is employment prospects, as Getnet Tadele explains:

> In this case, one can understand that a mother who has nothing to eat on her own, and strives to survive by way of working as a maid, is highly prone to abandon her child, because nobody wants to hire her if she carries her small baby. Moreover, employers usually fire their maids when they get pregnant. This situation suggests that they cannot keep their children and they would be forced to abandon them. (302)

The difficulty being both a good mother and a good worker is another reason provided by childfree women to justify their choice (Kelly; Baker). Domestic servants and street beggars, having no means to survive, prioritize work over motherhood, which is frequently unwanted. Becoming a mother limits women's possibilities of employment. As Joanne Minaker explains, the traditional standards of good motherhood as "self-sacrificing" (128), "staying at home" (126) as well as being a "full-time mother" (127), are unattainable for these Ethiopian workers, not only because of their social status but also because of their unwillingness to sacrifice themselves and their career for the unwanted child. The street beggar, as discussed in the case study above, would have considered keeping the unwanted child if she had had a baby boy because she saw him as a future partner in her street business. She perceived the baby girl as useless and problematic in her street career.

Concluding Remarks

In this chapter, I have discussed the practice of infant abandonment by Ethiopian domestic servants and street beggars and presented this practice as a form of voluntary childlessness. As Braelin Settle and Krista Brumley have noted, most studies on voluntary childlessness are focused "on childfree women who are white, married, college educated, and upper-middle class, with little religious affiliation, and who hold nontraditional gender beliefs" and rarely on "women of color, unmarried women, or lower-income women" (4). In writing this chapter, I have aimed to contribute to the scarce literature on the experiences of domestic servants and street beggars, whose voices are rarely heard. Not justifying the practice, I believe that infant abandonment comprises maternal resistance against the paternalistic government apparatus to control women (see Minaker). By abandoning their unwanted infants, women protest against forced sex, enforced pregnancy, and enforced motherhood. They want to interrupt the unwanted process of mothering and remain childfree.

Works Cited

Alemayehu, Kidane. *My Journey with the United Nations and Quest for the Horn of Africa's Unity and Justice for Ethiopia.* RoseDog Books, 2017.

Assefa, Dawit, et al. *Harmful Traditional Practices for the Ethiopian Health Center Team. Training Module Developed in Collaboration with the Ethiopia Public Health Training Initiative, the Carter Center, the Ethiopia Ministry of Health, and the Ethiopia Ministry of Education.* Awassa College, 2005.

Baker, Maureen. "Motherhood, Employment and the 'Child Penalty.'" *Women's Studies International Forum*, vol. 33, no. 3, 2010, pp. 215-24.

Basten, Stuart. *Voluntary Childlessness and Being Childfree. The Future of Human Reproduction: Working Paper #5. June 2009.* Oxford & Vienna Institute of Demography, www.spi.ox.ac.uk/fileadmin/documents/ PDF/Childlessness_-_Number_5.pdf. Accessed 12 Dec. 2020.

Belete, Yohannes Mersha. "Challenges and Opportunities of Female Domestic Workers in Accessing Education: A Qualitative Study from Bahir Dar City Administration, Amhara Region, Ethiopia." *International Journal of Sociology and Anthropology*, vol. 6, no. 6, 2014, pp. 192-99.

Boswell, John. *The Kindness of Strangers: The Abandonment of Children in Western Europe from Late Antiquity to the Renaissance.* University of Chicago Press, 1988.

Colom, Alejandra. "Forced Motherhood in Guatemala: An Analysis of the Thousand Days Initiative." *Privatization and the New Medical Pluralism: Shifting Healthcare Landscapes in Maya Guatemala*, edited by Anita Chary nd Peter Rohloff, Lexington Books, 2015, pp. 35-49.

Donath, Orna. "Choosing Motherhood? Agency and Regret within Reproduction and Mothering Retrospective Accounts." *Women's Studies International Forum*, vol. 53, 2015, pp. 200-9.

Dorgan, Kelly A. "All Hail the Militant Mom : Love and War in the Foster-to-Adopt Home." *Mothering in the Third Wave*, edited by Amber Kinser, Demeter Press, 2008, pp. 140-51.

Edwards, Anne. "Women and Deviance." *The Other Half: Women in Australian Society*, edited by Jan Mercer, Penguin Books, 1980, pp. 291-312.

Edwards, Beverly, et al. "Findings of a Study Exploring Homeless Street Females in Addis Ababa, Ethiopia: A Need for Community Based Programs." *International Journal of Gender and Women's Studies*, vol. 3, no. 1, 2015, pp. 42-50.

Endale, Derseh. *The Ethiopian Famines, Entitlements and Governance. Woking Paper No102. August 1992.* World Institute for Development Economics Research of the United Nations University, 1992.

Erulkar, Annabel, and Abebaw Ferede. "Social Exclusion and Early or Unwanted Sexual Initiation among Poor Urban Females in Ethiopia." *International Perspectives on Sexual and Reproductive Health*, vol. 35, no. 4, 2009, pp. 186-93.

Fennell, Julie "'It Happened One Night': The Sexual Context of Fertility Decision-Making." *Population Association of America. 2006 Annual Meeting Program.* 2006.

Fuchs, Rachel G. *Abandoned Children: Foundlings and Child Welfare in Nineteenth-Century France.* State University of New York Press, 1984.

Gillespie, Rosemary. "When No Means No: Disbelief, Disregard and Deviance as Discourses of Voluntary Childlessness." *Women's Studies International Forum*, vol. 23, no. 2, 2000, pp. 223-34.

Graham, Melissa, and Stephanie Rich. "Representations of Childless Women in the Australian Print Media." *Feminist Media Studies*, vol. 14, no. 3, 2014, pp. 500-18.

Hamel, Marie-Eve. "Ethnic Belonging of the Children Born out of Rape in Postconflict Bosnia-Herzegovina and Rwanda." *Nations and Nationalism*, vol. 22, no. 2, 2016, pp. 287-304.

Inhorn, Marcia C. *Cosmopolitan Conceptions: Ivf Sojourns in Global Dubai.* Duke University Press, 2015.

Kelly, Maura. "Women's Voluntary Childlessness: A Radical Rejection of Motherhood?" *Women's Studies Quarterly,* vol. 37, no. 3-4, 2009, pp. 157-72.

Kifle, Abiy. *Ethiopia—Child Domestic Workers in Addis Ababa: A Rapid Assessment. July 2002.* International Labour Organization, International Programme on the Elimination of Child Labour (IPEC), 2002.

Kitzinger, Sheila. *Women as Mothers.* Random House, 1978.

Mercer, Jan. "The Sexist Society: An Introduction." *The Other Half: Women in Australian Society,* edited by Jan Mercer, Penguin Books, 1980, pp. 23-31.

Mills, Melinda, et al. "Why Do People Postpone Parenthood? Reasons and Social Policy Incentives." *Human Reproduction Update,* vol. 17, no. 6, 2011, pp. 848-60.

Minaker, Joanne. "The Space Between: Mothering in the Context of Contradiction." *Moms Gone Mad: Motherhood and Madness, Oppression and Resistance,* edited by Gina Wong, Demeter Press, 2012, pp. 124-40.

Misganaw, Alemayehu C., and Yalew A. Worku. "Assessment of Sexual Violence among Street Females in Bahir-Dar Town, North West Ethiopia: A Mixed Method Study." *BMC Public Health,* vol. 13, 2013, pp. 825-25.

Molla, Tebeje. "Higher Education Policy Reform in Ethiopia: The Representation of the Problem of Gender Inequality." *Higher Education Policy,* vol. 26, no. 2, 2013, pp. 193-215.

Nattrass, Nicoli. *The Moral Economy of Aids in South Africa.* Cambridge University Press, 2004.

Nnaemeka, Obioma. "Introduction: Imag(in)Ing Knowledge, Power, and Subversion in the Margin." *The Politics of (M)Othering: Womanhood, Identity and Resistance in African Literature,* edited by Obioma Nnaemeka, Routledge, 1997, pp. 1-25.

Nyamongo, Grace Bosibori. "Cultural Representation of Childlessness: Stories of Motherhood and Resistance." *Moms Gone Mad: Motherhood and Madness Oppression and Resistance*, edited by Gina Wong, Demeter Press, 2012, pp. 108-23.

Ombelet, Willem, et al. "Infertility and the Provision of Infertility Medical Services in Developing Countries." *Human Reproduction Update*, vol. 14, no. 6, 2008, pp. 605-21.

Pande, Amrita. "The 'Sweat and Blood' of Womb Mothers: Commercial Surrogates Redefining Motherhood in India." *South Asian Mothering*, edited by Jasjit Kaur Sangha, Demeter Press, 2013, pp. 135-49.

Panter-Brick, Catherine. "Nobody's Children? A Reconsideration of Child Abandonment." *Abandoned Children*, edited by Catherine Panter-Brick and Malcolm T. Smith, Cambridge University Press, 2000, pp. 1-26.

Parker, Ben, and Abraham Woldegiorgis. *Ethiopia: Breaking New Ground*. Oxfam, 2003.

Pruitt, Sandi L. "The Number of Illegally Abandoned and Legally Surrendered Newborns in the State of Texas, Estimated from News Stories, 1996-2006." *Child Maltreatment*, vol. 13, no. 1, 2008, pp. 89-93.

Quesada, James, Laurie Kain Hart, and Philippe Bourgois. "Structural Vulnerability and Health: Latino Migrant Laborers in the United States." *Medical Anthropology*, vol. 30, no. 4, 2011, pp. 339-62.

Ransel, David L. *Mothers of Misery: Child Abandonment in Russia*. Princeton University Press, 2014.

Rich, Adrienne. *Of Woman Born: Motherhood as Experience and Institution*. 10th anniversary ed. Norton, 1986.

Seto, D. "Children Born of Wartime Sexual Violence and the Limits of Existence." *Peacebuilding*, vol. 3, no. 2, 2015, pp. 171-85.

Settle, Braelin, and Krista Brumley. "'It's the Choices You Make That Get You There': Decision-Making Pathways of Childfree Women." *Michigan Family Review*, vol. 18, no. 1, 2014, pp. 1-22.

Shaw, Rachel Louise. "Women's Experiential Journey toward Voluntary Childlessness: An Interpretative Phenomenological Analysis." *Journal of Community & Applied Social Psychology*, vol. 21, no. 2, 2011, pp. 151-63.

Singh, Susheela, et al. "The Estimated Incidence of Induced Abortion in Ethiopia, 2008." *International Perspectives on Sexual and Reproductive Health*, vol. 36, no. 1, 2010, pp. 16-25.

Stevens, Margot E. H. "Rape-Related Pregnancies: The Need to Create Stronger Protections for the Victim-Mother and Child." *Hastings Law Journal*, vol. 65, no. 3, 2014, pp. 865-97.

Tadele, Getnet. "Child Abandonment: Five Dramatic Cases of Mothers in Addis Ababa." *Medische Antropologie*, vol. 12, no. 2, 2000, pp. 292-307.

Tadesse, E., et al. "Illegal Abortions in Addis Ababa, Ethiopia." *East African Medical Journal*, vol. 78, no. 1, 2001, pp. 25-29.

Team, Victoria. "'God Gives Us Sons, but the Government Takes Them Away': Ethiopian Wars and Motherwork." *"New Maternalisms": Tales of Motherwork (Dislodging the Unthinkable)*, edited by Roksana Badruddoja and Maki Motapanyane, Demeter Press, 2016, pp. 44-65.

Team, Victoria, and Eyob Kamil Hassen. "Climate Change and Complexity of Gender Issues in Ethiopia." *Systemic Crises of Global Climate Change: Intersections of Race, Class and Gender*, edited by Phoebe Godfrey and Denise Torres, Routledge, 2016, pp. 314-26.

Tessema, Gizachew Assefa, et al. "Trends and Causes of Maternal Mortality in Ethiopia during 1990–2013: Findings from the Global Burden of Diseases Study 2013." *BMC Public Health*, vol. 17, 2017, p. 160.

The University of Nottingham. *Child Abandonment and Its Prevention in Europe*. Nottingham, The University of Nottingham, 2012.

The World Bank. "Fertility Rate, Total (Births Per Woman)." *The World Bank*, data.worldbank.org/indicator/SP.DYN.TFRT.IN. Accessed 12 Dec. 2020.

van der Sijpt, Erica. "The Pain and Pride of 'Angel Mothers': Disappointments and Desires around Reproductive Loss in Romania." *Medical Anthropology*, vol. 37, no. 2, 2017, pp. 174-87.

Veevers, J. E. "Voluntary Childlessness." *Marriage & Family Review*, vol. 2, no. 2, 1979, pp 1-26.

Wada, Tsehai. "Abortion Law in Ethiopia: A Comparative Perspective." *Mizan Law Review*, vol. 2, no. 1, 2008, pp. 1-32.

Walker, Ellen L. *Complete without Kids: An Insider's Guide to Childfree Living by Choice or by Chance.* Greenleaf Book Group Press, 2011.

Wojcicki, Janet Maia. "'She Drank His Money': Survival Sex and the Problem of Violence in Taverns in Gauteng Province, South Africa." *Medical Anthropology Quarterly,* vol. 16, no. 3, 2002, pp. 267-93.

Section III

Analyzing Popular Culture, French Literature, and the Hebrew Bible on Otherhood

Chapter Seven

Queering Cristina Yang: Childfree Women, Disrupting Heteronormativity, and Success in Failed Femininity

Joselyn K. Leimbach

"Progress looks like a bunch of failures."
—Meredith Grey, *Grey's Anatomy*, Season 10, Ep.11

If motherhood is treated as the ultimate sign of successful femininity and the culmination of womanhood, how do we conceive of women who actively choose to forego this reproductive imperative? How are conceptions of womanhood tied to the reproductive imperative depicted in popular culture? What happens when normative boundaries are transgressed and a woman who is childfree by choice gains visibility in the public eye? Although women who remain childfree by choice have gained increasing visibility since the mid-to-late 2000s— spearheaded by a rise in widely read news-lifestyle hybrid blogs[1] as well as by increasing acknowledgement from celebrities addressing their decision to remain childfree[2]—compulsory motherhood remains the cultural norm for women. In fact, the very visibility of being childfree as an option for women and efforts to normalize and legitimize this choice point to its continued deviance from gendered and sexual expectations.

The ideologies and disciplines that enforce this compulsion are visible not only in the presumption of reproduction for married and middle-age women but in the limited cultural depictions of women who are proactively and vocally childfree by choice. In "Mediated Representations of Voluntary Childlessness, 1900–2012," Julia Moore and Patricia Geist-Martin address this lack of visibility: "The lack of fictional voluntarily childless characters [occurs in two ways]; those who can be identified in books, television, or film often end up having children or are never explicitly identified permanently and voluntarily childless, leaving their childbearing status open to interpretation" (234). Cultural representation remains invaluable for marginalized populations. Invisibility in the pop culture sphere, for example, delegitimizes performances of nonconformity, treating these individuals as unworthy of recognition while reinforcing structural oppressions and justifying the status quo. By avoiding explicit identification and creating space for multiple interpretations, media depictions permit dominant cultural readings that reinforce structures of inequality even as the portrayal alludes to the inclusion of marginalized populations. Referred to as "window service," cultural producers incorporate subtexts available to marginalized audiences, which goes unnoticed by audiences whose identities and experiences mirror normative standards (Frejes 199). This strategy caters to and privileges normative perspectives while enticing marginalized populations hungry for recognition.[3] This history of invisibility, obscured representation, and ongoing stigmatization makes centring the perspective of a woman explicitly childfree by choice in a mainstream television show a significant development in the visibility and legitimization of this performance of womanhood.

This explicit representation is found in the portrayal of Dr. Cristina Yang, a brilliant cardiothoracic surgeon on ABC's *Grey's Anatomy* (2005–ongoing). At the end of season seven, when discussing an unwanted pregnancy to her husband Dr. Owen Hunt, she states "I don't want one [a child]. I don't hate children. I respect children. I think they should have parents who want them" ("Unaccompanied Minor"). Yang's unambiguous proclamation on *Grey's Anatomy*—a show in its seventeenth season, specifically tailored to women audiences, and on one of the top three broadcast television networks in the United States (U.S.)—provides a previously unseen visibility for this experience and identity. Given the show's longevity, the complexity of the story arch involving Yang's desire to remain childfree addresses both the stigmatization of women who are childfree by choice and the legitimacy of this option. In so doing, *Grey's Anatomy* expands definitions of womanhood to incorporate alternative definitions of success that do not require procreation.

Grey's Anatomy incorporates a large constantly evolving cast that centres around the personal and professional lives of the doctors working at a hospital in Seattle, Washington. While Yang, a heterosexual Korean American woman, conforms to some of the most enduring stereotypes associated with her gender, race, and sexuality, there's something queer about her performance that challenges the viability of simplistic stereotypes by altering how the terms themselves are defined. My use of the term "queer" in this chapter emphasizes challenges to normative boundaries—in this case, the demands of womanhood, heterosexuality, and racialization—rather than delimiting its use to same-gender desires. To queer an ideology functions as a strategy of resistance by making a naturalized and normalized concept strange; it involves disrupting the normalization of behaviours or identities, challenging and undermining the hierarchies they are based on. The other side of the equation, employed here, is to look at those aspects that are conventionally or historically treated as nonnormative and redefine our relationship to what is normative. In this sense, I'm interested in exploring the ways in which the notion of motherhood has been intricately tied to definitions of womanhood and how a childfree by choice narrative can be integrated into the enduringly successful primetime soap opera *Grey's Anatomy*. Analyzing pop culture texts provides important insights into discursive constructions of nonnormative identities and behaviours in an institution (media) that simultaneously reflects and constructs cultural norms. Seeing a popular and well-known character choose to be childfree by choice not only legitimizes this experience for those who identify as such but also makes childfree by choice a visible option to those who may not have previously imagined being childfree as a possibility.

The use of queer in this context relies upon an altered relationship to normative assumptions associated with how we define and value particular identities and behaviours. For instance, in "Non-Motherhood," Gayle Letherby and Catherine Williams queer women's relationship to reproduction and explain the political implications of the distinction between childless and childfree:

For many people, "childless" implies a person with something missing from her life, whether she is described as being "childless" in a "voluntary" or "involuntary" manner, although the former women are more often viewed as selfish while the latter frequently incur pity. Either way, mothers are seen as "proper" women, while women without children are perceived as "improper" and treated as "other." They are also treated as childlike rather than fully adult. Feminist rhetoric has simplified women's experiences through its emphasis on women's "choice." Although women's recent and hard-won "right to choose" among reproductive technologies and abortion has posed a challenge to the patriarchal myth that motherhood is women's inevitable destiny, "choice" in this respect is impossible for women who discover they are unable to have children. On the other hand, the "childfree," as a description of women who are "voluntarily childless," implies a positive choice not to have children. Many people consider this a selfish option. The word "childfree" also has association with the word "carefree," which in turn implies a childlike state. Thus, women who have no children are considered to have no responsibilities and thus to be like children themselves. (723)

Childfree rhetorics reject the assumption that something is missing as implied in the use of the word "childless." In this instance, one experiences freedom from children rather than mourning their absence. Rejecting this language disrupts the presence of children as the norm for women and works towards challenging the stigmatization of this identity. The rhetoric of "free by choice" emphasizes individual agency and queers cultural demands that dictate and presume desire for children. Although this linguistic turn is a significant strategy to redefine the status of women who do not conform to the mandates of compulsory reproduction, as Letherby and Williams note, the cultural implications of this choice are not so quickly or easily diminished.

Mirroring dominant perceptions of voluntarily childfree women, Yang's choice is interpreted by others, specifically her husband, as personally selfish and/or professionally too driven, a temporary phase to be outgrown, which suggests the previously discussed immaturity or indicates a deeper psychological trauma associating childfree women with a pathological problem. Each presumed motivation reinforces the deviancy of the desire to be childfree. The implications of these rhetorics suggest that her life lacks significance and depth because of her childlessness. The show's overall depiction of Yang's desire to remain childfree balances between conveying the validity of her decision and positioning her in relation to parallel narratives of characters who are involuntarily childless, which intermittently challenges and reinforces hegemonic failures of women who do not conform.

Over the course of her ten seasons (2005-2014), Yang had both a miscarriage and an abortion. Her proven fertility positions her in a privileged position associated with a nondisabled body, as compared to other characters who desire children yet have issues with infertility or are unable to reproduce on their own. Yang's early season-three narrative, in which she miscarries prior to a planned abortion, is sandwiched by the plot lines of those whose investment in reproduction is thwarted by infertility (e.g., colleague Dr. Addison Shepard) and other complications, which, for example, impede an adoption by Joe, the owner of the show's main bar, and his boyfriend. In these comparative narratives, Yang's desire to prioritize her career over motherhood, a decision that later proves inconsequential due to a miscarriage, depicts her as selfish in the face of others whose financial and emotional investment in having children remains unfulfilled. These competing narratives, intentional or not, reinforce hegemonic constructions of women and the reproductive imperative. In fact, while Yang's miscarriage is not directly related to her career, it becomes most apparent while she is in the operating arena, drawing a correlation that posits her career as the cause of her miscarriage. Yang's reproductive fertility and her choice to reproduce should not, however, be confused with a simplistic understanding of privilege as pure advantage, since this status effectively limits her appropriate options as a woman in a culture of compulsory reproduction. Although Yang is privileged to have the option to choose to be childfree, this agential performance marginalizes women who actively and consciously remain childfree in a culture of compulsory of procreation.

This chapter explores Cristina Yang's failure to conform to gendered expectations through her active pursuit of a childfree life. According to neoliberal demands, a departure from and disloyalty to societal norms constitutes failure. While her decision making relies on neoliberal ideals of individualized success based on a meritocratic system, her choices distinguish her from gendered definitions of success that, for women, require reproductivity. Yang's adherence and loyalty to one set of hegemonic demands for a successful career as a surgeon result in her inability to conform to alternative and conflicting demands required to achieve success as a middle-class, middle-aged, and able-bodied heterosexual woman. In *The Queer Art of Failure*, Jack Halberstam asserts "where feminine success is always measured by male standards, and gender failure often means being relieved of the pressure to measure up to patriarchal ideals, not succeeding at womanhood can offer unexpected pleasures" (4). Under these conflicting demands Yang performs a failed womanhood, as she is unwilling to achieve the requirements of this status and identity. Yet Yang's desires and decisions cannot be interpreted through frames of appropriate white heterosexual womanhood signifying her failure to meet normative standards. Yang's failed womanhood is further evidenced by her inappropriate emotional responses that contextualize her explicit choice to remain childfree at the expense of her marriage. Yang's alternative performance of womanhood queers singular definitions of success for women by revealing and disrupting naturalized standards obscured within normative gender constructions. If only those who conform to normative demands of womanhood can achieve success through reproduction, then we limit who has the capacity to achieve a desirable outcome and be a successful woman. When we reject the treatment of nonconforming behaviours, goals, and desires (i.e., childfree women) as failed, we legitimize alternative performances of successful womanhood.

At its start, *Grey's Anatomy* constructed a post-oppression world, seldom affected by systemic power imbalances based on gender, race, class, sexuality, or ability. While this neoliberal bent shifted in 2015 to highlight systemic critique by incorporating concerns associated with US activist movements (Black Lives Matter, #MeToo, etc.), as well as highlighting systemic inequity exacerbated by the coronavirus in 2020, central female characters perform a narrative of personal success or failure through dating, marriage, divorce, and motherhood.[4] Yang disrupts this narrative by explicitly, actively, and permanently choosing to remain childfree. Her decision—conventionally portrayed as antithetical to heteronormative mandates for a woman's happily ever after—highlights alternative definitions of success that challenge an otherwise single trajectory.

The postfeminist ideologies of the early seasons highlight the simultaneous failure and success of feminism, suggests that feminist diligence is no longer required and depend upon the show's cloaking of structural oppressions by including highly visible examples of minority success. During Yang's tenure, *Grey's Anatomy* minimized recurring microaggressions and institutional obstacles, and the presence of racialized characters occluded prevailing oppressions and upheld systemic claims to a post-oppression culture. This method of inclusion is critiqued in Patricia Hill Collins' *Black Sexual Politics* to justify claims to a post-oppression society: "A meritocracy requires evidence that racial discrimination has been eliminated. The total absence of Black people [or any person of colour] would signal the failure of color blindness. At the same time that Blackness must be visible, it also must be contained and/or denuded of all meaning that threatens elites" (178). The inclusion of a few characters with marginalized identities—particularly those central to the show's narrative who meet white, heteronormative, and middle-class respectability politics—reinforces that identity no longer plays a significant role in achieving or impeding success. This inclusion upholds claims that the system is already equitable and that there is no need for further critique.

Although the first episode ("A Hard Day's Night" 27 Mar. 2005) points to the disproportionate lack of women in the in-coming class of surgical interns, when issues of discrimination do exist, they are performed by a single individual. Early in the series, fellow intern Alex Karev personifies misogyny, even as he is later redeemed as a kind and supportive friend. Racist microaggressions are also portrayed when Izzie Stevens, another intern in Yang's cohort, presumes Yang's ability to speak Chinese, although Yang is of Korean descent. The significance of acknowledg-ing these microaggressions cannot be understated in an era when the mention of enduring systemic racial, gendered, sexual, and classed inequalities is simultaneously highlighted and obscured in the U.S. This emphasis on an individual as the source of inequality masks structural barriers that limit access to science, technology, engineering, and mathematics (STEM) programs through gendered socializations that undermine women's involvement in these fields and unequal socioeconomic structures that disproportionately limit people of colour and working-class populations' access to resources required for admittance to high-caliber institutions and higher education. Positioning gender, race, and class as a relative nonissue to entry reinforces the show's assertion of a just and equitable world.

Although there are several episodes dedicated to the difficulties of the various female surgeons (and only the female surgeons) to balancing work and motherhood, these concerns are generally resolved relatively quickly. Instead, the show's depiction of motherhood most often revolves around the difficulties they face in becoming mothers (e.g., Dr. Addison Montgomery, Dr. Meredith Grey, and Dr. April Kepner). This recurring theme positions women who have successfully pursued intensive, historically male-dominated careers as being involuntarily childless through their own carelessness, rather than normalizing alternative bodily configurations or forms of motherhood, reinforcing the normativity and desirability of an idealized, able body and hides the difficulties of balancing a career and children.

Most female characters delay pregnancy and motherhood during their internships, a time constructed in the show as an extended adolescence. The only central character whose narrative deviates from this timeline by including pregnancy is Cristina Yang. Unlike most of the female protagonists who become pregnant, Yang chooses to forgo motherhood. Perhaps because of the seeming void cause by Yang's choice to remain childfree, her narrative, at times, revolves around this decision in the same way that other women's plot lines emphasize their desire for, or journey towards, motherhood. Although the show normalizes motherhood as the pinnacle of female success, Yang's decision to remain childfree and her choices to pursue this decision, including having an abortion, make visible an underrepresented population affected by contemporary encroachments on reproductive rights by pronatalist discourses and policies. Although the show acknowledges the potential consequences for women who choose to be childfree, the most significant repercussions again centre upon the acts of a single individual and obscure systemic marginalization and delegitimization of women who are childfree by choice.

Although systemic oppressions are obscured, evolving gendered expectations that simultaneously uphold gendered hierarchies are central to Yang's depiction. The relationship dynamics between Yang and her husband balance contemporary contradictions between claims for women's increasing equity in the workplace and the continuing demands for women to remain grounded in the domestic sphere. This contradiction becomes particularly apparent considering shifting definitions of idealized masculinity that balance rugged individualism and emotional intelligence. In essence, men are now encouraged to incorporate nurturing and emotionality, which are traditionally associated with femininity, to perform a new, evolved masculinity in their idealized gender performance, while women remain confined by older conventions of femininity and constructions of womanhood that often requires professional sacrifice in the pursuit of personal fulfillment.

Not only does compulsory motherhood presume reproductivity as the only path to feminine maturity, it also incentivizes motherhood and disciplines women who choose to be childfree. Dorothy E. Roberts asserts as follows: "Women experience tremendous pressure, both systemic and ideological, to become mothers. Motherhood is virtually compulsory for women: no woman achieves her full position in society until she becomes a mother" (34). The presumption of motherhood affects women's relationship to education, career, law, medicine, marriage, family, etc. The primacy of reproduction impacts cultural perceptions of individual success as well as the validity and maturity of adulthood. Achieving motherhood grants increased social status, even as individual identity must shift to accommodate the demands of this position.

This singular heteronormative narrative is critiqued by Sarah Ahmed in *The Promise of Happiness*, who asserts that social constructions of happiness rely upon individual choices that espouse not personal preference but the limits of what we should be inclined toward (199). Inclination suggests that whereas free citizens may be offered several options, successful and appropriate choices are limited by propriety and acceptability defined by identity politics. Under this frame, happiness is based on an individual's proximity to the social ideal (53). Success and happiness are, thus, framed only in relation to a communal definition, wherein only the assessment by others legitimizes the decisions made. Conforming to the most acceptable choices reinforces the propriety of the choice made. Only poor choices result in negative consequences and so are conceptualized as the result of individual action rather than structures of power that discipline nonconformity.

In effect, certain choices limit access to success. For women, the pursuit of success in one area (career) often undermines the possibility of success in another (family). Depending on the cultural demands, prioritization of a goal that interferes with the performance of normative expectations results in ultimate failure. Yang can choose to commit her life to her career, becoming a successful surgeon and achieve greatness in the professional realm, but always at the expense of normative interpretations that perceive her performance of womanhood as failed. She is interpreted as too dedicated, unwilling to compromise, and focused on her career to achieve feminized success in the private sphere.

The threat of refusing conformity is compounded for racialized subjects, who are interpreted through normative white understandings of affective experience. In "Feeling Brown, Feeling Down," Jose Esteban Muñoz asserts "minoritarian affect is always, no matter what its register, partially illegible in relation to the normative affect performed by normative [read white] citizen subjects" (679). Racialized individuals' affective experiences and performances are silenced and untranslatable through epistemic violences that position the most privileged as the norm. Although Muñoz focuses specifically on the experience of Chicano populations, his emphasis on the impact of otherness recognizes a broader range of racially marginalized individuals whose experiences do not directly translate or correlate to normative whiteness.

The affective experiences and motivations of populations of colour are only ever understood using a frame of reference that relies upon an invisible and privileged whiteness. This results in the invisibility of racially marginalized individuals' experiences. This lack of recognition is compounded by the inability to recognize an alternative affective perspective. A singular interpretation of affect does not allow racially marginalized individuals to be heard or understood. Representation is reliant upon a dehumanized representation of otherness, not a lived experience, to define normative boundaries. This limitation is particularly detrimental to how women of colour are understood in relation to emotion, since conventional white heteronormative cisfemininity requires emotional intelligence as a foundation for appropriate per-formances of womanhood.

Throughout the series, Yang is depicted as exceptionally skilled in the operating room but unwilling or unable to express emotion according to normative standards of white cisfemininity. Early in the series, Yang's affect is treated as a significant barrier to becoming a truly great surgeon. Her lack of nurturing interferes with an emotional connection to patients. Yang's seeming disconnect from emotion cannot account for the ineffable characteristics associated with patient care. This becomes particularly evident when she is compared to and eventually mentored by the well-rounded and "emotionally mature" Dr. Preston Burke—the Black heteronormative head of cardiothoracic surgery—encompasses both body and spirit in his medical practices and becomes Yang's mentor and lover. It is only through Burke's guidance in appropriately performing a balance of gendered characteristics, the constructed masculinity of technical skill and the constructed femininity of emotional support and spiritual connection, that Yang finds the balance necessary to achieve professional success.

Yang's narrative development is compared in early seasons with fellow intern Dr. Izzie Stevens, a white former model who performs feminine nurturing. Stevens is often critiqued for her undue emotionality, culminating in a series of poor decisions that directly resulted in the death of her fiancé. The comparison between the two characters provides two extremes in which notions of femininity are placed in tension and competition with each other while functioning in a masculinized professional arena. Stevens's display of emotions, paired with both her earlier career as a model and having given up a child for adoption, positions her as the personification of conventional femininity. Stevens's emotional investment is often interpreted as caregiving that helps in her interactions with patients and improves her performance, but it also hinders her ability to successfully perform the masculinized logic and technique of medicine that distinguishes the profession from the emotion and nurturing of feminized nursing. Although Stevens's emotions are both a help and hindrance, Yang is characterized as her opposite. Yang conveys emotions in private interactions between a few trusted individuals, yet her professional countenance is often characterized as robotic and emotionless. In so doing, Yang overly conforms to the masculinized expectations associated with her role as surgeon. Yet just as Stevens's emotions both help and hurt her career, Yang also experiences negative repercussions for the perceived emotionlessness of her interactions. Associations with a robot construct Yang as a perfectionist who performs beyond human imperfections through her focus and attention to detail that obscures the big picture, including the humanity of her patients. Significantly, robots are limited to the commands of their programming, therefore robots do not challenge the demands placed upon them. Symbolically, representing Yang as a robot positions her as simultaneously super- and subhuman. If Yang's robotic performance is relegated to her career, then she cannot meet the nurturing requirements of white, middle-class, and heterosexual femininity required for a successful performance of womanhood.

Yang's career also parallels Alex Karev another member of the first intern cohort. Karev, a white, working-class, and seemingly mediocre student, conveys a surface apathy that ultimately conceals his underlying investment in the success of his career and positive outcomes for his patients. Karev's seeming lack of emotion is depicted as a defense mechanism that shields his insecurities, whereas Yang's emotionlessness denotes an excess of care but for an inappropriate object. Yang's emphasis on surgery and skill development is conveyed as selfish as opposed to the selflessness that prioritizes care for patients. This emphasis on the self parallels the neoliberal emphasis on individual success and achievement. However, since the imagined neoliberal citizen is inevitably a white cisgender able-bodied man, when performed by Yang's inappropriately gendered and racialized subject, the requirements for masculine professional success shift resulting in her feminized failure.

Yang's decision to remain childfree allows her to succeed as a driven and ambitious surgeon but is positioned as a failed married and mature woman, a status defined by the biological imperative to reproduce. The concomitant success and failure of Yang mirrors the demands of neoliberal choice unrestrained by identity and attendant systemic oppressions. Given her token status as the only significant recurring character of Asian descent during her tenure, Yang could have been portrayed as the personification of the model minority. Yang is conveyed as a driven, ambitious perfectionist who achieves whatever she sets her sights on. In fact, the show seems to suggest this possibility in the discussion of her academic success, a PhD in biochemistry from Berkeley and an MD from Stanford, where she graduated first in her class. This emphasis on Yang's intelligence and aptitude could have undermined recognizing the dedication she puts into her work and reinforced depictions of individuals of Asian descent as inclined towards mental labours over physical, perpetuating the mind-body divide. Although Yang does prioritize her career, her personal relationship—especially with Meredith Grey, who becomes her emergency contact and "her person" for emotional support—rejects simplistic binaries and challenges naturalized feminine competition. Ultimately her choice to remain childfree contributes to her ability to facilitate Meredith Grey's maternal success and provides alternative performances of family that are not determined by biological or legal legitimization.

Yang's Asian American race and upper-middle class status legitimize her reproductive decisions and are significant contributors to interpreting her childfree choice. Historically, questions related to which bodies should reproduce have centred around white, middle-class women. Although Yang does not conform to privileged whiteness, her accelerated class and education position her in the realm of idealized mother. Yang's refusal to engage in the losing game that requires professional women to be superwoman who can balance career and family is interpreted via two competing discourses. The first, perpetuated by her husband, requires reproduction for women. The second rejects the requirement for both, which is embraced by Yang.

Given white, heteronormative standards, Yang is consistently depicted in a manner that will not allow her to meet dominant require-ments for success. When we conceive of alternative performances of gender, sexuality, and race as failure, we, as a culture, lack the imagination to challenge normative limits. Queering the concept of failure emphasizes the existence of alternative goals and paths to success that are no more or less valuable than the route that has been historically required; in so doing, we disrupt understandings of failure and the negative values associated with nonnormative performances. Interpreting Yang's motives, desires, and goals through normative ideologies limits recognizing her successes and confines her affective performances to normative frames. These confines are reproduced in outside translations of her decision to remain childfree. For the rest of this chapter, I will focus on Yang's relationship with Owen Hunt to explore the dynamics of active and agential choices to be childfree in the form of abortion. Neoliberal ideologies of post-oppression are reinforced in *Grey's Anatomy*'s engagement with the politics of childfree by choice wherein social constructions endemic to cultural demands are obscured in favour of a problematic individual—in this case Yang's on-again, off-again significant other, Dr. Major Owen Hunt.

Yang's nonnormative affect is contrasted by a sexual relationship with a successfully masculine figure. Hunt is characterized by an excess of masculinized patriotism in the form of military service. The result of his battlefield experiences requires him to incorporate conventionally feminized characteristics, including perceived emotional intelligence and therapy due to PTSD. Part of his balancing of masculine and feminine characteristics includes a heightened valuing of the heteronormative nuclear family and prioritizing of children. Although Yang's emotional incapacitation often takes the form of withdrawal, Hunt's emotionality is framed through highly masculinized violence. Yang's rejection of motherhood is also countered by Hunt's desire/ requirement for reproduction. Her refusal to conform to static definitions of womanhood is deemed a failed performance according to these normative standards, while the shifting manhood/masculinity of her romantic partner is positioned as the twenty-first century man. In this depiction, men and hegemonic masculinity associated with male bodies are permitted the freedom and privilege to evolve and progress to encompass aspects of femininity that are not treated as weakness or a lack but rather as acknowledging and dismantling the limitations of hegemonic masculinity, further strengthening and valuing this position. In contrast, Yang's attempt to incorporate characteristics associated with masculinity in her professional and personal life are, as previously discussed, portrayed as excessive and inappropriate.

Yang's decision to remain childfree is made explicit when she becomes unintentionally pregnant while married to Hunt. In a conversation following the initial revelation Hunt attempts to convince her to carry the pregnancy to term.

Hunt: I could take time off. ... stop saying no. I'm telling you I want this I can do this. This does not have to be your problem. It'll be my problem. You wouldn't even...

Yang: What? Notice? It'll be a baby. I'm not a monster. If I have a baby, I'll love it.

Hunt: That's the problem, that you'll love it. That's a problem we can work with.

Yang: Are you even listening me?

Hunt: Yes. I'm just trying to figure out some kind of compromise.

Yang: Okay, but you know what? There is no compromise. You don't have half a baby. I don't want one. It isn't about work. It isn't a scheduling conflict. I don't want to be a mother.

Hunt: Do you love me ... Do you trust me? ... You'd be a great mother.

I know you don't believe me, but it is true. ("Unaccompanied Minor")

Hunt rhetorically positions a child as a problem to be solved. In fact, it is not the pregnancy that is the problem but Yang's relationship to and emotional engagement with the pregnancy that is problematic according to his perspective. When Yang acknowledges her potential emotional investment in a baby, she becomes the problem to be solved. Hunt's argument cannot recognize how Yang would be exponentially affected by the physical demands of pregnancy, in addition to cultural expectations for childcare and the stigma of the bad mother should she agree to let him raise the child on his own. Regardless of the potential repercussions should Yang carry the pregnancy to term, it's hard not to look past Hunt's request that Yang function as a walking womb; in this instance, she is valued only for her reproductive capacity and is stripped of her humanity. This point was addressed in an earlier conversation in the same episode when Hunt claims: "I don't love the incubating potential of your womb. I love you." Although this may be his intent, by positioning Yang as superfluous to the child-raising experience and by taking the responsibilities upon himself, he is, in fact, prioritizing her biological reproductive capacity over her desire to be childfree and to make decisions free of coercion.

Even though Yang denies that work affects her decision, her position as a resident in relation to Hunt's status as an attending and effectively her boss, cannot be ignored. The power imbalance places her in a more vulnerable location regarding her career trajectory. This concern, often ignored in *Grey's Anatomy*'s world, comes to fruition when she is passed over for a promotion when Hunt is tasked with choosing chief resident and is denied consideration to avoid appearances of favouritism. Prioritizing Hunt's professional desires and logic is mimicked in this scene when he asks her to prioritize his judgment over her own, even as he ignores her desires. In his final statement, Hunt equates her love for him as conditional based on carrying the pregnancy to term. His belief that she will be a good mother counters not her fear of being a bad mother but her lack of desire for a child. Using this logic to justify her continued pregnancy implies that it is this lack of desire that already positions her as a bad mother according to Hunt. His inability to comprehend Yang's perspective in the face of his own desires remains a recurring theme over the course of the following season.

Yang's emphasis on her own desires and judgment over and above

Hunt's is depicted as undermining the foundation of their relationship. In fact, her decision to be childfree counters cultural mandates to such an extent as to be unimaginable in Hunt's mind. After Yang has an abortion, the couple attempt marriage counselling to deal with the aftereffects of the abortion on their marriage. Taking place in the context of therapy, the following scene shows Hunt's demand for an understandable, or what he deems legitimate, motivation for Yang's desire to be childfree.

Yang: There is no deeper reason.

Hunt: There has to be.

Yang: There is no deeper reason. I wasn't abused. I don't have a dark secret. I wasn't mugged by a baby. I don't want kids.

Hunt: Nobody doesn't want kids.

Yang: People can not want kids. It's a thing.

Hunt: That is not a thing.

Yang: Well, it's my thing.

Hunt: You're going to change your mind. You're going to change your mind in three years or five. You're going to change your mind about having a baby, and then it's going to be too late. And you're going to regret it.

Yang: I will know and understand that I made a choice. It is my choice.... I choose medicine. I choose me. I choose that over the remote possibility that I might one day want a child. And by the way, it's okay to never want kids. Some people don't ever want kids. ("Have You Seen Me?")

Mirroring the dominant perceptions of voluntarily childfree women, Yang's choice is interpreted by Hunt as caused by a deeper psychological trauma, presenting it a pathological problem that reinforces the nonnormativity of the desire.

Her marginalization is bolstered by his inability to recognize remaining actively and permanently childfree as a legitimate choice. By claiming "it's not a thing" and "nobody doesn't want kids," Hunt positions Yang's desires as inconceivable. This choice is further positioned as a phase that will pass. As if, in three to five years, she will develop into a mature woman who finally knows what he has known all along. That she wants children. That her desires conform to normative standards about what fulfilling heteronormative adult womanhood looks like. That the goals and desires she currently has—to prioritize herself, to become the best doctor she can be, and to do what she loves for a living—are immature, shallow, and unfulfilling. That he knows better than she does what is in her best interest and what her true desires are. And in those three to five years, when she will have aged from her early thirties to her late thirties, all of her reproductive potential would have been lost. The assumptions put forth in this scene reveal that this man, depicted as in touch with his emotions and who values family above his own career, assumes not only that he is entitled to his desires but that he can also refuse to respect those who do not share his wants or needs. His privilege is conveyed in his utter certainty of his correctness. That in the face of her irrationality, he will triumph.[5] This delineation that positions her desires as immature relies upon a definition of maturity associated with the primacy of male whiteness that mirrors the dominant discourse by positioning racialized individuals, and women in particular, in a perpetual state of arrested adolescence.

The rhetorics that bolster and uphold compulsory motherhood seen in the depiction of Cristina Yang are powerful and seek to dehumanize and punish those who will not comply. Ultimately, compulsory motherhood positions reproduction as the pinnacle of women's experiences. Hunt makes this clear when he proclaims: "I believe your life can be bigger than you think it is. I know you can contain more than you think you can…. Cristina Yang, I imagine such a huge life for us" ("Unaccompanied Minor"). In the context of discussing his desire for a family and discussing the possibility of Yang continuing an unwanted pregnancy, Hunt situates all other possible accomplishments as paling in comparison to having a child. In this assertion, reproductive lives are intrinsically worth more than nonreproductive ones, in part because they expand beyond the individual and create a bridge to the future. Using biological reproduction as the only measure of value, Yang's life lacks significance and depth regardless of her future accomplishments.

Yet Yang performs an agential childfree womanhood that rejects definitions that limit successful womanhood to motherhood. In fact, we can see how alternative definitions of fulfillment and success for women can exist on a grand scale when Yang reimagines her future and longevity in relation to a lifesaving technique she develops. Speaking to her intern in charge of overseeing patients, she says, "This trial is my baby.... Don't let my baby die" ("You Be Illin'"). In this narrative, Yang's contribution to the world is reimagined not as biological reproduction but as intellectual and medical advancement. Her focus on her career creates the opportunity to impact not just her biological descendants but to create a lineage of survivors whose lives were improved and prolonged because of her labour.

According to Ahmed, "Queer and feminist histories are the histories of those who are willing to risk the consequences of deviation" (91). *Grey's Anatomy*'s depiction of Cristina Yang as a woman who is explicitly, actively, and agentially childfree by choice conveys competing ideologies representative of the diversity of discourses present in contemporary culture. One frame represents marriage and reproduction as the ultimate goal for women. Perhaps unsurprisingly, this rhetoric is depicted through a white, heteronormative, and cismale character. Representative of a dominant discourse that privileges these identities, womanhood is valued and defined by the characteristics inaccessible to this population— reproduction. The consequences of Yang's refusal are seen in her divorce from Hunt. Although the two are depicted as being romantically and sexually attracted to each other, neither's willingness to meet the reproductive demands of the other proves fatal for their marriage. This interpretive failure of womanhood must, according to the intersecting heteronormative structures of power, result in a failed heterosexuality. This definition and hierarchy of value prove problematic when rejecting alternative options and choices as legitimate and valuable. When a single narrative is depicted as the only path to a successful life, any variation must be seen as failure. Yet if we reconceive of our relationship with normative demands and recognize opportunities to explore different paths, then we queer relationships to failure and cultivate a multitude of successes.

According to Christian Agrillo and Cristian Nelini, "The spontaneous decision not to have children can be found only in Western society whereas monogamist couples in non-industrialised societies are expected to have children" (355). This observation conveys women in Western cultures as accessing a greater degree of choice but does not account for the ways in which the performance of this contingent privilege can and often does result in stigmatization and marginalization. Yang's privilege and ability to choose to remain childfree, regardless of the consequences of this decision, is highlighted by her access to resources that epitomize rhetorics of free choice, which are often inaccessible to populations marginalized by socioeconomic status or access to birth control technologies. Ultimately, these privileges and access do not protect against the repercussions of challenging normative demands, but they can mitigate the consequences.

In most senses of the hegemonic definition of woman, Cristina Yang fails to conform to societal demands—be it her prioritization of women friends over male romantic partners, her inappropriate emotionality, or refusal to reproduce. *Grey's Anatomy* provides a unique portrayal and an alternative definition/vision of and for women in the twenty-first century. Women need not appropriately perform emotionality or have children in order to be successful as a woman. Yang's racialized and gendered emotional enactment highlights the existence of femininities impacted by race, class, education, etc. This is further enhanced by the conspicuous portrayal of Yang as childfree that counters most represent-ations of women in dominant media. Even within the show's diegetic, Yang remains an exception to the rule of compulsory reproduction.

Perhaps this requirement to interpret alternative performances of womanhood as failed is a cultural requirement to reinforce the naturalized association of womanhood with the female body. Monique Wittig in "One is Not Born a Woman" critiques the use of biology to naturalize and affirm gender roles, as "it holds on to the idea that the capacity to give birth (biology) is what defines a woman" (Wittig 10). This definition not only justifies hierarchies of gender but delimits who can be included under this banner. The compulsion that exists simultaneously with the conflation of womanhood and motherhood invalidates alternative performances of womanhood. By maintaining boundaries that effectively limit who can and should be understood as a successful woman, naturalized hierarchies of white, cisgendered reproductive heteronormativity are maintained and reinforced. However, Yang's rejection of biological essentialism cultivates alternative definitions of womanhood divorced from the presumed capabilities of the female body and opens space for a multitude of experiences that can and must be incorporated into definitions of womanhood.

Yang bounces between and balances a multitude of normative

expectations. Yet even as she excels at meeting the expectations associated with a single norm—her chosen career path—the terms of a successful performance, as interpreted by others, shift. The intersections of Yang's childfree by choice ciswomanhood, Korean American ethnicity, heterosexuality, ability, profession, etc. cannot be adequately understood or valued using hegemonic ideologies. The strength of *Grey's Anatomy* lies in its ability and willingness to convey a multitude of perspectives, often in conflict with one another. This creates space to cultivate alternative systems of value that undermine seemingly static ideological mandates, disruptions that reverberate beyond the singular example explored here.

Appendix

Character	Played by	Seasons	Significance
Burke, Preston	Isaiah Washington	2005 – 2007	Cardiothoracic surgeon, Yang's mentor and fiancé, leaves Yang at the altar
Grey, Meredith	Ellen Pompeo	2005 – ongoing	General surgeon, Member of the first intern cohort, Yang's primary emotional support, experiences infertility, adoption, and motherhood
Hunt, Owen	Kevin McKidd	2008 – ongoing	Trauma surgeon, former military, married to and divorced from Yang, desires children
Karev, Alex	Justin Chambers	2005 – 2020	Pediatric surgeon, member of the first intern cohort, known for his abrasive personality
Kepner, April	Sarah Drew	2009 – 2018	Trauma surgeon, experiences death of first child due to osteogenesis imperfect
Shepard, Addison	Kate Walsh	2005 – 2012	Neonatal surgeon, experiences infertility

Stevens, Izzie	Kathrine Heigl	2005 – 2012	Surgical resident, former model, member of the first intern cohort, chose adoption as a teenager
Yang, Cristina	Sandra Oh	2005 – 2012	Cardiothoracic surgeon, member of the first intern cohort, had a miscarriage during relationship with Burke, married to and divorced from Hunt, childfree by choice
Joe	Stephen W. Bailey	2005 – 2010	Owner of Emerald City Bar, where the doctors drink after work, experiences complications trying to adopt children with his boyfriend, Walter

Endnotes

1. *Huffington Post* is perhaps the most visible online source of articles on childfree by choice and has an extensive catalog of pieces centering childfree perspectives. In the five months between May 2016 and September 2016, childfree-explicit articles included "How Childfree Seniors Can Take the Future into Their Own Hands" (9/20/16); "'First Day of School Pic' Alternatives for the Childfree" (9/14/16); "5 Things Childfree People Want You to Know"(8/17/16); and "The Real Problem with being Childfree and Unmarried in Your Mid-Thirties" (5/26/16), which highlights the continued stigmatization of those who are childfree.

2. Chelsea Handler announced "No Kids for Me, Thanks" in the *New York Times* (4/3/15), along with numerous other celebrities, who have been vocal about their childfree by choice status. *Refinery 29,* a woman-centred lifestyle website, recently ran "15 Celebrities Who Never Had Kids and That's Okay" (7/22/16). However, the article does not distinguish between how gender affects this decision for men and women or for those who are childfree by choice relative to those who are involuntarily childless, blurring the active decision to

remain childfree with those whose narratives frame their childlessness from a variety of alternative perspectives.

3. Fred Frejes's work focuses on tailoring advertising to LGBTQ+ communities. Although sexually marginalized populations' histories of oppression are distinct from women who are childfree by choice, similar strategies have been used by dominant popular culture producers to allude to communities with stigmatized identities, even as they avoid potential backlash from explicit support.

4. Given the group dynamic, narrative character, and longevity of *Grey's Anatomy*, definitions of centrality are subjective. For the purpose of this chapter, definitions of centrality involve individualized storylines in which they are the core figure rather than supporting the narrative of an already established character's plotline and remain significant for multiple seasons. Other factors also influence motherhood narratives, including the character's age and, perhaps most significantly, her status within the hospital hierarchy.

5. Significantly, for a doctor, Hunt ignores the availability of assistive reproductive technologies and the possibility of adoption should Yang change her mind.

Works Cited

Agrillo, Christian, and Cristian Nelini. "Childfree by Choice: A Review." *Journal of Cultural Geography*, vol. 25, no. 3, 2008, pp. 347-63.

Ahmed, Sara. *The Promise of Happiness*. Duke University Press, 2010.

Almendrala, Ana. "5 Things 'Childfree' People Want You to Know." *Huffington Post*, 17 Aug. 2016, www.huffingtonpost.com/entry/first-day-of-school-pic-alternatives-for-the-child_us_57d85291e4b0a5cd12d74187. Accessed 13 Dec. 2020.

Collins, Patricia Hill. *Black Sexual Politics*. Routledge, 2005.

Dixon, Laura. "How Childfree Seniors Can Take The Future into Their Own Hands." *Huffington Post*, 20 Sept. 2016, www.huffingtonpost.com/laura-dixon/childfree-seniors_b_11981716.html. Accessed 13 Dec. 2020.

Donnelly, Erin. "15 Celebrities Who Never Had Kids and That's Okay." *Refinery 29*, 22 July 2016, www.refinery29.com/2016/07/117410/childfree-celebrities-without-kids#slide. Accessed 13 Dec. 2020.

Frejes, Fred. "Advertising and the Political Economy of Lesbian/Gay Identity." *Sex and Money: Feminism and Political Economy in the Media*, edited by Eileen R. Meehan and Ellen Riordan, University of Minnesota Press, 2002, pp. 196-208.

Gershon, Ilana. "Neoliberal Agency." *Current Anthropology*, vol. 52, no. 4, 2011, pp. 537-55.

Halberstam, Jack. *Queer Art of Failure.* Duke University Press, 2011.

"Have You Seen Me Lately?" *Grey's Anatomy*, written by Shonda Rhimes and Austin Guzman, directed by Tony Phelan, Shondaland, The Mark Gordon Company, and ABC Studios, 2012.

Kozak, Liz. "'First Day of School Pic' Alternatives for the Childfree." *Huffington Post*, 13 Sept. 2016, www.huffingtonpost.com/entry/first-day-of-school-pic-alternatives-for-the-child_us_57d85291e4b0a5cd12d74187. Accessed 13 Dec. 2020.

Letherby, Gayle, and Catherine Williams. "Non-Motherhood: Ambivalent Autobiographies." *Feminist Studies*, vol. 25, no. 3, 1999, pp. 719-28.

Moore, J., and P. Geist-Martin. "Mediated Representations of Voluntary Childlessness, 1900–2012." *The Essential Handbook of Women's Sexuality*. Ed. Donna Marie Castaneda. Santa Barbara, CA: Praeger. 2013. 233-251.

Muñoz, José Esteban. "Feeling Brown, Feeling Down: Latina Affect, the Performativity of Race, and the Depressive Position." *Signs*, vol. 31, no. 3, 2006, pp. 675-88.

Roberts, Dorothy E. "Mothers Who Fail to Protect their Children: Accounting for Private and Public Responsibility." *Mother Troubles: Rethinking Contemporary Maternal Dilemmas*, edited by Julia E. Hanigsberg and Sara Ruddick, Beacon Press, 1999, pp. 31-49.

"Unaccompanied Minor." *Grey's Anatomy*, written by Shonda Rhimes and Debora Cahn, directed by Rob Corn, Shondaland, The Mark Gordon Company, and ABC Studios, 2011.

Wittig Monique. "One is Not Born a Woman." *The Straight Mind and Other Essays*. Beacon Press, 1992, pp. 9-20.

"You Be Illin'." *Grey's Anatomy*, written by Shonda Rhimes and Zoanne Clack, directed by Nichole Rubio, Shondaland, The Mark Gordon Company, and ABC Studios, 2014.

Chapter Eight

Mothers, Interrupted[1]: Reframing Motherhood in the Wake of Trauma in Contemporary French Women's Writings

Nathalie Ségeral

The two narratives included in this study challenge normative discourses on motherhood at both ends of the spectrum—the mother and the childless woman. They are both articulated around a destructive mother-daughter relationship, which combined with a history of family trauma is depicted as preventing the main female character from experiencing the so-called maternal instinct and from finding fulfillment in motherhood. Both narratives draw on their authors' personal experiences in various ways. The first one, Françoise Guérin's *Maternité* (*Motherhood*) (2018), with its deceivingly simple title, is a 465-page fictional narrative told entirely in the second-person singular; it recounts a thirty-four-year-old woman's experience with motherhood, from the few weeks preceding conception until her daughter is about six months old. In the same vein as Éliette Abécassis's *Un Heureux* Événement (*A Happy Event*), it challenges stereotypical depictions of motherhood and deals with the inner dilemmas brought about by the birth of a child. Guérin draws on her experience as a clinical psychologist specializing in the mother-infant bond. Upon its release, *Maternité* was hailed as breaking the last remaining taboo on femininity, that of motherhood as the ultimate fulfillment.

The second narrative is a work of autofiction by Jane Sautière, titled *Nullipare* (Nulliparous), which is a term commonly used in French medical discourse to refer to a woman who has never borne a child. *Nullipare* examines the tensions between trauma, memory, and (non) motherhood. Sautière's work—as well as the work of Linda Lê, Malika Mokeddem, and Cécile Wajsbrot—represents an emerging trend in contemporary Francophone literature: the reclaiming of a desire to remain childless and the need to write a manifesto-like text about it, in the context of traumatized memory. Sautière's *Nullipare* helps to redefine the notion of motherhood by questioning its founding principles and by using literature as a means of exposing her narrator's choice not to procreate in the context of a society—France—that currently prides itself for having one of the highest birth rates in Europe as a result of a social policy that heavily emphasizes motherhood as the ultimate fulfillment.[2]

Casting this literary process in a different light from Natalie Edwards's *Voicing Voluntary Childlessness: Narratives of Non-Mothering in French*,[3] this chapter argues that although these texts can, in some ways, be read as feminist manifestos for childlessness or against the maternal instinct, they are complicated by issues of (post)memory. According to Edwards, women writers like Lê and Sautière, who devote their autofictional narratives to their childlessness, present the reader with "nuanced and reflective representations.... Neither simply states their past as the reason for not producing children and both refuse a facile connection between past and future, inheritance and legacy" ("Deliberately Barren?" 36). However, without reducing these writers' choices to a traumatic past, it seems difficult to discuss their texts without a close analysis of the unusually violent mother-daughter relationship they depict, which also constitutes a central narrative to Guérin's *Maternité*. Refusing motherhood, therefore, appears as closely linked to a rejection of the mother figure and the mother tongue (or the "Name of the Mother," as a counterpoint to Lacan's "Name of the Father"), which eventually amounts to a rejection of the burden of memory, of origins and of trauma.

In this perspective, rejecting motherhood is ultimately presented as a carefully thought decision not to pass on the weight of one's past, with the child being cast as a living memorial instead of an opening towards the future. Yet what can appear, in Lawrence Langer's terms, as a "choiceless choice"[4] is also far from being an avowal of victimhood. It is quite the opposite insofar as, in Sautière's text, the choice not to procreate is upheld as a way of reclaiming agency over her story and of re-embodying her childless body through literature. Guérin's narrative recounts a similar scenario to Sautière's story, with opposite results in the two sisters: one, the main character, decides to become a mother regardless of her complete lack of biological drive to motherhood, whereas her older sister hopes to counter the family malediction by adopting instead of having a biological offspring.

This chapter, thus, explores the arguments of Sautière's narrator for choosing not to procreate, thereby re(en)gendering memory through non-motherhood, challenging idealized notions of "roots[5]" and seeking a new kind of post-menopausal normalcy (see Edwards 2015 for a discussion of the re-appropriation of the narrator's post-menopausal identity in Sautière). Yet it also studies the psychiatric disorders and inner dilemmas encountered by Clara and her sister Maud on the road to motherhood in *Maternité*. I will show that the texts included here can be read as attempts at reappropriating one's story and, therefore, at moving beyond victimology in a complicated memory context through challenging the trope of motherhood as the ultimate fulfillment of femininity.

In *Mothers: An Essay on Love and Cruelty*, British professor and psychoanalyst Jacqueline Rose starts from what she terms "a simple argument": "Motherhood is, in Western discourse, the place in our culture where we lodge, or rather bury, the reality of our own conflicts, of what it means to be fully human. It is the ultimate scapegoat for our personal and political failings, for everything that is wrong in the world, which it becomes the task— unrealizable, of course—of mothers to repair (I)." American feminist Adrienne Rich argued as early as the 1970s that all women participate in the concept of motherhood—the childless woman to the same extent as the mother, insofar as they are nonetheless defined in relation to motherhood and to heteronormative patriarchy. Drawing on her essay, Rose includes in her study several literary, historical, mythological, and real-life instances of the opprobrium to which women have been subjected as mothers, being turned into society's scapegoats for many contemporary ills. According to Rose, this is highlighted by the current British media discourses around the migrant crisis, whereby the migrant single mother is depicted as seeking asylum in order to live on welfare with her offspring. Rose also reminds the reader that childless women have not been spared the same stigma, as they are often blamed for being too sexual—as opposed to the mother's body, which is supposed to be invisible, just like her very being. Rose takes after Rich's suggestion that "without the testimonies of childless or 'unchilded' (Rich qtd. in Rose) women, as she prefers to name them, we would all suffer from spiritual malnutrition" (Rose 102). Thus, she also includes childless women in her thorough study of the ambivalence of motherhood in contemporary Western societies.

Namely, Rich highlights "every woman's participation in the experience and institution of motherhood," since "the 'childless' woman and the 'mother' are a false polarity, which has served the institutions both of motherhood and heterosexuality" (qtd. in Hirsch, *The Mother/Daughter* 202). In this perspective, this new trend in French literature—women writers reclaiming, through literature, their desire for childlessness—can be read as a way of inscribing new narratives of motherhood in the context of a society which still heavily emphasizes motherhood as the ultimate fulfillment. France seems to place a heavier emphasis on motherhood as several other European countries as a result of a trend started at the time of the Nazi Occupation of France, when Pétain, the head of the Vichy government under occupied France, replaced the French motto "liberté, égalité, fraternité" (freedom, equality, fraternity) with "travail, famille, patrie" (work, family, fatherland) or, more accurately, "motherland." He also created Mother's Day as a way to encourage women to have more children and focus on the domestic sphere. As Sautière remarks, in the eyes of the patriarchal French medical discourse, only women's bodies are labelled according to their procreative choices: "Nullipare: je me demande s'il existe un mot semblable qui désignerait un homme qui n'aurait pas d'enfant. Je comprendrais qu'il n'y ait rien" (Childless: I wonder if a similar word exists for men who have not had children. I would understand if there's none) (Sautière 13).

Sautière's text appears to be autobiographical, as the first-person female narrator is depicted as identical to the author in age, circumstances and profession; however, as Edwards points out, the absence of explicit or complete identification could put it in the autofictional category. Even though Guérin's and Sautière's texts deal with different personal and historical traumas, and different experiences of (non)motherhood, these narratives are particularly well suited to being read dialogically, in that both end up revolving around strikingly similar issues. These two women writers also converge in their use of the trope of the castrating or infanticidal mother in order to challenge stereotypical discourses and perceptions on and of motherhood. Sautière's writing is a means to reappropriate her story of childlessness, which she feels has been silenced by the dominating master discourses, and to reclaim her childless woman's body. At the other end of the spectrum, Guérin's narrative also places the body at the centre of the narrative, echoing Rose's criticism of the invisibility of the maternal body and making the mother's (and infant's) body hypervisible in its most appalling and gruesome aspects. The theme of infanticide—a central subplot to both texts that goes against the usual, idealized discourse of motherhood as being the last vestige of humanity in situations of extreme trauma—provides these women writers with a gendered discourse that highlights the sexed subjectivity of their experience of trauma.

In her Foreword to *Beloved*, Toni Morrison explains that motherhood—defined by the fact of being a mother to one's child, as opposed to the fact of merely giving birth—constitutes a central stake in women's writings of slavery. As Morrison explains, the experience of slavery and freedom is fundamentally gendered, insofar as, for a woman slave, being a mother implies being free, that is, free to mother her own child. Morrison explains that her main character, Sethe, a former slave, fully endorses the consequences of her choosing infanticide.[6] In this respect, not only is Sethe depicted as having chosen infanticide out of free will (which contradicts the dominating discourse according to which she lost her mind temporarily, since a mother cannot deliberately decide to kill her child), but infanticide becomes the paradoxical condition of her accession to freedom. The theme of infanticide, albeit metaphorical, is also an essential tool in Guérin's and Sautière's vindications. As far as Guérin's main narrator and her sister are concerned, they must first symbolically kill the child whom they could have had, in various ways, so as to be able to give birth to themselves as mothers and women; Clara must also overcome her infanticidal impulses before being able to develop a bond to her own child; for Sautière, the sacrifice of the child whom she could have had allows for her liberation from the burden of her dead brother and sister, thus escaping what she terms "la reproduction macabre" (macabre reproduction) (Sautière 49) passed on to her by her mother.

According to Marianne Hirsch, who also heavily relies on Rich's text on motherhood, postmemory[7] consists of the transgenerational transmission of Holocaust trauma and generally occurs through the mother-daughter relationship (characterized by greater affective proximity than that between a mother and a son). It mostly refers to the memory and identity dilemmas encountered by Holocaust survivors' descendants. In Sautière and Guérin, the rejection of motherhood underscores a rejection of their own mother figures, which, as the texts unfold, amounts to a crisis of memory, of origins, and of trauma. Thus, rejecting motherhood becomes a refusal of transmission. In her essay titled "Material Histories of Transcolonial Loss: Creolizing Psychoanalytic Theories of Melancholia?" Elizabeth Constable argues that expressing the Other's trauma requires moving away from traditional psychoanalytical theories to develop a new definition of trauma. As far as historical trauma is concerned, it originates in society and, therefore, can no longer be expressed through the movement from one idea to another, as Freud would think, but "from one body to another" (Constable 120). That movement from one body to another is central to my argument, insofar as the women writers included here are trying to literally reembody their stories, which they feel have been silenced by master historical narratives and of which they feel dispossessed. This reembodiment occurs through a variation on the theme of both the mother's and non-mother's body in both texts. Furthermore, that movement from one body to another also characterizes postmemory, in which trauma is physically passed on from the mother to her daughter. Constable states that "When communities de-realize the past in order to 'go on,' history remains non-history... Children bear and take on the unresolved affective states of their parents' generation, and unmourned loss can reverberate as buried affect from generation to generation" (33-34). Constable's position also echoes Hirsch's notion of postmemory. In the texts studied here, choosing to be childfree is, thus, complicated by issues of memory and, arguably, postmemory. I am here extending the notion of postmemory to other traumas to demonstrate how, in the works of Sautière and Guérin, rejecting motherhood reveals a rejection of the author's own mother figure, which amounts to a crisis of memory as the narratives unfold. Thus, remaining childfree becomes a refusal to pass on the burden of one's past and preserving one's unborn child by sacrificing them. Building on Adrienne Rich's statement, according to whom the mother-daughter plot is "the great unwritten story" (qtd. in Hirsch, "Mothers and Daughters" 225), Hirsch sets out to rewrite that silenced plot. In a kind of parody, Guérin and Sautière seem to challenge Hirsch by implying that the mother-daughter plot is "poisoned," as Cécile Wajsbrot states in *Mémorial*, another autofictional narrative in which the female narrator experiences her childlessness as liberating in a heavily charged context of Holocaust postmemory. It is a "poisoned" plot in that it only seems to bring about suffering, and, as a result, that plot had better be silenced forever. In fact, throughout these two narratives, it quickly becomes obvious that a parallel story is being told, behind the main discussion of the choice whether to become a mother or not. This running subtext is the story of a (failed) mother-daughter relationship—centred on metaphors of "de-membering" and oblivion, thereby echoing these writer-narrators' attempts at reembodying their stories.

We will, thus, see the ways in which these narratives revolve around a rewriting of Hirsch's mother-daughter plot, in which the mother figure becomes a symbol conveying at once trauma and the burden of the past and in which the disruption of the traditional genealogical order by trauma allows for new networks of sisterhood outside of family. However, the rejection of the mother figure is also expressed through a metatextual analysis of the desire to remain childless or the desire to kill one's child, which runs through both narratives. Both texts can be read through three overarching, recurring issues: the rewriting of the mother-daughter plot through the lens of trauma, which is expressed through the rejection of an unsatisfactory and/or toxic mother figure; the refusal of motherhood as a literal expression of the refusal to transmit; and the blurring of traditional lineages. The common trope of childlessness and destructive maternity to which these writers resort can be seen as constituting a new voice of women's writings dealing with the sexed subjectivity of trauma and challenging accepted notions of gender. In the wake of Melissa Benn, who, in 1998, "argued that post-feminism, 'self-contained to the point of arrogance,' had slammed the lid back on the demands and painful emotions of motherhood that had been opened up by 1970s feminism" (qtd. in Rose 126), Jacqueline Rose sees in today's attitude to motherhood a tragic step backward for feminism.

I. Françoise Guérin's *Maternité*: "To Whom or What Exactly Is a Woman Giving Birth?" (Rose 154)

In her fictional narrative, Guérin presents the reader with a fierce criticism of the maternal instinct as well as of society's and the medical corps' normative discourses towards mothers. Misunderstandings start when Clara is about to give birth, as the midwife asks her if she is planning to feed her baby. Clara is not yet aware that in the "temple of motherhood" (Guérin 133), to feed one's baby exclusively refers to breastfeeding. Guérin's word choice hints at the current normative discourses on motherhood having become a new religion, and the narrative is saturated with satires of the medical discourse as well as of the nurses' and pediatricians' ways of speaking. Guérin provides a vitriolic illustration of the terrible damage caused by the social incentive denounced by Rose that "a mother must live only for her child, a mother is a mother and nothing else" (78). Solely written in the "you" form, in a dry and concise style, the story follows Clara, a young woman obsessed with her professional success. We learn in the opening of the book that Clara graduated from a prestigious business school with the highest honours and that at thirty-four, she has already become a financial director, a promotion usually reserved for more senior employees. Clara suddenly decides to have a baby—as opposed to deciding to become a mother, as highlighted by the author's word choice—and her decision is presented as a negative choice, one made out of peer pressure, especially from her husband, who urgently desired to become a father. Thus, her decision to have a child is presented as a contradiction in terms, as she tells her husband: "J'arrête la pilule parce que j'ai décidé d'avoir envie de faire un enfant!" (I am going to stop taking the pill because I have decided to desire conceiving) (Guérin 27).

The second-person narrative, instead of creating a dialogical space, fosters a disturbing feeling of entrapment, further contributing to Clara's objectification, which is seen only from outside, as though she were deprived of any interiority. This uneasy, disturbing feeling is constantly reinforced throughout the narrative, as the reader is progressively granted access to Clara's inner life and discovers the sheer lack of motherly emotion or attachment she experiences during the pregnancy and once the baby is born. As Clara keeps sinking deeper and deeper into postpartum depression, her deteriorating mental state is emphasized by the fact that the baby is not named for three-hundred pages. It is only referred to as "the baby" or a variety of other epithets: "la petite sauvageonne" (the little wild one) (Guérin 306, 395); "une grosse dégueulasse" (a fat disgusting girl) (167); "sale petite garce" (dirty little bitch) (169); "pantin ensorcelé" (bewitched puppet) (237); "la petite tigresse" (the little she-tiger) (246, 287, 301); "bébé-fardeau" (burden-baby) (361); and "la jeune espionne" (the little spy) 385). The objectification of the pregnant woman is conveyed through Daphné, Clara's secretary: "Deux seins gonflés qui débordent du décolleté, un ventre proéminent et, détail incongru, un nombril saillant sous la tunique en jersey" (Two swollen breasts, a protruding belly and, incongruous detail, the salient navel under the jersey top) (Guérin 19). The expecting woman's dismembered body, reduced to a sum of mismatched body parts, culminates in the young mother's gradual desexualization, mirrored by the baby girl's paradoxical sexualization: "le petit être répugnant que tu as engendré. Un nourrisson avec des seins de mère et un sexe de femme... Une chimère troublante, capable de condenser, en un seul être, toutes les générations" (the disgusting little being to which you have given birth. A baby with motherly breasts and a woman's sex.... A disturbing chimera, able to condense all generations within one single being) (Guérin 180). The theme of the reversal of the traditional genealogical order is also central to Sautière's narrative of childlessness, as epitomizing the disruption of linear reality by trauma.

Guérin's text constantly emphasizes the embodied experience of motherhood, as if echoing Rose's argument that "the body *in extremis*— the body experiencing itself acutely *as* a body—is a human reality to which mothers cannot help but have access" (Rose 90). In the title of this section, I use the following quote from Rose's essay "On Mothers": "to whom or what exactly is a woman giving birth? It is often said that having a baby reintroduces a woman to her own mother" (154). Clara's difficult motherhood story clearly echoes this paradigm, in so far as even before pregnancy, she is depicted as practicing self-mutilation on a regular basis by biting her own tongue until it bleeds and by burning the inside of her mouth so that she becomes unable to speak or eat for a few days. As the narrative progresses, the reader discovers that this self-mutilation echoes a founding trauma in Clara's childhood, when she had needed stitches after severely biting her tongue while tripping after feeling humiliated in front of her classmates. The tongue issue becomes a metaphor for the silence behind which Clara has locked the mental suffering caused by a childhood at the hands of a psychotic mother. It is then presented as a natural consequence of Clara's experience with her own mother that she builds a wall of silence around herself once her baby is born. As Rose notes, "Perhaps what goes by the name of 'postnatal depression' is a way of registering griefs past, present and to come, an afront to the ideal not least because of the unbearable weight of historical memory and/or prescience it carries" (185). Just like Clara's voice as a child had been silenced by an abusive and controlling mother, her own voice as a mother is then silenced both by society's refusal to hear the disturbing narratives surrounding motherhood that do not corroborate the instinct myth and by herself, having internalized these conflicting injunctions. As a result, she projects onto her newborn daughter her own refusal to acknowledge her past griefs, with the baby becoming the embodiment of the past traumas that she is desperate to forget: "La faire taire, la faire taire à tout prix, pour ne pas entendre ce qui, depuis toujours, hurle en toi" (To make her shut up, to make her shut up at all cost, in order not to hear what has been screaming within you forever) (Guérin 200).

The character of Maud, Clara's sister, embodies a different response to the traumatic mother-daughter relationship experienced by both sisters during their childhood. Maud is first presented as being affected by unexplained sterility (Guérin 33), but it eventually turns out that she has willingly chosen not to procreate and to, instead, adopt two little orphans from Africa, for fear of reproducing the destructive maternal pattern. Maud was convinced that becoming an adoptive mother would protect her against the biological destiny of toxic motherhood, which she feels has been ingrained in her by her own mother figure. However, she confesses to her sister that one's challenges with motherhood trump biological genealogy. Maud's character serves to further underline the constructed notion of motherhood and the lack of a biological instinct, contrary to the promises held by the popular master discourse: "Être mère, t'a-t-on répété, c'est tellement naturel.... Ne devrais-tu pas te fier à ton instinct?" (You have been told many times that being a mother is such a natural thing.... Shouldn't you just trust your instinct?) (Guérin 149). Devoid of the usual sublimation of the embodied experiment of pregnancy and motherhood, Clara's perception of her pregnant self becomes a distorted monstrous vision: "Tu ne vois plus que son effarante rondeur, un monstre tendu entre le monde et toi, une singulière anomalie" (All you can see is how terrifyingly big your stomach has become, a monster standing between you and the world, a puzzling anomaly) (Guérin 102).

Ultimately, as Clara finally seeks psychotherapeutic help to overcome depression and develop a bond with her daughter, she gradually develops a sense of belonging to a transnational and transhistorical community of women who silence their traumatic experience of motherhood as a social construct—or, rather, a shattering of one's former self, outside of the realm of the promised "maternal insctint": "Vous êtes des milliers, silencieuses, honteuses. Des milliers à ne rien oser révéler de la chute vertigineuse que constitue, pour vous, la maternité" (There are thousands of you, silent, shameful. Thousands of women who do not dare reveal the dizzying fall that motherhood is for you) (Guérin 296). The sense of belonging she develops is quite different from the maternal instinct upheld by society's discourse but propels her into the community of the struggling mothers, the silenced multitude whose voices are stifled by the dominant discourses:

Se sentir appartenir.... À présent, tu les vois défiler, celles qui forment l'incommensurable peuple des mères. Elles sont là, elles marchent, silencieuses, à tes côtés. Toutes différentes mais comme elles te ressemblent!

Il y a celles qui n'ont eu de mère que le nom. Que le non.[8] Celles qui, abandonnées à leur sort de bébé, ont grandi comme le lierre qui s'accroche où il peut. Celles qui ne perçoivent même pas dans quel incessant mouvement de répétition elles sont enfermées. Celles qui se débattent, jour après jour, avec la débâcle des souvenirs. Celles qui n'ont de mémoire qu'un corps énigmatique traversé de symptômes.

Tu songes avec mélancolie à celles qui se sont sacrifiées. Celles qui ont fui, fauté, failli. Celles qui, perplexes à l'heure de donner la vie, n'ont pu dévier de la trajectoire que l'autre ancestral avait tracée pour elles. Et celles qu'une obscure logique a poussées dans le gouffre.

(To experience a sense of belonging.... Now, you can see them marching, those who constitute the infinite people of mothers. They are there, they are marching, in silence, next to you. All different and yet, they resemble you so much!

There are those who were only mothers by name. Only the "no." Those who, left alone to their fates as babies, grew up like ivy that clings to whatever it can. Those who do not even perceive in which permanent compulsion of repetition they are locked. Those who struggle, day after day, with the debacle of memories. Those who can only remember an enigmatic body possessed by symptoms.

With sadness, you think about those who have sacrificed themselves. Those who ran away, committed terrible acts, or failed. Those who, skeptical at the time of giving life, were not able to deviate the trajectory that the ancestral Other had drawn for them. And those that a dark logic pulled into the abyss.) (Guérin 452)

The function of this long diatribe is to reinscribe Clara into an alternative community of women who never experienced the maternal instinct. These women all had to struggle in various ways to survive within a society that has erected as its last, unbreakable taboo the supposedly natural aspects of the traumatic transition from being a woman and an independent human being to suddenly existing only for others and forgetting all sense of her selfhood. Guérin's book denounces the schizophrenic expectations of motherhood as they stand in most contemporary Western societies.

II. Jane Sautière's *Nullipare*: Disembodying Deadly Motherhood through Anorexia and Childlessness

Quoting French feminist philosopher Elisabeth Badinter, Rose remarks that mothers are desexualized in the public discourse, since "[a] mother is a woman whose sexual being must be invisible" (Rose 36). She continues: "Nor is the childless woman immune from sexual taint.

'Surely,' as one journalist summed up a common presumption about the declining birth rate in twenty-first century France, 'a woman who refuses to be a mother enjoys lovemaking rather too much?'" (qtd in Rose 37). In her autobiographical narrative *Nullipare*, Jane Sautière seeks to re-sexualize the childless woman and re-appropriate her childless, menopausal body, which mirrors Guérin's narrative of the inner dilemmas of motherhood in several ways.

Sautière was born in 1952 in Teheran and spent her childhood and adolescence there, before moving to France and working in prisons. Her Iranian nanny would only speak to her in Farsi, which she considers her mother tongue, since she recurrently highlights the maternal characteristics of her nanny and her immense suffering when they were separated, as opposed to her biological mother's coldness and remoteness. In the same vein as Lê's *À l'Enfant que je n'aurai pas*, Sautière's *Nullipare* grants a central position to the unborn child figure and offers the reader a reflection on the choice of remaining childfree. Thus, Sautière presents her text as "un livre sur ce qui s'est absenté, l'enfant non né, qui existe comme ce qui n'a pas eu lieu existe, car il y a une existence des choses qui n'ont pas eu lieu") (a book on what has gone missing, the unborn child, who exists just like what has not happened exists, since things that have not happened do exist[9]) (Sautière 100). This text, thereby, paradoxically grants existence to, and embodies, her never-born child. Reflecting on her new essence as a childless woman, now that she is past menopause, she adds that "Je me retourne maintenant vers ce que je ne peux pas changer. Pour toujours je serai une femme sans enfants" (I now look back on what I cannot change. I will forever be a childless woman) (Sautière 103).

However, as the narrative unfolds, it becomes obvious, as is the case in Guérin's text, that the narrator is telling the story of her tumultuous and complicated relationship to her own mother, whereby the issue of remaining childless is intertwined with the narrator's attempt at coming to terms with the fact that she was born after two dead children (both apparently dead from tuberculosis) as well as her attempt at recovering from anorexia. From the opening onwards, Sautière likens the issue of non-motherhood to that of origins: "Une femme de nulle part, irrecevable quant à la question des origines (ce sont bien les origines que la descendance questionne, comment l'ignorer?")" (A woman from nowhere, unacceptable when it comes to the question of origins [and having descendants inevitably interrogates one's ancestry, or origins—how could anyone not know that?]) (Sautière 13). Bearing a child amounts to inscribing oneself within a lineage, and through this refusal to have descendants, the author rejects her ancestry. The association of childlessness with place-lessness is brought to mind by the disturbing sound similarities between the French words "nullipare" (used to designate a woman who has never born a child) and "nulle part" (nowhere).

Rose argues that "one reason why motherhood is often so disconcerting seems to be its uneasy proximity to death" (24). This is especially salient in Sautière's narrative, in which it eventually becomes clear that the narrator's desire to remain childless conceals a refusal to pass on a painful, traumatic past. In this perspective, the narrator recalls her childhood spent in Teheran and the trauma of her classmates sent to camps (Sautière 22), along with the feeling of uprootedness she experienced upon moving to France and being suddenly separated from her Iranian nanny and the Farsi language. Then, she moves on to evoke her first encounter with narratives about the Holocaust and, more specifically, narratives about French women publicly shamed and chastised for having slept with German soldiers,[10] intertwining history and fiction:

> Moi, peut-être quatorze ans, peut-être entendant pour la première fois parler des femmes tondues. Je me souviens du jour où j'ai su pour les camps. Je me souviens exactement comment ça a coupé ma vie en deux.... Je me souviens de la cave de Nevers, oui, ça très bien, le film *Hiroshima mon amour* et la séquestration dans la cave, je m'en souviens.

> (I was perhaps fourteen, hearing perhaps for the first time about the shaved women. I remember the day when I heard about the camps.[11] I remember exactly how it cut my life into two... I remember the cellar in Nevers yes, I remember very well, the film *Hiroshima mon amour* and the forced confinement in the cellar, I remember this well.) (Sautière 121)

This revelation is depicted as having had a tremendous impact on the narrator's life, since the phrase "ça a coupé ma vie en deux" (it cut my life into two parts) is extremely strong. She goes on to draw a parallel between herself and Marie, her adopted cousin, whereby the childless woman is likened to the traitor, the woman who collaborated during the Occupation by having sexual intercourse with German soldiers. More exactly, the childless woman is ostracized in the same manner as the woman suspected to have slept with a German would be shaved in public upon France's "Liberation": "Sachant comme elle, et dans le même silence imposé par la messe de l'ordre, qu'elle était née en pleine Occupation d'un Allemand et d'une Bretonne" (Knowing, just like she did, and in the same silence imposed on us by the orderly mass, that she had been born during the Nazi Occupation of France, of a German father and a mother from Brittany) (Sautière 122). This instance creates a sisterhood in historical ostracism. A further parallel is drawn between the childless woman and the sentenced woman whom Sautière encounters every day in her work in jails (Sautière 20), insofar as both the childless woman and the convict are considered outcasts.

Lastly, the narrator's decision to remain childfree is constantly brought back to her specific position within her family's genealogy:

Je suis fille d'une femme qui a perdu deux enfants avant de peiner à me donner la vie…. Je suis née de cette peine, de cette hésitation ultime à redonner enfant à un homme nouvellement épousé. Née de l'horreur de désirer et la vie et donner la vie lorsqu'on a, apocalypse de la faute, survécu à la mort de ses enfants.

(I am the daughter of a woman who lost two children before finally, painstakingly, giving me life…. I was born from that grief, that ultimate hesitation to give another child to a new husband. Born from the horror of desiring life and to give life when one has, apocalyptical sin, survived the death of one's children.) (Sautière 47)

In this perspective, giving life, or giving birth, equates to giving death, especially when the narrator refers to her choice not to have children as "l'absence de la reproduction macabre" (the absence of deathly reproduction) (Sautière 49). Ultimately, her childlessness is paradoxically depicted as a lifelong pregnancy: "Oui, le deuil de ce qui n'a pas eu lieu, être mère, est un processus particulier. Nullipare, part nulle. Je suis avec en moi l'enfant que je n'ai pas eu, une place vide et peuplée" (Yes, mourning for what has not happened, to be a mother, is a particular process. Childless, less than a child. I am with, in me, the child I have not had, a place at once empty and populated) (Sautière 50).

Gradually, the close, literal link between non-motherhood, anorexia, and the dead children of the narrator's mother is disclosed (Sautière 86-87); namely, the narrator explains that: "J'ai tant voulu ne pas avoir de corps.... Ne plus manger, fuir l'incorporation. Refuser de manger, c'est évidemment refuser la procréation, refuser l'enfantement, refuser ce qui fait corps, refuser de comprendre ce que nourrir veut dire" (I desired so much not having a body.... To stop eating, to escape embodiment. Refusing to eat obviously amounts to refusing procreation, refusing to bear a child, refusing what embodies, refusing to understand what feeding means) (Sautière 138).

The narrator recounts spending her adolescence and young adulthood haunted by the ghosts of her dead siblings, which prompted her descent into anorexia as a means of sacrificing herself so as to bring her dead siblings back to life, in the hope to retain the appearance of a little girl. In so doing, she ponders over the tragic irony of the fact that "Je donnais vie aux enfants morts de ma mère, pour pouvoir me libérer du poids de la mort" (she was giving life to [her] mother's dead children, so as to be able to free herself from the weight of death) (Sautière 89), which results in a reversal of traditional lineages that becomes even more obvious towards the end of her mother's life, when the narrator eventually becomes at once her mother's daughter and her mother's mother:

> J'ai vu ma mère dépérir et sombrer. Elle est devenue vieille et tout à fait folle, perdant totalement la mémoire.... J'étais là, j'étais enfin sa fille. Sa fille, mais aussi sa mère. Cette bascule insensible du grand âge qui fait des enfants les parents de leurs parents, si troublante pour chacun, l'était un peu moins pour moi, habituée à l'anarchie généalogique.

> (I saw my mother waste away and sink. She became old and quite insane, losing her memory completely.... I was there, I was finally her daughter. Her daughter, but also her mother. That slow shift of old age that turns children into their parents' parents, which is so unsettling for each of us, was a little less unsettling for me, as I was used to genealogical anarchy.) (Sautière 98)

Going further than most narratives of voluntary childlessness, because of her unusual family history, Sautière notes that by becoming her mother's mother during her mother's last moments, she ultimately became "la mère d'une enfant au bord de la mort, selon la malédiction initiale" (the mother of a child on the verge of dying, according to the original malediction) (Sautière 99), thus closing her narrative of childlessness on a very dark note

In the same vein as Linda Lê, the self-proclaimed "eternal daughter," Sautière eventually views her childlessness as a way to "rester fille pour que ma mère ait toujours une fille. Comme si, moi-même devenue mère, j'aurais cessé d'être sa fille. J'aurais cessé d'être exclusivement sa fille" (remain a daughter so that my mother never ceases to have a daughter. As if, by becoming a mother, I would have stopped being her daughter. I would have stopped being solely her daughter) (Sautière 111). Thus, it is here the narrator herself who is cast as a sacrificial figure. In Sautière's text, infanticide is omnipresent in the background, as a subtext running through her entire manifesto for childlessness. Namely, the narrator reports some of the actual cases of infanticide which she has encountered over the course of her career as a prison education coordinator. She highlights the tragic irony and ambivalence of motherhood in the following instance: "Une collègue doit organiser les obsèques d'un bébé de dix mois, mort des maltraitances de sa mère. Elle est submergée par la femme qui lui dit que son enfant est mort dans ses bras, et qui, dans la foulée, déplore que la poussette de sept mille balles soit maintenant inutilisable" (A colleague has to organize the funeral of a ten-month-old baby killed by his abusive mother. She is overwhelmed by that woman who is telling her how her child died in her arms, lamenting that the seven thousand French francs stroller is now useless) (Sautière 82). Furthermore, the narrator hints at her own metaphorical infanticide, i.e., her desire to disappear through her anorexic body or the symbolical murder of the child she could have had so that she can remain alive, thereby fulfilling what she sees as the family prophecy, or the family curse. This is particularly salient in the following remark: "C'est quand même quelque chose qu'il faille que cela se produise la mort des enfants que je n'ai pas eus, alors que je ne suis pas 'de la famille', que je reste dans la mienne où les enfants meurent tous sauf un—moi" (It is quite telling that the death of the children I have not had has to happen, while I am not "part of the family," I remain in my own family in which children all die except for one—myself) (Sautière 80). Language thus becomes performative and enacts both the narrator's necessary and metaphorical killing of the children she could have had and her inability to create her own family.

Eventually, the narrator grants the childless woman a new position within a transnational historical lineage; in lieu of a blood lineage, the childless woman is reinscribed within the history of ostracized women and becomes part of a sisterhood with other sacrificed women who have been historically marginalized: "Femmes prises dans l'Histoire, avec les autres, les lapidées, les martialement violées, les brûlées au titre des intégrations qui n'ont pas lieu" (Women caught up in History, with the other ones, the women stoned to death, the women raped during wars, the women burnt in the name of integrations which never took place) (Sautière 125). This sisterhood echoes the closing of Guérin's narrative, whereby Clara eventually recovers from postnatal depression and is able to create a bond between her daughter and herself by replacing her fate within a long historical lineage of tormented motherhood, whose narratives had been silenced by the totalitarian discourses on motherhood as the ultimate fulfillment of femininity. Whereas Sautière grants a place to the childless woman—pursuing her initial comment on the homophony between "nullipare" (childless) and "nulle part" (nowhere)—Guérin grants a body to the disembodied mother upheld by dominant narratives, thus focusing her narrative on the physical experience of pregnancy, motherhood, and caring for a newborn.

Conclusion

Thus, as Rose argues, "to put it at its crudest, a mother can suffer, she can be the object of heartfelt empathy, so long as she does not probe or talk too much" (15). I have argued that Sautière's *Nullipare* and Guérin's *Maternité* both allow for a de-objectification of women as mothers—be it the actual mother or the childless woman. Both narratives re-sexualize their narrators in their motherhood or their voluntary childlessness and give a voice to the voiceless. The themes of voluntary childlessness and infanticide—whether metaphorical or actual, be it Sautière's never-born child or Guérin's narrator's infanticidal impulses—enable these two women writers to reclaim those silent (his)stories in order for their female narrators to work through the initial trauma and move beyond the burden of the past. Sautière and Guérin repeatedly highlight the blurring of genealogical and gender boundaries brought about by family, historical and personal traumas, as well as exile, such as the Holocaust and immigration to France from Iran, along with a toxic mother-daughter relationship. It is worth noting that the central theme of both narratives seems to be the ultimate liberation of the woman fixated in her biological position as a daughter passively receiving the burden of traumatic memory and is depicted as happening through the choice either to remain childfree or to struggle through postnatal depression and eventually create a maternal bond through the psychoanalytic talking cure.

Both texts resort to the trope of motherhood as a social construct rather than instinctual to metaphorically express the narrator's traumatized memory and the refusal to pass it on in a paradoxical context of disembodiment. This corporeal writing, or writing through the body, gives rise to a metaphorical reembodiment via a crystallization of trauma on the female body, which allows these writers to regain agency. Sautière's childless female narrator and Guérin's depressed, unattached mother character contribute to redefining the notion of motherhood by challenging its very founding principles and accepted motifs through tropes that enable them to re(en)gender memory through a vindication of non-motherhood and of motherhood as nonnatural.

In 2009, Michael Rothberg denounced the ethical issue of the child figure being placed at the centre of the current discourses on trauma and memory by analyzing Michael Haneke's film *Caché*, dealing with the transmission of the trauma of the Algerian War of Independence and of the Holocaust (Rothberg 121). Sautière and Guérin's texts can be read as counterpoints to that issue. Their narrators' rejection of motherhood underscores a rejection of their own mother figures, which, as the texts unfold, amounts to a crisis of memory and of origins as well as to a rejection of the original trauma, going against the current politics of memory and idealization of roots discussed in Marianne Hirsch and Nancy Miller's *Rites of Return*.[12] Thus, the rejection of motherhood becomes a refusal of transmission (and of the burden of memory). Childlessness and its dilemmas become tropes used as a means to re(en) gendering memory through a crisis of motherhood in contemporary French literature, whereby the child becomes a metaphor of memory. In these narratives, trauma is depicted as affecting family relationships to such an extent that the child is no longer perceived as representing the future and a new beginning but becomes the bearer of the traumatic past and a living memorial through which the mother risks perpetuating her own trauma. Remaining childless amounts to discarding the child as a living memorial. Yet, paradoxically, Sautière does not depict her choice as being the necessary negative result of a psyche trapped in past family entanglements. Rather, devoting her autofictional narrative to her decision of remaining childless proves cathartic and enables the author/narrator to mourn her past trauma and overcome it, thereby claiming agency over her childless self. Furthermore, moving beyond Marianne Hirsch and Adrienne Rich, these narratives foreshadow a new wave of feminism, as they are no longer about freeing oneself from "the shackles of motherhood and daughterhood" (Hirsch, *Mother/Daughter* 129). Instead, their narratives are about embracing the eternal daughter position, or what I have called elsewhere the "child-mother" figure (Ségeral)—that is to say, the in-between-ness provided by literary creation and the possibility of re(en)gendering oneself through literature.

Endnotes

1. In this title, I am taking the liberty of paraphrasing the title of Susanna Kaysen's 1993 memoir, subsequently adapted into a film: *Girl, Interrupted*. It chronicles the author's eighteen-month stay at a psychiatric hospital at age eighteen.

2. This paper comes from a talk that I gave on 26 October 2013 at the conference titled "Motherhood in Post-1968 European Women's Writing: Cross-Cultural and Interdisciplinary Dialogues," at the University of London (United Kingdom).

3. Sautière, along with Lê, has recently gained the attention of Natalie Edwards in *Voicing Voluntary Childlessness: Narratives of Non-Mothering in French* and in "Deliberately Barren? The Rejection of Motherhood in Contemporary French Women's Life Writing." However, Edwards does not approach these narratives through the critical lens of (post)memory and trauma.

4. Langer coined the phrase "choiceless choice" in the context of Holocaust trauma to refer to the psychological dilemma of women who had to abort or kill their children in order to try to escape being sent to the gas chambers.

5. Contrary to recent studies, such as Marianne Hirsch and Nancy Miller's *Rites of Return: Diaspora Poetics and the Politics of Memory*.

6. "The heroine would represent the unapologetic acceptance of shame and terror; *assume the consequences of choosing infanticide*; claim her own freedom" (my emphasis, *Beloved*, xi).

7. Postmemory is a term coined by Hirsch ("Past Lives") to describe the experience of children and grandchildren of Holocaust survivors who inherit a trauma they have not directly experienced.

8. Here, the Lacanian pun of the French homophony between "Nom" (name) and "Non" (no) is impossible to translate.

9. My translation (all of Sautière's translations are mine).

10. When France was liberated from the German occupants from May to August 1945, women who had been suspected of sexual relationships with German soldiers were publicly shaved and had swastikas tattooed on their skulls or naked bodies, and there have also been instances where they were raped or even killed.

11. Here, Sautière refers to the Nazi death camps during the Holocaust.

12. According to Hirsch and Miller, *Rites of Return* stages "a dialogue between feminist and diaspora studies, offering a multifaceted paradigm of community that *acknowledges longings to belong and to return while remaining critical of a politics of identity and nation* (my emphasis, Hirsch and Miller 4).

Works Cited

Constable, Elizabeth. "Material Histories of Transcolonial Loss: Creolizing Psychoanalytic Theories of Melancholia?" *The Creolization of Theory*, edited by Françoise Lionnet and Shu-mei Shih, Duke University Press, 2011, pp. 112-41.

Edwards, Natalie. "Deliberately Barren? The Rejection of Motherhood in Contemporary French Women's Life Writing." *Australian Journal of French Studies*, vol. 52, no. 1, 2015, pp. 24-36.

Edwards, Natalie. *Voicing Voluntary Childlessness: Narratives of Non-Mothering in French*. Oxford: 2016.

Guérin, Françoise. *Maternité*. Albin Michel, 2018.

Hirsch, Marianne. "Mothers and Daughters," *Signs*, vol. 7, no 1, 1981, pp. 200-22.

Hirsch, Marianne. "Past Lives: Postmemories in Exile." *Poetics Today* 17.4 (1996): 659-686.

Hirsch, Marianne. *The Mother/Daughter Plot. Narrative, Psychoanalysis, Feminism.* Indiana University Press, 1989.

Hirsch, Marianne. Miller, Nancy K. *Rites of Return: Diaspora Poetics and the Politics of Memory.* New York: Columbia University Press, 2011.

Kaysen, Susanna. *Girl, Interrupted.* Turtle Bay Books, 1993.

Langer, Lawrence. "Gendered Suffering? Women in Holocaust Testimonies." *Women in the Holocaust,* edited by Dalia Ofer and Lenore Weitzman, Yale University Press, pp. 351-63.

Lê, Linda. *A l'Enfant que je n'aurai pas.* Nil, 2011.

Mokeddem, Malika. *Je Dois tout à ton oubli.* Grasset, 2008.

Morrison, Toni. *Beloved.* Knopf, 1987.

Rich, Adrienne. *Of Woman Born: Motherhood as Experience and Institution.* Norton, 1976.

Rose, Jacqueline. *Mothers: An Essay on Love and Cruelty.* New York: Farrar, Straus & Giroux, 2018.

Rothberg, Michael. *Multidirectional Memory: Remembering the Holocaust in the Age of Decolonization.* Stanford University Press, 2009.

Sautière, Jane. *Nullipare.* Paris: Gallimard, 2008.

Ségeral, Nathalie. *Reclaimed Experience: Gendering Trauma in Slavery, Holocaust, and Madness Narratives.* Doctoral dissertation. University of California, eScholarship, 2012.

Wajsbrot, Cécile. *Mémorial.* Paris: Zulma, 2005.

Zürn, Unica. *L'Homme-Jasmin. Impressions d'une malade mentale.* Paris: Gallimard, 1971.

Chapter Nine

Childlessness among Women in the Hebrew Bible: Reframing their Stories

Judith Dunkelberger Wouk

"Give me a child or I will die."
—Rachel to Jacob, Gen 30:1, [c. 1700 BCE])

"I felt ... outside of history because I had no child to give me a sense of continuity with the past or connection with the present. I felt ... apart from the human family, uprooted and ungrounded ... ashamed of myself."
—Lisle 59

"No woman in the Hebrew Bible is described as resisting motherhood."
—Brenner 57

"Those of us without children find the reality of our lives liberating."
—Lisle 245

S ome things do not change. But some things do. Childless biblical women, possibly even childfree by choice, do exist; let's bring them out of the confines of that narrative and into an ongoing story (Frymer-Kensky, *Reading* 333). If the spirituality of women is not coded to find the most fulfillment in the role of mother, how do we validate and celebrate the unique aspects of being female without reducing ourselves to wombs and breasts and being gender coded in societally rigid ways? (Goldstein 72). Let's include roles and role models, in both the private and public arenas, for women with various attitudes towards childbearing. Let's elucidate a deeper understanding of the interaction between femininity, motherhood, fertility, sex roles, and feminism (Basten).

Without a past to lean upon and a future to aspire to, we cannot have a meaningful present. This position does not mean agreeing with the past or accepting its authority; rather, it means becoming familiar with it, feeling a sense of belonging to it, and interpreting it to produce living meaning (Raveh xxiv). As Laurie Lisle writes, "It is important to place ourselves in historical perspective, to find relevant female ancestors" and, thus, "to enlarge the frame and connect to a feminine tradition outside of motherhood" (59). Ironically, in order to do so, I will examine the lives of biblical women from the point of view of their reproductive accomplishments. Procreation is a primary aspect of family and society in the Jewish tradition. It is the cornerstone of marital life, although companionship, fulfilment, and avoidance of sin (illicit sexual acts and fantasies) are also important (Biale 198).

Though striking characters, biblical women are not well fleshed-out individuals. The Bible tells us little of their backgrounds, their future, or their thoughts; we learn only their actions in a particular context, which reveals only those facts that serve the writer's agenda (Frymer-Kensky, *Reading* 333). The agenda of the originators of the Hebrew Bible was the long-term survival of the Jewish people. Primarily written between 922 and 722 BCE (Friedman 3-5) and compiled over several hundred years of political chaos, the stories that are canonized as the Hebrew Bible speak to a confused and despairing people (Callaway 9) in order to promote monotheism and patriarchal values at the expense of goddesses and independent women. The preoccupation with the reproductive capabilities of women during the early history of the Israelites relates to political and demographic concerns during the formation of a national identity (Setel 88). Fertility, in terms of both the family and land, constituted an imperative for survival for the Israelites (Knight 134). However, their religion moved away from the concept that fertility resulted from the activity of a goddess, identified as Asherah, Astarte, Ashtoreth, Ashtaroth (Judg 2:13) or the Queen of Heaven (Jer. 7:18, 44:15-19, 25; Frymer-Kensky, *In the Wake* 89). Gradually, the powers of creating and assuring childbirth, which had belonged to goddesses, were explicitly added to the Hebrew God's powers[1] (Frymer-

Kensky, *In the Wake* 97). Hosea, in a polemic against the ancient Canaanite religion, emphasizes God's control of fertility in general and female reproductive capability in particular. For Hosea, infertility results from trusting Canaanite deities (Hosea 2:4-5). He, thus, sets (religious) promiscuity in opposition to fertility. This echoes the connection in Hosea 1:2 between human harlotry and the land (Hosea 9:12; Setel 93).

The ideology of "be fruitful and multiply" (Gen. 1:28) makes sense given the harsh conditions and child mortality of the time. Complying with the pressure to procreate enhances a woman's social status and contributes to her family's security, prosperity, and labour power. Although frequent pregnancies diminish biological wellbeing, choosing a long life without children could mean forfeiting security and even life support in old age (Brenner 68).

Biblical women are shown primarily within the family, with family-oriented goals. The prime figure is the mother (Frymer-Kensky *In the Wake* 121), defined by her children. However, there is limited discussion in the Hebrew Bible of pregnancy, childbirth, or childrearing. Practical considerations, such as children performing work or caring for elders, is also largely absent (Meyers 97-98). Although they intervene at strategic points, the lives of mothers do not revolve around their children. Rather, the role of specific children is the focus. Biblical mothers derive their significance from famous sons. The role of the matriarchs is to bear the "children of the promise," and the stories that are chosen to be included trace how the right wife (from the viewpoint of the originators of the Hebrew bible) must be the mother of the heir, who must be the right son (Exum, "Mother" 74-75). The barren matriarch provides a threat that the needed son might not appear, providing an opportunity for God to intervene (Exum, "Mother" 76).

To biblical authors, the birth of a child is a metaphor for (or proof of) the power of God. A child is a token of God's love (Ochs 177) and favour; children are seen as a reward, and lack of them is seen as a punishment. Children are also a metaphor for the Israelites. The Hebrew words "h-d / orah," which literally mean a pathway that stops, occur in only two verses: Deborah's poem (Judg. 5) and Sarah's infertility (Gen 18:11). When pathways are cut off, both the Israelites and the women pursue new paths (Klitsner 154). The exodus from Egypt describes the emergence of a nation framed as the story of a birth. The dominated people are compared to a cunning woman struggling to survive (Raveh 56), and they emerge through the parted waters of the Sea of Reeds, which may be interpreted as representing a birth canal.

Examining these issues can serve as a tool for gender justice in the twenty-first century. Although biblical women make choices and influence the course of events—they are not passive and pitiful wives—women today increasingly claim agency over their lives as whole beings in ways that were not available to our ancestors.

One way to fulfil Rosemary Ruether's proposal for a feminist principle as "the affirmation of and promotion of the full humanity of women" (Russell 137) is to liberate the Bible from patriarchy.[2] From the ancient world to the present, scripture is being released from the prison of the past to speak to the living (Trible, "Postscript" 147). Our task now is to reinterpret ancient stories and imagine new relationships between the text and our experience (Thistlethwaite 102).

Many words describe the condition of being without children; barren, sterile, infertile, unfruitful, childless, and childfree are some of them. The term "childless" implies being explicitly without something which is naturally expected, like being homeless or friendless. "Childfree" is positive and implies emancipation from something by choice or good fortune, such as carefree or disease-free. At the same time, however, it implies freedom from something negative. In female physiology, the womb is either a "vacant emptiness" or the space for "radical openness" (Morell qtd. in Basten).[3]

In the Hebrew Bible, children are noted for their place in the line of descent. Thus, the importance is not a child per se, but a child who produces grandchildren. This means that one can be childless as a result of the absence of birth ("nullipara") or the early death of the spouse or children or both.

This chapter covers more than three thousand years. Although dating is controversial, events may have occurred as early as 3000 BCE (Teubal 72). Ancient Israel is usually dated from the middle of the second millennium BCE to the beginning of the second century BCE (Brenner 71). The Rabbinic Period spanned the turn of the millennium and lasted some five hundred years into the Common Era.

Being voluntarily childfree is not a traditional choice for Jewish couples. The Hebrew Bible has us believe that the choice exercised by Israelite women is exclusively prolife (of children and society at large) in order to carry out God's plan.[4] In the twenty-first century, many ancient concepts are being reframed. These include Sabbath practices, circumcision, diet, and the concepts of "mikvah" and "niddah," which are associated with ritual purity. An increasing number of women are now asking, "How can we manifest these concepts in a way that is relevant today?" and "How can we respect the reason behind the ancient rules by updating them within our personal conscience?" This chapter will discuss childlessness among women in the Hebrew Bible by reframing stories that include women that were called barren but who eventually give birth, and strong women whose lives do not include children, possibly by choice. They all can speak to us today.

Barrenness

Continuity, which is both a blessing and a burden, is gendered in the Hebrew Bible; although either partner may be infertile, the burden of transforming the condition falls to the woman. Divine intervention, too, affects the woman physically—God must "open the womb"—whereas the man is affected socially (Brenner 59). The male wish for posterity is depicted as basic and intrinsic but not as an instinct for fatherhood. Biblical texts dealing with procreation, sexual activity, and heterosexual desire should be read in light of this asymmetrical gendering and ideological preference (Brenner 55).

Motherhood in the Hebrew Bible is promoted as the goal of a woman's life, if not the sole reason for her existence. No biblical text explicitly discusses other options, such as contraception, abortion, or infanticide. There is nothing worse than being infertile (i.e., sonless), especially when her husband is not. Numerous narratives about mothers of future leaders and heroes provide instructive examples. Sometimes, this desire is presented as derived from the need to propagate the social group (e.g., Lot's daughters, Noah's daughters, Tamar, and Ruth). Otherwise, women's motivation in becoming mothers is represented as inherent, intrinsic, and innate—in short, women desire children (Brenner 56).

Close examination reveals two views of barrenness within biblical literature. One portrays childless women as cursed by God; barrenness is a sign of divine disfavour or punishment for sin. This view is found in scattered legal and poetic texts (e.g., Lev. 20:20-21; 2 Sam. 6:23; Job 18:19; Hos. 9:10-18; Prov. 30:15-16; Isa. 14:22). However, it is not presented strongly and the passages in which it appears are largely after the eighth century BCE (Callaway 16). The other view, found from

Genesis through Kings, offers no reason for the barrenness; God closed the womb for unknown reasons.[5] Moreover, these narratives tell the stories of individuals; they are not simply symbols but real women with names and specific situations (Callaway 17).

Desperate women, longing for children, go to great lengths—either directly or by a surrogate (male, female, or both)—to accomplish the goal of having a child that is attributed to them. In the stories that make it into the canon, these women succeed. Although the biblical narrative makes it clear that life and death outcomes, including pregnancy, come from God, seven[6] major biblical women, said explicitly to be barren, take action and eventually have (God gives them) at least one biological child—always a son. Two matriarchs, Sarah (Gen. 16ff) and Rachel (Gen. 30ff), try the same strategy—that is, female surrogacy through encouraging her husband to produce heirs with her handmaid (Hagar and Bilhah, respectively). When Rachel's maid becomes pregnant, Rachel (not Bilhah) names him Dan (Gen 30:6) because "God has judged me, and has also heard my voice and given me a son." Both Sarah and Rachel later become pregnant themselves.

Seeking a male surrogate ("baby daddy") is a strategy for women with no husband. He is often a family member through levirate[7] marriage or incest. When Judah's son Er (Gen. 38) dies, Judah's second son, Onan, "spills his seed" rather than provide offspring for Er's widow Tamar, which would have superseded his own claim to the first-born's double property share. When Onan dies, Judah returns Tamar to her father's house to wait for his remaining son, Shelah (Gen. 38:6-11). Neither married nor unmarried, she no longer belongs anywhere (Sawyer 59). When Judah does not follow through, Tamar takes action. She tricks him; without recognizing her, he gets her pregnant himself (Gen. 38:14-26), which brings her back into his family.

Lot's daughters, who are unnamed, recognizing that their father is growing old and there are no other men left, get him drunk and seduce him. Both become pregnant (Gen. 19:31-36; Antonelli 43). Noah's daughters, in the same predicament, use the same tactic: They get their father drunk and have sex to preserve their family line. Both have sons (Gen. 19:34-38).

Like Tamar, Naomi needs (another) son after her husband and both sons die. She cleverly arranges a levirate marriage for her widowed daughter-in-law Ruth. Ruth's child is identified as Naomi's—a miracle birth to a childless widow (Sawyer 83)—a type of surrogacy by both male and female.

Another biblical strategy for obtaining children is prayer.[8] Abram[9] tells God that since he is childless, a household servant will be his heir (Gen. 15:1-3), and God promises him many descendants (Gen. 15:2-6). When he has a child with Hagar (Gen. 11:30; 16:1-8), Sarai, still childless, tells Abram (Gen. 16:5) he should have prayed on behalf of both of them (Rashi qtd. in Antonelli 35). In the next generation, Isaac prays for his wife because she is barren. God grants his prayer, and Rebecca conceives (Gen. 25:21). A generation later, "Finally God remembers Rachel and heeds her and opens her womb,"[10] resulting in Joseph (Gen. 30:22-24).

In another story, Elkanah loves his wife Hannah, although God has closed her womb, and his other wife Peninnah has children (1 Sam. 1-2). Elkanah says, "Am I not better to thee than ten sons?" (1 Sam. 8), but Hannah beseeches God "to raise her into the empire of motherhood"; she vows that if God gives her a son, she will give him back to God (1 Sam. 10-11). God remembers her, and Hannah bears Samuel (1 Sam. 1:24-28).

The unnamed[11] wife of Manoah (Judges 13:2) is a barren woman. An angel tells her she will have a son and instructs her how to raise him. Manoah prays that the angel will teach them both (Judges 12:8), and the angel returns. The story affirms Manoah's wife as a person by not letting her husband steal the limelight, despite his efforts, and by attributing theological insight to her (Exum, "Mother" 82). She gives birth to Samson.

In the Gospel of Luke, Elizabeth, who is "of the daughters of Aaron" and her husband are "righteous before God" but childless. The angel Gabriel says to Zacharias, "Do not be afraid, your prayer has been heard. Your wife Elizabeth will bear you a son" (Luke 1:5–15). Elizabeth becomes pregnant and says, "God has shown his favor and taken away my disgrace among the people" (Luke 1:24–25). Her son is John the Baptist.

A third strategy is to attract divine attention through hospitality. It is during their reception of guests that Sarah overhears that she will be "a mother of nations" (Gen. 17:15-21; Gen. 18:1-15). Does Abram believe God had punished them with childlessness for a previous offence to a passing guest (Ochs 107-108)? A Shunamite woman is rewarded with a child for being hospitable to the Prophet Elisha (2 Kings 4:8-37). Elisha asks, "What can we do for her?"; his servant Gehazi responds that she has no son. Elisha tells her that she will bear a son. She has not asked for this; if she prays or feels empty, it does not say. She later seems unengaged by her child's needs; only after he dies does she fight for his life. It was Elisha's whim and now is his responsibility (Brown, "Shunamite" 159).

Temporary Abstinence

The Hebrew Bible never mentions deliberate prevention or cessation of childbearing; in later elaborations by the rabbis, this is seen as inappropriate, and the person who ends it is a hero. Miriam, sister of Aaron, twice attempts to bring separated couples together. One succeeds; the other does not. When she is a child, the pharaoh decrees death to newborn males. Her father, Amram, proclaims that all couples should separate to avoid bearing children destined for death.[12] Miriam brings her parents, and the other couples, back together, using three arguments: The pharaoh's decree would kill only male children while her father's action would affect both boys and girls; the pharaoh is evil and no one will obey him, whereas they respect her father and will do as he says; and the pharaoh's decree kills children in this life, whereas her father's action would prevent children from being born and thus eventually entering the life to come. Amram rewards Jochebed and Moses is born (Babylonian Talmud Sotah 12a; Labowitz 110; Raveh 63).

Much later, described in Numbers 12, Miriam is punished by God for talking against Moses "because of his Cushite wife." Usually interpreted as racist, it could equally mean that Moses's wife[13] confided to her sister-in-law that Moses is so concerned with his spiritual tasks that he neglects his family, and Miriam tries to mediate. God supports Moses (Num. 12:1-10). Whatever the relationship between Moses and his wife, there are no more children.[14]

Rules

The Hebrew Bible makes it clear that the power of life and death rests with God (Setel 88-89). Reproduction is the province of God, divorced from any control on the part of women (Setel 93), or men for that matter (Sawyer). Despite this, or perhaps to implement it, the insistence on children is reinforced by a series of rules. For example, rules that prohibit intercourse during menstruation lead to maximum fertility, as ovulation usually occurs between menstrual periods.

The commandment, "Be fruitful ('go forth') and multiply"[15]—the Hebrew God's first command as interpreted by the rabbis—is a central tenet of historical, and modern, Judaism. The biblical world is created to be inhabited (Isa. 45:18) by both people and animals. Playing by the rules attracts God's blessings on Israel, which always include fecundity[16] or the absence of barrenness[17] (Carlebach). Breaking the rules, such as sex with an unacceptable partner (e.g., an uncle's or a brother's wife), leads to both being childless (Lev. 20:20–21). The punishment of the adulteress is sterility (Dolansky 79). More importantly, Genesis 38:9 forbids "wasting seed" (through withdrawal or masturbation). The implications of this on procreation are self-evident.

Sometimes, the explanation is ex post facto. Rebecca's childlessness is attributed to her decision to leave home to marry Isaac without waiting to mourn her father, who in this interpretation has suddenly died. Her brother Laban's blessing,[18] interpreted as mockery, leads to her barrenness (Gen. Rabbah 60:12).

The commandment to procreate applies only to (Jewish) men. Women are excluded from the legal duty to bear children (Biale 198)—they must be willing, not commanded. For women, procreation is an act of choice and free will (Antonelli 9) under religious law.[19] This is based on Judith, wife of R Hiyya (third-century BCE), who after suffering agonizing pains in childbirth appears in disguise before her husband (an adjudicator) and asks, "Is a woman commanded to propagate the race?" He replies, "No." She promptly drinks a sterilizing potion. The prevailing view is that to be "fruitful" means to have one son and one daughter, from the Biblical verse "male and female He created them" (Gen. 5:2; Isaacs).

Contraception

Female contraception is never mentioned (Brenner 69), so there are no specific biblical laws regulating or proscribing either birth control or termination of pregnancy, although both are widely discussed in later Jewish traditions (Knight 134). Contraception is known from ancient Egypt, Greece, Rome (Knight 134), and, by inference, Israel (Brenner

71). In addition to celibacy/abstinence and infanticide, from the middle of the second millennium to the beginning of the second century BCE (Brenner 71), three main methods of avoiding childbirth were available: chemical substances, mostly plants; mechanical prevention; and abortion, including inducement of premature labour. Such plants as pomegranates, saffron, Queen Anne's lace, juniper, rue, ferula, and myrrh were often shared among women (Knight 134) to prevent or end pregnancy. The "cup of roots" sterility potion appears in several places in the ancient writings. Salt, egg barley, sleeping on the ground, bloodletting, and crying were said to be detrimental to sexual potency (Carlebach).

Suppositories of cotton, wool, honey, gum, or crocodile dung were known (Knight 134) as mechanical barriers. Most rabbinic rulings on contraception are based on a Talmudic passage that permits (requires?) the use of a contraceptive tampon by minor, pregnant, or lactating women (Beraita of the Three Women, Yev. 12b; Jakobovits; Isaacs). Voluntary miscarriage is obliquely mentioned (Brenner 70; Dolansky 79). Abortion is implied for woman suspected of adultery (Brenner 69); abortifacients such as pennyroyal and saffron could have been used (Knight 134).

Although divorce is discouraged, there is one specific exception: ten years[20] of marriage without offspring (Biale 202). However, for a childless but otherwise happy couple, it is accepted that the obligation of procreation is neither enforceable nor paramount (Gen. Rabbah 17:7; Baskin 128).

Ancient Near East literature includes, for example, provisions for adoption (Callaway 16). On the other hand, the sole law in the Hebrew Bible dealing with childlessness is the Levirate (Deut 25:5-10).

Reinterpreting the Matriarchs

Three biblical matriarchs (Sarah, Rebecca, and Rachel) are called barren in Genesis, spending long periods expressing a longing for children. Biblical scholar Savina Teubal does not take this at face value; she interprets it in light of their cultural context (e.g., Mesopotamian tablets, artwork, and legends prevalent in the area at the time). Teubal sees these matriarchs as members of a matrilineal social order in which women participate extensively in decision making within their matrifocal community (Teubal 68). Her thesis is that their childlessness is voluntary. She interprets their actions in light of the tradition of ancient Middle Eastern priestesses dedicated to ensuring the fertility of the land and of the people by mating with the secular/religious leader. This rite, called *hieros gamos*, requires them to forego personal biological fertility (Teubal 82). As Rigoglioso put it, "Teubal's argument that Sarah's statement "the lord has kept me from having children" in Genesis 16:2 is not a lament about her biological barrenness but rather a reference to the religious laws she had to follow that forbade her from procreating (*The Mystery Tradition* 49).

As society increasingly adopted patriarchal values, the matriarchs sought to perpetuate the customs of their mothers. Thus, any interest in having a child was to further her own line rather than her husband's[21] (Teubal 33). Childless matriarchs chose to preserve the customs of their matrifocal tradition even after they moved to Canaan[22] (Teubal 65). These practices were abolished only slowly (Teubal 53).

Sarah, Rebecca and Rachel are all portrayed as conceiving due to divine intervention after ten to thirty years of childlessness.[23] As the practice of monotheism consolidated, only one God remained available to ensure pregnancy. This patriarchal God, usually transcribed Jehovah, has neither spouse nor offspring (Teubal 131). Abraham, as the intermediary between his God and his community, is rewarded with the land of Canaan (Gen. 17-18; Teubal, 135). Sarah, in contrast, directly represents a goddess; her reward is thus for officiating in the ceremony of *hieros gamos* to ensure the fertility of the land and wellbeing of its people (Teubal 135). Sarah's consorting with both Pharaoh and Abimelech,[24] both political alliances from which she and Abraham emerge wealthy, fits this pattern. As a priestess, the issue of ritual sexual union is not progeny but bountiful harvests. As a religious and political professional, she is paid handsomely for officiating in the sacred marriage ritual[25] (Teubal 131).

The characteristics Sarah shares with her avatar goddess are childlessness and having more than one ritual husband (Teubal 131). Did the goddess that Sarah embodied come with her from Mesopotamia to Canaan? When Sarah wishes to have an heir(ess), she follows Mesopotamian rules that govern the conduct of women in particular religious groups, who are forbidden to have children of their own: she uses a surrogate. This explains why she is recorded as (initially) barren

(Teubal 37). The Babylonian law for priestesses—that if the pregnant servant becomes uppity she can be treated badly—applies to Hagar's expulsion as well, indicating that Sarah's childlessness is due to her status rather than an organic cause (Teubal 104; Rigoglioso, *The Mystery Tradition* 52).

The people who migrate to Canaan are Terah, his son Abram, his daughter-in-law Sarai, and his grandson Lot (Gen. 11-13; Teubal 8). The text says twice that Sarai has no child. Why the redundancy? Some say the repetition emphasizes the all-encompassing nature of her condition— that is, absolutely barren, having no child whatsoever. Others say the opposite: the redundancy limits Sarai's infertility (i.e., though barren now, she will not be forever). Alternatively, the repetition may be a dramatic technique to challenge us to revise our assumptions about procreation (Gen. 29:31; 30:22; 1 Sam. 1:5; Klitsner 114).

Rachel's sister/cowife Leah has four sons when Rachel begs Jacob to give her children (Gen. 30:1). If Rachel is a priestess, God has withheld children by the stricture against childbearing. Rachel, using almost the same exact words as Sarah, sends her maid to her husband to "bear on my knees and through her, my house too will be built up" (Teubal 52, 106). Rachel is not concerned that her husband have sons; he already does. She is observing the same rule as Sarah and for women of religious rank in Babylonia (Teubal 52).

The recurring mention of barrenness is especially significant in light of the primary purpose of marriage in a patriarchal world—providing a man's family with male heirs. It seems unlikely that three generations of women married to patriarchs would have similar medical conditions. Since childless women are regarded as useless and the continuation of their marital status is regarded as undesirable and even immoral (Patai)— and that they follow the rules for priestesses[26]—may explain why the matriarchs' husbands do not leave them. The narratives of the Sarah tradition represent a nonpatriarchal system struggling for survival in isolation in a foreign land. These women are in control of their bodies and their spiritual heritage (Teubal 139-40). In identifying with a goddess, they choose to remain childless for decades and choose to conceive, late in life, because of the circumstances of exile (Teubal 140).

Prophets[27] and Others

Of the four named woman prophets in the Hebrew Bible, one has a husband, and one may have a husband; for the other two, the Hebrew Bible makes no mention of a husband. They live influential lives, without being said to have (or want) children. Miriam the Prophet occupies a central place in biblical lore, without being depicted as the supportive partner of a heroic male (Brown, "The Well" 43). She is never called a wife or mother, although her life from early childhood to death is told. She helps the pharaoh's daughter rescue her brother Moses and dances with the women when they escape Egypt. When she challenges Moses's leadership and is banished, the people refuse to move until she returns. Jewish tradition, however, cannot tolerate Miriam's status as single and childfree, so it matches her with an identified man. The first-century historian Josephus selects Hur, a Judean nobleman, as her husband (Trible, "Miriam"). Rabbinic sources marry her to Caleb, a spy sent by Moses (Numbers 13-14), with Hur as her son (Trible, "Miriam").

Huldah the Prophet, wife of Shallum, is asked by Hilkiah, a priest in the time of King Josiah, to validate a scroll found in Solomon's Temple. Under her own authority, she speaks in the name of God (Camp 96), authenticates the book, and predicts destruction (2 Kings 22:20). In nine verses (2 Kings 22:13-20; 2 Chronicles 34:22-28), the narrative shows that Huldah is accustomed to speaking the word of God directly to high priests and royal officials, who come to her in supplication. Huldah also teaches publicly in the school (Targ. to 2 Kings 22:14). Her husband's background is included but not whether they have children.

Even less is known about Noadiah the Prophet. She appears only once (Neh. 6:14), in reference to opponents seeking to intimidate Nehemiah, governor of Yehud (c 444 BCE). The context implies that Noadiah has high status (Eskenazi 132), and she is probably not young. Nothing is said about her family.

Deborah, a major judge in Biblical Israel, with authority to call people to war as well as to prophesize, is introduced as "eshet lappidot" (Judges 4-5). Usually translated as "wife of Lappidoth," these words may also mean "woman of torches," fiery woman, or even redhead. Deborah accompanies Barak, the Israelite general, to battle. Barak destroys every Canaanite except Sisera. Jael, the wife of Heber the Kenite (Judg. 4:17-22; 5:6, 24-27), "most blessed of women," but not a prophet, invites the defeated Sisera in, feeds him, and then kills him with a tent peg (Frymer-Kensky 2000, 97-98).

When the greater world of national battles intrudes into her domestic space, Jael becomes known as one of the so-called mothers of Israel (Frymer-Kensky, "Jael" 97-98). Deborah's victory song, possibly the earliest poem in the Bible from late twelfth-century BCE, describes the chaotic conditions that exist until "you arise, Deborah, / arose as a mother in Israel" (Judg. 5:7). The phrase may indicate that her arbitration powers are parental; "Mother" is an honorific title for a protector in the community (Hammer and Shere 120). Another possibility is that Deborah administers God's plan, like the matriarchs (Frymer-Kensky, "Jael" 65-67). Whether either Deborah or Jael is a biological mother is not stated.

Both Deborah and Jael break all maternal moulds. They do not consider themselves dead without children; on the contrary, each embraces life to the fullest (Klitsner 155). Far from showing sympathy towards another woman, Deborah taunts Sisera's mother waiting in vain for her son, portraying her as the quintessential enemy.[28] Jael kills a man. The stealthy heroine of the prose account and fierce warrior of Deborah's poem are both dramatic inversions of motherhood. One offers maternal nurturing before she strikes and the other stands with the slain foe between her legs in a grim parody of birth (Frymer-Kensky, Apocrypha 97-98).

Judith also kills a man. When her people are in trouble, she volunteers to save them, and cuts off the head of the enemy General Holofernes. The Book of Judith is deuterocanonical[29] (not part of the Hebrew Bible). At the start of the story, Judith is a widow; at the end, she refuses to remarry (Judith 8; 16:22). At her death, she distributes her wealth among her family and her husband's (Judith 16:24), which implies she has no children. Her genealogy is traced apart from her husband's, and her identity is distinct from his. Judith chooses her own way of life. Requiring neither the material support of a man nor a male partner to provide her with a child, Judith's piety is not prompted by any obvious need (Sawyer 93). She is childless and does not seek to change this situation.

Delilah, said to cause Samson's downfall, is not bound to any man. She conducts her love affair with Samson and her business affairs with the lords of the Philistines without a father, brother, or husband as mediator (Sawyer 67). There is no mention of children.

Interrupted Lives/Uncompleted Stories

A number of young, childless women appear in the Hebrew Bible, play their part, and disappear from the story. We do not know how long they live or whether they remain childless, voluntary or otherwise. Later extrapolations imply an early death, attribute a celibate life, or match them with biblical men, often by identifying them with a named wife.

The childlessness of Michal, daughter of Saul, is explicit: She had no children to the day of her death (2 Sam. 6:23). She marries David for love before he is king (1 Sam. 18:20) and helps him escape her father (1 Sam. 19:11-17). Then, separated for years, both remarry. After Saul's death, David, now king, demands and receives Michal back (2 Sam. 3:13-15). Michal's childlessness is not accounted for in the biblical text. Later interpretations say her second marriage is never consummated. Perhaps, David confines her and shuts her away, as he did with some of his other wives (2 Sam. 20:3). Or is she punished for criticizing King David for dancing? (2 Sam. 6:20; Schwartz and Kaplan 104-105). A more politico-religious explanation, given the function of children in furthering the family line, relates to Michal's role in the dispute for the kingship between her father, Saul, and her husband, David. In this view, Saul blocks David from claiming the kingship through Michal by marrying her to another man, and David wants her back to legitimize his own claim. Her lack of children is necessary theologically; God's rejection of Saul precludes his descendants ruling over Israel.

How, then, could David give the Gibeonites "the five sons of Michal, Saul's daughter whom she bore for Adriel" (2 Sam. 21:8-9)? Some say this refers to Adriel's wife/Michal's sister Merab (Exum, "Michal"). Others say that Merab died and Michal brought up (not bore) the children (1 Sam. 18:17-19).

Vashti, the wife of the Persian King Ahasuerus, refuses to show off her beauty at a drunken feast (Esther 1:10-12). The king issues a commandment "that Vashti come no more before king Ahasuerus" and a decree that every man should rule in his own house (Esther 1:22). Later, after his anger subsides, he remembers Vashti and what she had done and what he had decreed about her (Esther 2:1). Then Vashti disappears from the story. Is Vashti executed, either at once (Midrash Tehilim, on Ps. 22:26) or later? Or does Ahasuerus, regretful (Esther Rabbah 5:2), allow her to live in obscurity (Meir; Hyland)? Vashti's successor, Esther, cleverly manages to save her people without alienating her husband. Although the achievements of her uncle Mordecai are recorded, after she exerts authority to confirm the "words of peace and truth" (Esther 9:29-30), nothing further is said of her. Did Esther and (non-Jewish) Ahasuerus produce children? One tradition asserts that Esther used a resorbent to prevent pregnancy; another has her miscarry (Esth. Rabbah 8:3). Additional traditions maintain that Esther becomes the mother of Darius or of Cyrus (Kallah Rabbati 2:15; Meir).

Batya/Bithia ("daughter of God") is called only "Pharaoh's daughter" in Exodus 2:5-10. She saves the infant Moses, who becomes her son without, however, losing his identity as a Hebrew. There is little about her in the biblical text, neither whether she already has children nor whether she does subsequently. However, in her story, as elaborated later, she converts, marries, and has children (Kadari).

Dinah (Gen. 34) has sex with Shechem, who then proposes marriage. Her father, Jacob, agrees, but her brothers kill Shechem and take Dinah away. Then Dinah disappears. Does she remarry? Does she live hidden away by her brothers? Does she die of a broken heart (Adelman 29)? Later stories have Dinah marrying various men (Kadari), with or without children. In another account, pregnant by Shechem, Dinah gives birth to Asenath (who later becomes Joseph's wife) in Egypt where Potiphar's childless wife raises Asenath as her own (Pirkei de-Rabbi Eliezer 37; Midrash Aggadah, Gen. 41:45; Kadari).

Jephthah's (nameless[30]) daughter (Judges 11:30-39) is his only child. Jephthah vows that if successful in battle, he will sacrifice whatever first comes out of his house. It is his daughter. He cannot withdraw the vow, but he grants his daughter's request for time to "bewail her virginity" with her friends (Judges 11:37). Two months later her father "did to her as he had vowed" (Judges 11:39). Some rabbinic commentators say Jepthah's daughter is not killed but rather becomes devoted to God and is forbidden to marry (Zondervan).

Conclusion

Both from the Hebrew Bible and from later elaborations, the stories of biblical women, promoted as role models for subservient housewives praying for a family, still have an impact today. It is important to put these stories into context. The motif of the barren matriarch giving birth to a hero or divine child is a literary creation of the biblical author(s), reinterpreting ancient traditions about the birth of sons into a pattern of barrenness and subsequent fertility (Callaway 17, 30). Biblical authors may also have added barrenness to the patriarchal narratives to underline the dependence of Israel on divine grace rather than achievement (Callaway 31). Later commentators elaborate on these themes.

With childlessness out of the closet (Notkin xv), can twenty-first-century women learn something different from our biblical predecessors? Might some biblical women have (silently) been content with their childfree lives either permanently (e.g., Miriam and Judith) or until there was some intervention (e.g., the Shunamite, the wife of Manoah, and the matriarchs)? Despite the emphasis in the Hebrew Bible on motherhood, there are lessons for contemporary women who choose to remain childfree. Some biblical women chose to have children towards the end of long and active lives. Others live their entire lives childfree and contribute to their society by means other than reproduction. Both exhibit agency over their lives and the lives of those around them.

Many biblical narratives pivot on the emotionally charged issue of women's fertility. A woman who attaches exclusive significance to her reproductive success risks undervaluing herself as a human and being under esteemed by others. The commandment to multiply is not a goal in itself. It is one, but only one, means to spiritual fulfillment and covenantal continuity (Klitsner 133); there are numerous other ways to be fruitful.

Biblical stories redeem childless women by giving them children. Early (male) commentators married childless biblical women off to redeem them. Let's write new commentaries with new endings.

Endnotes

1. Men appropriate the power of childbirth and transform it from something concrete and physical into something abstract and symbolic; from something individual into something collective; from the birth of a single, mortal human into the birth of an eternal collective (nation/state); from a birth by a woman into a birth without women; and from individual birth giving life to birth of the collective by taking life. Men, thus, give birth to society and

establish a masculine dynasty that transcends the fate of individual death (Raveh 72).

2. A male deity using female vehicles to accomplish his plan reinforces, not undermines, the patriarchal worldview, leaving the power of the male deity triumphant and assured (Sawyer 13).

3. In her book *Virgin Mother Goddesses of Antiquity*, Marguerite Rigoglioso elaborates on this theme by pointing out that virginity represents not sterility but inviolable and sovereign creative power. Similarly, in her blog, Rigoglioso points out the following: "The womb is available for more than bringing children to our planet … beyond pulling souls into incarnation, the womb is a storehouse and a conduit for miracle level interventions" ("Why?").

4. Mothers are indispensable to the literature of patriarchy; they furnish God with a chance to interfere and prove his ability to change the situation (Brenner 57).

5. Some scholars suggest that infertility humbles the matriarchs, who are imagined as great beauties. Others explain childlessness as a benefit, which allows a woman freedom; she is not subject to the demands of her offspring (Baskin 133). One text (Gen. Rabbah 45:4) suggests that the matriarchs were infertile so their husbands could enjoy their beauty unimpaired. Thus, infertility as punishment and as reward are juxtaposed (Baskin 133).

6. The number seven comes from Hannah's invocation (1 Sam. 2:5), "while the barren woman bears seven" being read as "on seven occasions has the barren woman borne" (Baskin 136). Five are always Sarah, Rebecca, Rachel, Manoah's wife, and Hannah. The others are variously Leah; the personified future Israel/Zion (Isaiah 54:1); the Shunamite, Michal, and Elizabeth mother of John the Baptist.

7. A childless widow marries her deceased husband's brother.

8. Only God can open a womb, according to a divine calculus beyond human understanding. The only role humans can play is prayer (Baskin 134). Exegetical tradition stresses the efficacy of prayer and the value of suffering (Baskin 132).

9. God later tells him he will be father of many nations, gives instruction for the Covenant and circumcision, and changes his name to Abraham (Genesis 17). Sarai becomes Sarah at the same time.

10. Gen.25:21 is inserted with no link to an earlier tradition and no further mention. Isaac prays and Rebecca's womb opens; there is no attempt by Rebecca to solve her problem, no mention of anguish, and no hint of human conflict over her barrenness (Callaway 30).

11. Identified in rabbinic tradition as Hazelelponi from 1 Chronicles 4:3.

12. With one son and one daughter, he has met the minimum requirement.

13. Zipporah, whom he married in Midian, or possibly another woman.

14. Moses's sons Gershom and Eliezer rejoin their father in the desert, then disappear from the Hebrew bible. Numbers 3:1 begins "These are the descendants of Moses and Aaron" but only lists Aaron's four sons.

15. Technically the commandment of procreation comes from Genesis 9:1, addressed to Noah and his sons, and Genesis 35:11, addressed to Jacob. Genesis 1:28 is a blessing, not a commandment (Biale 279). The blessings of fruitfulness given at creation (Gen. 1:28)— and later to Noah (Gen. 9:7), Abram/Abraham (Gen. 12:2-3, 15:5, 17:4-8), Isaac (Gen. 26:3-5) and Jacob (Gen. 28:13-15)—are renewed in the covenant blessings of Deut. 28:1-4, contingent on Israel's obedience. The Covenant Code concludes with the promise that none will be barren in Israel (Exod. 23:26, Deut. 7:14), an ancient Semitic treaty blessing. In the Holiness Code in Leviticus 26, the blessing of fruitfulness is promised (Callaway 15; Baskin 120).

16. I will look on you with favor and make you fruitful and increase your numbers (Lev. 26:9). The LORD will grant you abundant prosperity in the fruit of your womb, the young of your livestock and the crops of your ground (Deut. 28:11).

17. And none will miscarry and be barren in your land (Exod. 23:26); You will be blessed ... none of your men or women will be childless, nor will any of your livestock be without young (Deut. 7:14).

18. May you increase to thousands upon thousands; may your offspring possess the cities of their enemies (Gen. 24:60).

19. Even with no religious obligation, the barren wife fails to fulfill the primary expectation of her social role; children assure a wife's position in her home (Gen. R. 71:5; Carlebach). The importance of children in securing a woman's status as well as the divine role in fertility is elucidated in Genesis (Rabbah 71:1; Baskin 130).

20. After Sarah who waits ten years before proposing that Abraham have a child with Hagar (Brenner 56).

21. Sarah and Rachel each speak of providing herself with heirs (Teubal 79). Sarah indicates her intention to regard her maid's child as her own offspring, not her husband's (Teubal 33). A literal translation of "perhaps I shall have a son through her" is "that I shall be 'built up' by her," referring to lineage or succession (Teubal 33). One characteristic of the matriarchs' kinship group is ultimogeniture (succession of the youngest). Sarah and Rebecca provide themselves with heirs according to this rule, regardless of their husband's preferences (Teubal 67); Sarah banishes Ishmael, and Rebecca chooses Jacob over Esau (Teubal 65, 95).

22. The reason for their childlessness could have been pragmatic rather than religious-cultic (Brenner 68).

23. Although the encouragement of childbirth is vital to Israel's survival, and with miscarriage and death in childbirth being common, "the whole enterprise was too doubtful and precarious to take place without divine supervision" (Frymer-Kensky, *In the Wake* 97).

24. Angels predict Sarah's pregnancy. She meets Abimelech. She bears a son (Gen. 21:1-7).

25. In Genesis 20:1-16, Abraham introduces Sarah as his sister to King Abimelech, whose household is then beset with infertility. Sarah returns to Abraham along with livestock, servants, and one thousand pieces of silver. The text reports that Abraham then prays to God, who heals Abimelech, his wife, and his female slaves so they have children again.

26. Rigoglioso argues that Abraham was not Sarah's husband in the usual sense but rather her consort (*The Mystery Tradition* 51).

27. The rabbis identify (*Megillah* 14a) seven prophetesses: Sarah, Miriam, Deborah, Hannah, Abigail, Huldah, and Esther. They, thus, exclude Isaiah's wife and Noadiah and include Sarah,

Hannah, Abigail, and Esther (Mariottini). Isaiah's wife, who is not named, has both a husband and children (Mariottini). Abigail gives birth to King David's second son. The accomplishments of many of these women are found in Jill Hammer and Taya Shere (61-65).

28. Sisera's mother anticipates a girl or two (the literal translation of the Hebrew is "womb-girl") for every man (Judges 5:30), alluding to sexual favors. Instead, the two "wombs" who greet him are Deborah and Jael. Rather than gratifying the sexual appetite of Sisera, they remove his head. By laughing at the gruesome death of her enemy, Deborah derides conventional motherhood as embodied by the woeful mother of Sisera (Klitsner 156).

29. Scripture to Catholic and Eastern Orthodox Christians but apocrypha to Protestants.

30. Called Sheilah in legend (Ochs 85).

Works Cited

Adelman, Penina, editor. *Praise Her Works: Conversations with Biblical Women.* Jewish Publication Society, 2005.

Antonelli, Judith S. *In the Image of God: A Feminist Commentary on the Torah.* Jason Aronson Inc., 1997.

Baskin, Judith R. *Midrashic Women: Formations of the Feminine in Rabbinic Literature.* Brandeis University Press, 2002.

Basten, Stuart. "Voluntary Childlessness and Being Childfree." *The Future of Human Reproduction: Working Paper #5.* Oxford and Vienna Institute of Demography, 2009.

Biale, Rachel. *Women and Jewish Law: An Exploration of Women's Issues in Halakhic Sources.* Schocken Books, 1984.

Brenner, Antalya. *The Intercourse of Knowledge: On Gendering Desire and "Sexuality" in the Hebrew Bible.* Brill, 1997.

Brown, Erica. "The Well Dried Up: Miriam's Death in the Bible and Midrash." *All the Women Followed Her: A Collection of Writings on Miriam the Prophet and the Women of Exodus,* edited by Rebecca Schwartz, Rikudei Miriam Press, 2001, pp. 42-52.

Brown, Erica. "Shunamite Woman." *Praise Her Works: Conversations with Biblical Women,* edited by Penina Adelman, Jewish Publication Society, 2005, pp. 156-64.

Callaway, Mary. "Sing, O Barren One: A Study in Comparative Midrash." *Society of Biblical Literature Dissertation Series 91.* Scholars Press, 1979.

Camp, Claudia V. "Huldah." *Women in Scripture: A Dictionary of Named and Unnamed Women in the Hebrew Bible, the Apocryphal/ Deuterocanonical Books, and the New Testament,* edited by Carol Meyers, William B. Eerdmans Publishing Company, 2000, pp. 96-97.

Carlebach, Alexander and Judith R. Baskin. "Barrenness and Fertility." *Encyclopaedia Judaica,* 2nd ed. The Gale Group, Jewish Virtual Library, 2008, www.jewishvirtuallibrary.org/barrenness-and-fertility. Accessed 25 Dec. 2020.

Dolansky, Shawna. *Now You See It, Now You Don't: Biblical Perspectives on the Relationship Between Magic and Religion.* Eisenbrauns, 2008.

Eshkenazi, Tamara Cohn. "Noadiah." *Women in Scripture: A Dictionary of Named and Unnamed Women in the Hebrew Bible, the Apocryphal/ Deuterocanonical Books, and the New Testament,* edited by Carol Meyers, William B. Eerdmans Publishing Company, 2000, p. 132.

Exum, Cheryl. "Mother in Israel: A Familiar Figure Reconsidered." *Feminist Interpretation of the Bible,* edited by Letty M. Russell, Westminster Press, 1985, pp. 73-85.

Exum, J Cheryl. "Michal: Bible." *The Encyclopedia of Jewish Women,* Jewish Women's Archive, jwa.org/encyclopedia/article/michal-bible. Accessed 25 Dec. 2020.

Friedman, Richard Elliott. *The Bible with Sources Revealed: A New View into the Five Books of Moses.* HarperOne, 2003.

Frymer-Kensky, Tikva. *In the Wake of the Goddesses: Women, Culture and the Biblical Transformation of Pagan Myth.* Fawcett, 1992.

Frymer-Kensky, Tikva. "Jael." *Women in Scripture: A Dictionary of Named and Unnamed Women in the Hebrew Bible, the Apocryphal/Deutero-canonical Books, and the New Testament,* edited by Carol Meyers, William B. Eerdmans Publishing Company, 2000, pp. 97-98.

Frymer-Kensky, Tikva. *Reading the Women of the Bible: A New Interpretation of their Stories.* Schocken Books, 2002.

Goldstein, Elyse. *Seek Her Out: A Textual Approach to the Study of Women and Judaism.* UAHC Press, 2003.

Hammer, Jill, and Taya Shere. *The Hebrew Priestess: Ancient and New Visions of Jewish Women's Spiritual Leadership.* BenYehuda Press, 2015.

Hyland, J. R. "What the Bible Really Says: Chapter 12: Whatever Became of Vashti." *Humane Religion,* 1998–2016, www.all-creatures. org/hr/what-12.htm. Accessed 25 Dec. 2020.

Isaacs, Rabbi Ronald H. "Procreation and Contraception." *Every Person's Guide to Jewish Sexuality.* Jason Aronson Publishers. Excerpted and reprinted with permission by *My Jewish Learning,* www.myjewishlearning.com/article/procreation-and-contra ception/. Accessed 25 Dec. 2020.

Jakobovits, Immanuel. "Birth Control." *Encyclopaedia Judaica.* The Gale Group, Jewish Virtual Library, 2008, www.jewishvirtuallibrary. org/birth-control. Accessed 25 Dec. 2020.

Kadari, Tamar. "Dinah: Midrash and Aggadah." *The Encyclopedia of Jewish Women,* Jewish Women's Archive, jwa.org/encyclopedia/ article/dinah-midrash-and-aggadah. Accessed 25 Dec. 2020.

Klitsner, Judy. *Subversive Sequels in the Bible: How Biblical Stories Mine and Undermine Each Other.* Jewish Publication Society, 2009.

Knight, Douglas. *Law, Power and Justice in Ancient Israel.* John Knox Press, 2011.

Labowitz, Shoni. *God, Sex and Women of the Bible: Discovering Our Sensual Spiritual Selves.* Simon & Schuster, 1998.

Lisle, Laurie. *Without Child: Challenging the Stigma of Childlessness.* Ballantine Books, 1996.

Mariottini, Claude. "The Seven Prophetesses of the Old Testament." *Claude Mariottini,* 16. Dec. 2013, claudemariottini.com/2013/12/16/ the-seven-prophetesses-of-the-old-testament/. Accessed Dec. 25 2020.

Meir, Tamar. "Esther: Midrash and Aggadah." *The Encyclopedia of Jewish Women,* Jewish Women's Archive, jwa.org/encyclopedia/ article/esther-midrash-and-aggadah. Accessed 25 Dec. 2020.

Meyers, Carol. *Rediscovering Eve: Ancient Israelite Women in Context.* Oxford University Press, 2013.

Meyers, Carol, editor. *Women in Scripture: A Dictionary of Named and Unnamed Women in the Hebrew Bible, the Apocryphal/Deuterocanonical Books, and the New Testament.* William B. Eerdmans Publishing Company, 2000.

Notkin, Melanie. *Otherhood: Modern Women Finding a New Kind of Happiness.* Penguin Group, 2014.

Ochs, Vanessa L. *Sarah Laughed: Modern Lessons from Wisdom and Stories of Biblical Women.* McGraw Hill, 2005.

Raveh, Inbar. *Feminist Readings of Rabbinic Literature.* Translated by Kaeren Fish. Brandeis University Press, 2014.

Rigoglioso, Marguerite Mary. *The Mystery Tradition of Miraculous Conception: Mary and the Lineage of Virgin Mothers.* Bear and Company, 2021.

Rigoglioso, Marguerite. *Virgin Mother Goddesses of Antiquity.* Palgrave Macmillan, 2010.

Rigoglioso, Marguerite. "Why Your Womb, Why Now?" Seven Sisters Mystery School, November, 2020, www.sevensistersmysteryschool. com/why-your-womb-why-now/. Accessed Dec. 25 2020.

Russell, Letty M, editor. *Feminist Interpretation of the Bible.* Westminster Press, 1985.

Russell, Letty M. "Authority and the Challenge of Feminist Interpretation." *Feminist Interpretation of the Bible*, edited by Letty M. Russell, Westminster Press, 1985, pp. 137-46.

Sawyer, Deborah F. *God, Gender and the Bible.* Routledge, 2002.

Schwartz, Rebecca, editor. *All the Women Followed Her: A Collection of Writings on Miriam the Prophet and the Women of Exodus.* Rikudei Miriam Press, 2001.

Schwartz, Matthew B., and Kalman J. Kaplan. *The Fruit of Her Hands: A Psychology of Biblical Women.* William B Eerdmans Publishing Company, 2007.

Setel, T. Drorah. "Prophets and Pornography: Female Sexual Imagery in Hosea." *Feminist Interpretation of the Bible*, edited by Letty M. Russell, Westminster Press, 1985, pp. 86-95.

Teubal, Savina J. *Sarah the Priestess: The First Matriarch of Genesis.* Swallow Press, 1984.

Thistlethwaite, Susan Brooks. "Every Two Minutes: Battered Women and Feminist Interpretation." *Feminist Interpretation of the Bible*, edited by Letty M. Russell, Westminster Press, 1985. pp. 96-110.

Trible, Phyllis. "Miriam: Bible." *The Encyclopedia of Jewish Women*, Jewish Women's Archive, jwa.org/encyclopedia/article/miriam-bible. Accessed 25 Dec. 2020.

Trible, Phyllis. "Postscript: Jottings on the Journey." *Feminist Interpretation of the Bible*, edited by Letty M. Russell, Westminster Press, 1985, pp. 147-50.

Zondervan. "Jephthah's Daughter: The Woman Who Was Sacrificed for an Oath." *Bible Gateway,* 1988, www.biblegateway.com/resources/all-women-bible/Jephthah-8217-s-Daughter, Accessed 25 Dec. 2020.

Afterword

Judith Dunkelberger Wouk

Fifty-some years ago, as an aspiring anthropologist in a PhD program at the University of Pittsburgh, I submitted a proposal for a thesis on voluntary childlessness. However, life had other plans for me; I married and moved to Canada. Instead of a PhD, I ended up with a law degree from Dalhousie University in Halifax, Nova Scotia, and a career in the Canadian federal public service rather than in academia. However, I never gave up my earlier vision. When I joined the team that created this volume, after the initial stages, it was a dream come true; academic bookends to my (mostly) nonacademic life.

So, in this Afterword, I ask, "Where do we go from here?" These chapters contain suggestions about two types of needs: the need for more research with more inclusive but more precise definitions of the concepts being explored and the need for policies in the workplace and in society in general that support the entire range of women's reproductive choices, including the choice not to have children. Of course, just as there is diversity among childfree people, so there is diversity among researchers; any individual author may agree or not with any of these recommendations.

Diversity of Research and Definitions

Many of the authors in this volume mention deficiencies in the current research, citing the diversity of the category of people who are childfree by choice. In their chapter in this collection, Stuart Gietel-Basten et al. point to numerous studies that have identified a clear inadequacy in considering childlessness in a binary fashion. The chapter by Victoria Clarke et al. notes that an inclusive, intersectional framework and ethos for future research encourages researchers to focus on the full diversity of the childfree population, without losing sight of the importance of giving voice to women's experience. All of the chapters make the point that the population of people without children is demographically diverse. From these chapters we learn that women without children may:

- never have married; be married, be separated, divorced or widowed; or be living in a common-law relationship;
- temporarily or permanently live alone, or with siblings, parents, other family members, chosen family, friends, hired caregivers, strangers or in a polyamorous family with one or more co-wives and/or husbands. Nonbiological (adopted, fostered, step-) children may also be part of their household;
- have children in their lives whom they influence or even have responsibility for raising. They may have professional roles working with children as professors, journalists, psychologists, caregivers, or physicians. They may influence young people through teaching, writing, or by example. They may have a special relationship with a particular child, such as a godchild or the children of friends and other family members. For example, Cassandra Chaney, in her chapter, recognizes Black women who are voluntarily childfree and who are stable social mothers to children that are not biologically their own;
- have one or more partners who are anywhere along a continuum of sexual identity;
- be sexually active or not, and that sexual activity may be by choice, not by choice, or both;
- come from a large multigenerational family with a history of taking care of others or may have never been in contact with an infant or young child;
- have any type of spiritual belief, degree of religiosity, religious identity, or religious affiliation, including subcategories within a religion;
- have completed education ranging from one or more post-secondary degrees to little or no formal schooling;
- be of any race, colour, ethnic or national origin, or age;
- live in an area that is urban, suburban, or rural as well as in a country with more or fewer economic resources;

- have various physical, intellectual, and psychological abilities;
- have various degrees of income and financial stability and have a wide range of occupations;
- be originally from or currently a member of any socioeconomic class;
- live in a place where a pronatalist government incentivizes motherhood through support for families or even penalizes households without children or one in which every family is required to support themselves;
- be part of a rising or falling demographic;
- become or remain childfree, temporarily or permanently, because they are celibate, biologically unable to conceive or carry a child, take action to prevent pregnancy, or reach menopause without having conceived. Or they have been pregnant and become childfree as a result of abortion, stillbirth, infanticide, neglect, abandonment, adoption, death of a child, returning a surrogate child to biological parents, or turning a child over to be looked after by their parents or distant relatives; and
- have responsibility for, and receive attention and love from, one or more pets; they may tend other growing things, such as flowers or vegetables.

There is also great diversity in both the societal contexts and reactions to women without children. If they live alone, they may feel isolated, or they may have a life filled with neighbours, friends, and coworkers. They may feel regretful, lonely, marginalized, and depressed or be content and fulfilled. They may be a part of a socially privileged group and expected to reproduce, or they may be from a group for whom having children is often criticized and not deemed appropriate, such as women with a disability, women who are poor, single, lesbian, or outside the age range (e.g., teenagers or postmenopausal women). Women without children have had a wide variety of life experiences. They may have had loving parents or not. They may have had a happy childhood or a history of abuse.

The attitudes of the society in which they live also vary. Women without children, in many places, are rejected as sociocultural misfits and deviants; they are stigmatized as social outcasts and barren waste, devalued, denigrated, and seen to be selfish and self-absorbed. Or they may benefit from a changing society that increasingly gives women access to higher education, greater social mobility, freedom to choose whether to continue a pregnancy, access to income and opportunity, and access to contraceptives.

In addition, women without children react to societal pressures in different ways. They may be outspoken feminists or environmentalists, or they may not politically active. Some childfree people affiliate with childfree communities and groups, and others do not. Some proclaim their choice about not wanting children; being childfree is a radical statement of a lifestyle. Others embrace being childfree as only one aspect of their identities; they see it as a nonissue or even reject telling their parents or in-laws of the decision. Some actively resist normative ideals, such as strong gendered roles and pronatalist understandings that conflate being a woman with being a mother. Others negotiate and manage the stigma associated with being childfree. Others still, at least to some extent, perceive themselves as they are perceived by others—as deviant and failures as women.

Support for Childfree Women

Creating public policies to support childfree women is a challenge for two reasons. For one, it often conflicts with other policy goals. As well, given the great diversity of this population, women without children do not have uniform needs. All policies need to be examined through a natalist lens as well as a feminist one to avoid negative outcomes for childfree women. As Amy Blackstone points out in her chapter, "What these women's reflections teach us is that the choice not to have kids is one that is made in the context of competing and sometimes contradictory ideas and ideals. In the end, as with most all of life's major choices, it is complicated." On a global scale, women's issues, including childfreedom, need to gain more visibility. All policies should value and include women, whether or not they have given birth and/or raised children. These include promoting educational opportunities for women, creating more stable jobs with pensions, and achieving global sustainability to maintain a healthy world for all.

One major requirement to support women who want to be childfree is easy access to contraceptives, sterilization, and pregnancy termination, including education on how to use them properly, without undue questioning of the woman's motives and decisions by medical or religious personnel. As Victoria Team points out in her chapter, infant abandonment in developed countries is uncommon due to improved access to contraceptive technologies and termination services, as well as the availability of state-organized adoption services.

Efforts must also be made to deconstruct the negative image of women without children and promote roles to women other than motherhood. One way to do this is through including more positive images of childfree women in popular culture. For example, Joselyn Leimbach's chapter introduces Dr. Christina Yang, a fictional cardiothoracic surgeon on the TV series *Grey's Anatomy*. Dr. Yang reimagines futurity and longevity by developing lifesaving medical techniques; she contributes to the world not through biological reproduction but through the intellectual and medical advancements she makes. Rather than biological descendants, she wants to create a lineage of survivors, whose lives are improved and prolonged because of her labour. In my own chapter, I explore the long history of childfree women by reframing Biblical role models, including Miriam—whose life story is told in the Hebrew Bible from childhood to death, without mention of either husband or children—and Sarah, who may have refrained from having children early in life because she was a priestess.

In her chapter, Nathalie Ségeral speaks of "the in-between-ness provided by literary creation, the possibility of re(en)gendering oneself through literature." Literature can highlight paradox. In relation to this, Segeral quotes the novelist Toni Morrison, who states that motherhood (defined by the fact of being a mother to one's child, as opposed to the fact of merely giving birth) constitutes a central stake in women's writings of slavery. In Morrison's novel *Beloved*, the main character, Sethe, a former slave, chooses to kill her daughter instead of seeing her become enslaved, which becomes the paradoxical condition of her accession to freedom. Gillian Alban, in *Medusa Gaze in Contemporary Women's Fiction: Petrifying, Maternal and Redemptive*, similarly reframes the theme inherent in the slave mother's dilemma represented by Sethe. Trapped in dehumanising slavery, she exerts the ultimate Medusa power over her daughter by killing her in order to prevent her return to slavery.

In the same vein, Victoria Team, in her chapter, advocates reframing actions of mothers towards children they have given birth to; she concludes that abandoning a newborn could be considered as the will to become childless—that is, free from care for the unwanted child. Abandonment could also be seen as a form of maternal resistance against the paternalistic government apparatus that aims to control women.

In terms of policy formulation, Helene Cummins's chapter argues that changes in social policy are essential. She notes that cohorts of single women are grouped in workplace policies; widowed, separated, and/or divorced women are considered together, despite large variations between women with dependents, married women, and childfree women. Cummins maintains that the lives of these women need to be addressed politically in order to create policies that meet their needs.

Family structures are changing, especially in industrialized countries. Society is moving towards a social responsibility model of the family, in which household and family members may be, but are not assumed to be, congruous; spousehood is not automatically identified with parenthood; and all dependency relations are socially recognized, regardless of whether they are between kin or nonkin. What is required is an analytical framework that is capable of accommodating the existing diversity of family types. Policies that privilege one family type over other types should be discouraged (Eichler).

Specifically, policymakers need to be aware of the following concepts:

- Do not assume that a woman without children doesn't have obligations towards others. In the workplace, this requires flexibility. Employment legislation and collectively bargained union contracts should include flextime and scheduling, including paid family leave and benefits for care for elderly, sick or challenged siblings and other family or nonfamily members.

- On the other hand, do not assume that everyone has family members or friends to care for them; long-term care and support for adults/seniors who need it must be available. Victoria Clarke et al. point out the need to reconceptualize older childless people as a social resource rather than as a burden. It is important to note that raising children is not a guarantee that they will be able or willing to care for an aging parent.

- Taxation laws, insurance, and mortgage requirements should not penalize women with nontraditional family arrangements.

- Childfree women should not be required to stay longer at the job, work overtime, or work weekends to offset the childcare responsibilities of their peers.

Beyond these specific suggestions, above all, in order to become a more just society, the ability to delink concepts becomes critically important. This volume has critiqued the use of several words and terms, such as mother, motherhood, womanhood, femininity, adult status, maturity, parent, parenting, parenthood, lineage, family, and community as well as sterility, infertility, childless, childfree, voluntarily childless, and childfree by choice. These concepts must be delinked from ideas of success as well as normative ideas about the family.

Many of these concepts need to be reframed as well. As Julie Anne Rodgers puts it in this volume, "It is vital, therefore, that we, as a society, accept this life choice as legitimate and overhaul the prejudicial way that the woman without child is configured in the cultural imagination." In summary, both the experience of motherhood and that of childfreedom can be either actively sought after or not; each can be a positive or negative experience.

More is needed in order to support women's reproductive choices in the workplace and in society in general. This book focuses on the choice to be childfree, within this larger context.

I will finish this Afterword, as I began, with a personal comment. What do I want my legacy to be, as a woman, now in my senior years, without children? Certainly, this book is an important part of my legacy. I would also like to be remembered for my passion for drumming, my advocacy of natural burial, my spiritual contributions as a Kohenet Hebrew priestess, and my work for the maternal gift economy and for peace.

Works Cited

Alban, Gillian. *The Medusa Gaze in Contemporary Women's Fiction: Petrifying, Maternal and Redemptive.* Cambridge Scholars Publishing, UK, 2017.

Eichler, Margrit. *Affidavit of Dr. Margrit Eichler in the Ontario Superior Court of Justice (Divisional Court) in the case of Halpern et al., and the Attorney General of Canada et al.* Court File 684/00, Sworn Nov. 15, 2000, discoverarchives.library.utoronto.ca/downloads/margrit-eichler-fonds.pdf. Accessed 23 Dec. 2020.

Notes on Contributors

Amy Blackstone is Professor in Sociology and the Margaret Chase Smith Policy Center at the University of Maine, where she directs Maine NEW Leadership, a residential institute that trains undergraduate women for roles in civic and political leadership. She studies childlessness and the childfree choice, workplace harassment, and civic engagement. Her work has been published in a variety of peer-reviewed outlets and featured in such media as the Katie show, Washington Post, USA Today, Huffington Post, The Walrus, and other national and international outlets. She is the author of *Childfree by Choice: The Movement Redefining Family and Creating a New Age of Independence* (Dutton, 2019).

Virginia Braun is a Professor in the School of Psychology, The University of Auckland, Aotearoa/New Zealand. She primarily works around gendered bodies, sex/uality, and health, as well as writing about qualitative research. She is co-author (with Victoria Clarke) of *Successful qualitative research* (2013, Sage), co-editor (with Victoria Clarke and Debra Gray) of *Collecting qualitative data* (2017, Cambridge). Currently she is writing a book on thematic analysis with Victoria Clarke for Sage Publications.

Cassandra D. Chaney, J. Franklin Bayhi Endowed Professor, is broadly interested in the dynamics of African-American family life. Under this umbrella, her interests are intimacy and commitment; narratives; the characteristics of stable marriages; the historic and contemporary salience of religion/spirituality; media (television, song lyrics, and films) portrayals; masculinity, femininity, motherhood, and fatherhood in Hip Hop; Blacks' historic and contemporary relationship with law enforcement; as well as critical examinations of individual and institutional racism in America. In 2012, Dr. Chaney published the book *Black Women in Leadership: Their Historical and Contemporary Contributions* (Peter Lang Publishers) with Dr. Dannielle Joy Davis. In 2019, she published the book *Police Use of Excessive Force against African Americans: Historical Antecedents and Community Perceptions (Policing Perspectives and Challenges in the Twenty-First Century)* (Lexington Books—An Imprint of Rowman & Littlefield) with Ray V. Robertson.

Victoria Clarke is an associate professor in qualitative and critical psychology at the University of the West of England, Bristol, UK. She has published three prize winning books—*Out in Psychology* (Wiley); *Lesbian, Gay, Bisexual, Trans and Queer Psychology* (Cambridge University Press); *Successful Qualitative Research* (Sage)—and numerous papers in the areas of LGBTQ and feminist psychology, family and relationships, appearance psychology, human sexuality, and qualitative methods. Her latest book is *Collecting Qualitative Data* (Cambridge University Press), co-edited with Virginia Braun and Debra Gray. She has developed an approach to thematic analysis with Virginia Braun that has become widely used in and beyond psychology (*www.psych. auckland.ac.nz/thematicanalysis*). Her current projects include writing a book on thematic analysis with Virginia Braun for Sage Publications.

Helene A. Cummins is a full professor of sociology at Brescia University College, Western University in London, Ontario. She received the first Award of Excellence in Teaching at Brescia University College and was nominated on two occasions for distinguished teaching at Western University. She is a former elected chair of the Department of Sociology and former associate academic dean at her university. She has published in *The Canadian Review of Sociology and Anthropology, Women's Studies International Forum, Advancing Women in Leadership, Identity: An International Journal of Theory and Research, The Canadian Geographer*, and *Journal of Rural and Community Development*, to name a few. She was elected chair of The Status of Women Committee for OCUFA. In 2016, she won The Status of Women Award of Distinction for OCUFA, which represents twenty-eight universities in Ontario, Canada. Her areas of expertise include gender and equity, sociology of the family, rural sociology, and ethics.

Judith Dunkelberger Wouk has degrees in anthropology and law. After a career as a Canadian federal public servant, she is now involved in political and spiritual activism. She has taught about lesser known women of the Bible, including Miriam, Jezebel, Delilah, Rachel and Teraphim and Judith. She has researched or published on paganism in Ottawa in the 1990s, the feminine divine, women and Judaism, religion in Latin America, and refugee protection in Canada.

Stuart Gietel-Basten is professor of social science and public policy, director of the Center for Aging Science, and associate dean of the School of Humanities and Social Science at the Hong Kong University of Science and Technology. Prior to this, he was associate professor of social policy at the University of Oxford. His research covers the links between population and policy, with a regional focus on Asia. In particular, he is interested in the emergence of low fertility across the region and the consequences of this in terms of population ageing and growth. He has been published in a number of major journals in demography and other social science subjects and is the author of *The "Population Problem" in Pacific Asia* (Oxford University Press, 2019) and *Why Demography Matters* (cowritten with Danny Dorling, Polity Press, 2017).

Nikki Hayfield is a senior lecturer in social psychology in the Department of Health and Social Sciences at the University of the West of England (UWE), Bristol, UK. Her research interests are focused on sexualities, relationships, and alternative families. In 2016, she conducted British Academy/Leverhulme funded research with Victoria Clarke, Sonja Ellis, and Gareth Terry focused on the lived experiences of heterosexual, lesbian, bisexual, and queer women who choose not to have children. Nikki has published on a range of topics, including childfree identities and bisexual and pansexual appearance and identities. She has also written about qualitative methods, including thematic analysis and insider/outsider research.

Joselyn K. Leimbach is a lecturer with the Institute for Women's Studies at the University of Georgia. She earned her PhD in Gender Studies from Indiana University (2014). Her work uses feminist and queer theory to explore intersections of gender, sexuality, and race in U.S. popular culture. Previously, she published "Strengthening as they Undermine: Rachel Maddow and Suze Orman's Homonormative

Lesbian Identities" in *In the Limelight and Under the Microscope* (Continuum 2011) as well as a piece cowritten with Brenda R. Weber, "Comedian, Covergirl, Conversationalist: Ellen's Incorporate Body," in *Hysterical! Women in American Comedy* (University of Texas Press 2017).

Naomi Moller is a senior lecturer at The Open University in Britain and a (part-time) psychotherapist working one-to-one with adults. Trained as a counselling psychologist, she has published in the areas of family and couple relationships, family and couple counselling, infidelity, attachment, eating disorders, weight stigma, and counselling and psychotherapy training. With Andreas Vossler, she edited *The Counselling and Psychotherapy Research Handbook* (Sage), and she has a strong ongoing interest in research methodology for therapeutic practice.

Jasmijn Obispo received her MSc in medical anthropology and sociology from the Graduate School of Social Sciences (University of Amsterdam), where she conducted an ethnographic study of drug use in nightlife settings. She is particularly interested in the intersection of (mental) health and social justice. This includes ontological and epistemological considerations of mental health and emotional wellbeing research, practices, and policies. Alongside her involvement in academia, she has worked for contemporary art institutions, such as the Hague Contemporary (The Hague, NL), Mediamatic (Amsterdam, NL), and Het Nieuwe Instituut (Rotterdam, NL).

Clare Ridd studied human sciences at the University of Oxford.

Julie Anne Rodgers is assistant professor in French at Maynooth University, Ireland. Her research (mainly in the field of French studies) focuses on the production and reception of maternal counternarratives and incorporates the study of a wide range of mothering experiences that do not correspond to the normative, patriarchal script of mother-hood. These include maternal ambivalence, postnatal and ongoing maternal depression, difficult pregnancies, and, of course, the choice to remain childfree. Julie has published widely on motherhood and mothering. She has published articles in *Francofonia*, the *International Journal of Canadian Studies*, the *Irish Journal of French Studies*, and *Women: A Cultural Review*. Julie has also previously published a chapter with Demeter Press on Lisa Baraitser and the ethics of maternal interruption in *Mothering and Psychoanalysis* (2014), edited by Petra Bueskens. In addition to her scholarship on motherhood and mothering, Julie is also mother to Harry, currently aged six.

Nathalie Ségeral is a lecturer in French studies at the University of Sydney. Prior to moving to Australia, she received a PhD from the University of California, Los Angeles and held a tenured appointment at the University of Hawaii at Mānoa (USA). Her research and publications weave together trauma theory and motherhood studies in contemporary women's writings of the French-speaking South Pacific, Rwanda, and the Holocaust. Her latest book-length publication is a French translation of David Chappell's *The Kanak Awakening: The Rise of Nationalism in New Caledonia* (Presses universitaires de la Nouvelle-Calédonie, 2017). Her forthcoming co-edited book (with Laura Lazzari) is titled *Trauma and Motherhood in Contemporary Literature and Culture* (Palgrave-McMillan, 2021). Her articles have appeared in *The Journal of Holocaust Research*, *Contemporary French and Francophone Studies*, *Jewish History and Culture*, *Sextant*, *Crossways Journal*, and *Women in French Studies*.

Victoria Team, MD, MPH, DrPH, is senior research fellow in the School of Nursing and Midwifery, Monash University, and in the Monash Partners Academic Health Science Centre, both in Australia. Her interests are medical anthropology, public health, and the translation of research evidence into policy and practice. Her current research projects focus on capacity building for pressure injury prevention. She is associate editor of the *Frontiers in Communication* and managing editor of *Medical Anthropology: Cross-Cultural Studies in Health and Illness*.

Sonia Yuhui Zhang is a Ph.D. student in the Anthropology Department at the New School for Social Research. She completed her BA in human sciences at the University of Oxford in 2017 and has worked with grassroots NGOs in China with a focus on rural development and internal migration. Her doctoral project looks at the relationship between loneliness and technology through ethnographic engagement with social roboticists in Japan.

Deepest appreciation to
Demeter's monthly Donors

DEMETER

Daughters
Rebecca Bromwich
Summer Cunningham
Tatjana Takseva
Debbie Byrd
Fionna Green
Tanya Cassidy
Vicki Noble
Bridget Boland
Naomi McPherson
Myrel Chernick

Sisters
Kirsten Goa
Amber Kinser
Nicole Willey
Christine Peets